CONTENTS

Intro		1
1:	Before the Future	7
2:	Soho Nights	21
3:	Party Party	35
4:	'No, I'm Sorry, But You Can't Come In'	49
5:	They Shoot Clothes Horses, Don't They?	73
6:	Electro Disco	89
7:	Tribal Britain	103
8:	Let's Go to Warren Street	115
9:	The Ballet Begins	131
10:	Aspiration, Aspiration, Aspiration	147
11:	The Face of the Decade	165
12:	Your Fifteen Minutes Start Now	183
13:	We'll Take Manhattan	197
14:	The Blitz Is Dead, Long Live the Blitz	213
15:	Mad About the Boy	231
16:	The Roaring 80s	255
17:	After the Dance	265

BLITZ

ROBERT ELMS

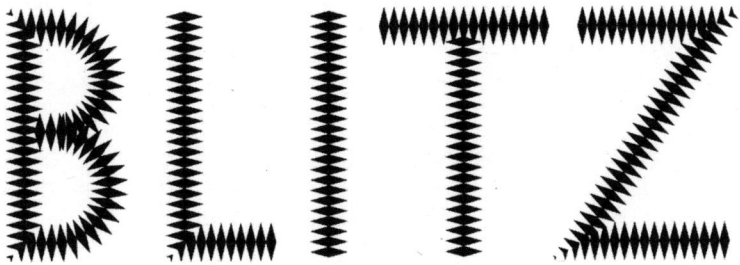

BLITZ

THE CLUB THAT CREATED THE 80s

faber

First published in the UK and USA in 2025
by Faber & Faber Ltd
The Bindery, 51 Hatton Garden
London EC1N 8HN

Typeset by Faber & Faber Ltd
Printed and bound by CPI Group (UK) Ltd, Croydon, CR0 4YY

Photographs © Graham Smith

A CIP record for this book
is available from the British Library

ISBN 978–0–571–39418–0

Printed and bound in the UK on FSC® certified paper in line with our continuing
commitment to ethical business practices, sustainability and the environment.
For further information see faber.co.uk/environmental-policy

Our authorised representative in the EU for product safety is
Easy Access System Europe, Mustamäe tee 50, 10621 Tallinn, Estonia
gpsr.requests@easproject.com

2 4 6 8 10 9 7 5 3 1

THIS BOOK
IS DEDICATED TO

Steve Strange Rusty Egan Princess Julia Melissa Caplan George O'Dowd
Jeremy Healy Kim Bowen Chris Sullivan Fiona Dealey Stephen Linard
Peter 'Marilyn' Robinson Stephen Jones OBE Christos Tolera Graham
Smith Graham Ball Steve Dagger Stevie Stewart David Holah Gary
Kemp Martin Kemp Simon Withers Ian Shaw Mandy D'Wit Duggie
Fields Darla Jane Gilroy Barry Bryan Ollie O'Donnell Philip Sallon
Jon Baker Willie Brown Michele Clapton Perry Haines Siobhan Fahey
Jimmy O'Donnell Michael Clark CBE Andy Polaris Andrew Logan
Midge Ure OBE Caryn Franklyn MBE Tony Hadley MBE Toyah
Willcox Dave Mahoney Electric Barry Lee Sheldrick Dinny Hall Jo
Strettell Polly Strettell Helen Robinson Cerith Wyn Evans Judith
Frankland Kevin Whitney Iain R. Webb Miss Binnie Steve Norman
Steve Lewis Rod Marsh Dangerous Jane Gary Wilkinson Myra Falconer
Emma Paolozzi Paula Pieroni John Maybury Martin Degville Richard
Ostell Scarlett Cannon Steve Marshall Steve 'Flid' Brown Sade Adu
CBE Reggie Massey Luciana Martinez Molly Parkin Kate Garner Paul
Sturridge Dylan Jones OBE Jo Hargreaves John Galliano CBE David
Claridge Carpet Head Billy Idol Pam Hogg Sir Grayson Perry CBE
Jeffrey Hinton Wilf Rogers Neil Matthews Pete the Murderer Steve
Beech Clare Thom Pinkietessa Braithwaite Lesley Chilkes Jane Chilkes
John Barclay Daryl Humphries Peter Doig John Keeble Richard Law
Bic Owen Naomi Gryn Michael 'Mac' McDermott Greg Davis Phil
Dirtbox Richard Burgess MBE Perri Lister Stephen Mahoney Lee
Barrett Billy Currie Wendy May Judy Blame Phil Bloomberg Frank
Kelly John 'J. J.' Connolly Mark Moore Don Devreaux Liz Fremantle
Vivienne Lynn Plug Box Plum Swede and me.

INTRO

For about eighteen months, as 1979 segued into a startling new decade, a small, musty, Second World War-themed wine bar in Covent Garden became the centre of the universe. The door to No. 4, Great Queen Street was the most important portal in London. If you could make it through there on a Tuesday night, you found yourself at the thrilling epicentre of a youth culture explosion of a kind this city had not seen since the Swinging Sixties: a nightclub which would come to define an era and whose influence is still reverberating today.

The 1980s, and all that they became, began a year early in the Blitz club, with Steve Strange deciding who would make it through the door and Rusty Egan spinning tunes to jive and flirt and pose and preen to. It was the hard core of 150 or so over-dressed, undervalued youngsters inside – those vain, arrogant, remarkably creative teenage misfits and macaronis* – who would go on to shape the decade and define so many aspects of the world we live in today.

I would guess that at least two-thirds of those Blitz kids – and they were indeed all kids, almost nobody over the age of twenty-one, almost all from working-class backgrounds, none of them privileged or monied – went on to become very successful in their chosen fields. Many became internationally prominent and plenty

* Pejorative 18th-century term for a fashionable, androgynous, overdressed fellow.

of them are still famous today. Nearly half a century later, I'm returning to the club's heyday in the pages of this book to reflect on how it happened.

Like a petri dish fizzing with alchemical reactions, or a pressure cooker of perpetual creativity, the realms of music, nightlife, fashion, design, art, dance and journalism were all ripped up and reshaped by this coterie of do-it-yourself dandy urchins dancing to a selection of epic electronic tunes and plotting to take over the world. Downstairs in the toilets, meanwhile, our collective sexual and gender mores were being tested to destruction. Boys will be girls and girls will be boys. Gender fluidity and bodily fluids.

The list of Blitz alumni covers just about every aspect of British cultural life, a remarkable number of them now sporting honours from OBEs to knighthoods, still more of them notorious and glamorous – stars of every kind. It is an incredible legacy, and I regularly bump into hugely successful people who I first saw dancing to 'Moskow Diskow' by Telex or applying eyeliner in the ladies' cubicle. Those days were so long ago that I've now also started going to their funerals.

But I still remember it vividly. What it felt like and smelled like to be there in that pulsating room after midnight pretty much every Tuesday for a year and a half. I was there with a truly remarkable cast of characters, writing the future as we went along. But I also recall what it was like outside that magical enclave in our grim and bitter land, torn by strife and riven by division.

All this has stayed with me because it was a truly defining period of my life. It formed who I was and who I would become. George O'Dowd and Gary Kemp, Siobhan Fahey and Sade Adu, Grayson Perry and Peter Doig, Dinny Hall, Dylan Jones, Chris Sullivan,

Michele Clapton, Michael Clark and John Galliano . . . They shaped and styled our world.

Once I set to writing this book, the memories came whooshing back. I think they are fairly reliable; they are certainly visceral, though time may have played tricks and hindsight will undoubtedly have played a part. Others will definitely remember things differently. The Blitz was full of giant egos (mine very much included), all of whom assumed that the room rotated around them. They will have their own Blitz memories, their own versions of events, their own analysis of what happened. This is mine.

I resisted the temptation to talk to lots of my fellow Blitz survivors; this is a personal narrative of how I saw it and felt it and lived it at the time. I wanted to reach back to become that stroppy, optimistic, overdressed young man again. But I still often speak to Chris Sullivan, Graham Ball and Gary Kemp. They are still close friends, and no doubt some of their memories are mixed in with mine. We lived this tumultuous time together and have since shared the stories so many times. Spandau's manager Steve Dagger has also been my confidant in this process. He was always the most clear-headed among us, the one who saw the possibilities and who can still recall the particulars. His help has been invaluable.

Looking at photos brings back some very specific moments and sensations, particularly those taken by Graham Smith, my arty mate from grammar school with a camera round his neck, who was there with us all the way and whose pictures grace this tome. His own book, *We Can Be Heroes*, with fantastic words by Chris Sullivan, is for me easily the best on this subject and the whole club scene of the 70s and 80s. It comes directly from the people who were there and I allowed myself to dip into that. With its ebullient but earthy imagery, flawless chronology and great storytelling, it plunged me right back into that maelstrom of extreme emotions and haircuts.

A few other photographers took shots, but they tended to be outsiders, and later there was a barrage of press coverage which largely got it wrong, always pointing their lenses at the most outrageous, the least authentic. Graham's pictures are special. His grainy black-and-white photos are strikingly evocative, raw, untutored but absolutely genuine, just like we were.

It is remarkable how young we all look, because it is remarkable how young we all were. To quote the title of Patti Smith's memoir, we were 'Just Kids'. But when I meet those grown-up Blitz kids today, when I bump into Rusty Egan or Stephen Jones, Fiona Dealey or Princess Julia, I still see those blazing brilliant youths of yore, still see the magic and the mischief in their eyes.

Even Graham almost never took his camera inside the Blitz; he was too busy doing what we were all doing, which was living it as large as our egos and our imaginations would allow. As well as there being few photos, there is almost no film or video evidence, little record of what actually went on at No. 4, Great Queen Street all those decades ago. Just the memories of some ageing New Romantics.

This was a pre-digital age, so it was not captured and chronicled much at the time; it was a purely lived experience. You had to be there, and if you were there, you had to be fully immersed; it was no place for part-timers or voyeurs. There was no shortage of exhibitionists at the Blitz, but all the furious posing and peacocking was just for ourselves. We did this – showing up and showing off, putting in so much effort, dressing to the nines – strictly for each other, not for wider consumption or financial compensation.

Nobody was trying to gain followers or get clicks and likes.

Social media didn't exist; social advancement didn't seem likely. For more than a year, the whole thing was out of sight and beneath the radar, until it all suddenly blew up and we became a national and even international news story. Before that, we were completely ignored by what is now termed the mainstream media, and even by the still-surviving alternative press and music press. Just a load of poseurs in preposterous outfits.

Talking of clothes – and inevitably I talk a lot about clothes in this book – I have a pretty accurate memory for what I wore and what others wore, a sign, I guess, of just what a vain and shallow man I am. Clothes, for me, work like an aide-memoire, a spear-collared, kipper-tied, fly-fronted, zoot-suited, cowboy-booted mnemonic. I can only remember outfits and song lyrics, both skills which have served me quite well.

But despite my very clear recall of specific items of clothing, I cannot guarantee that every one of the memories in this book is sartorially accurate. Sometimes I have quoted an example of what, say, Christos Tolera or Melissa Caplan were wearing on this or that occasion, and it may in fact have been on a different night that the low-rider outfit came out or that the tabard dress first appeared. I wanted to illustrate the kinds of garments, the outfits, the styles which were worn – and, believe me, *many* styles were worn. At the Blitz, a look lasted just one night.

I have also gone before and beyond the Blitz. Our story starts with the various trouser tribes and subsects which preceded Tuesday nights in Covent Garden, particularly the punks and the soul boys who were the progenitors of this cult with no name. Then it continues after the Blitz was no more, into the numerous clubs and bands, the designers, dancers, photographers and writers who emerged from that extraordinary milieu, from that little group of hardened hedonists and exhibitionists dancing together on a Tuesday night. The club was a catalyst for change, a motor for an age driven by pure, unfiltered teenage desire and wanton, egotistical energy. The 1980s would not have been the same without them.

For a long time, I wanted to escape that decade. It was great while it lasted, and I am not the least embarrassed – indeed, I'm very proud to have played my part – but to be forever linked to what you were wearing, saying and doing nearly half a century ago can be a little galling. I've done a lot of other stuff since and I am no longer that brash and arrogant young fellow in kung fu slippers, Black Watch tartan trews and a Basque beret waltzing into the offices of *The Face* magazine demanding they put my mates on the cover. But, in writing this book, I have reacquainted myself with him and his mates, with his fellow New Romantics. And I really like them.

I admire them for their boldness, their bottle and their brazen chutzpah, their carpe diem capacity to rise above the shitty conditions they were living in, the troubled times, the lack of money, the widespread animosity, the prejudice and even the violence they faced. I love them for being so bloody out there, so in your face, so in the moment, so determined to become whoever they wanted to be, that they became the future. Those Blitz kids were great kids.

This charismatic cabal of wayward young souls – gathered together for safety on the quietest night of the week, hidden away in a deserted part of town, dancing only after dark – discovered talents they never knew they had and pushed down walls with their collective will and individual elan. And they sure had fun along the way. *We* had fun along the way. The Blitz was a blast.

1
BEFORE THE FUTURE

t was a bad time to be a dead body, but a terrific time to be a teenager. That benighted winter, when 1978 morphed angrily into 1979 – the infamous winter of our supposed discontent – was played out against a festering backdrop of decomposing rubbish in the streets and cadavers in the morgue. Strikes and pickets, militants and marches, power cuts and shortages: a perfect time for taking liberties. What I really remember was the sweetly sulphurous stench of putrefaction wafting through the near-deserted night-time alleyways of our dimly lit West End playground. The noxious streets were ours, and oh what japes we had. Life was in grainy black and white, but we were in glorious technicolour.

On Tuesdays, we tried to waft too, attempting to be sylph-like in our movement and elegant in our comportment as we sashayed through Soho, down the Charing Cross Road, into Old Compton Street, with its mounds of mouldering restaurant detritus, shimmying past the shivering women working the corner. Decked out in our outrageous do-it-yourself finery, we were homemade macaronis, travelling in small groups for safety, parading on our litter-strewn catwalk, headed for a grotty basement with a disco ball and a Bowie tune or two. Headed for the glittering future.

It all began in Billy's, an old-time, low-life Soho dive on the corner of Dean and Meard Streets. Back in the 1930s, this had been the glamorous Gargoyle Club, home to elegant soirées featuring Noël Coward and Tallulah Bankhead, but now it was a dank basement beneath a grubby brothel called the Golden Girl, owned by a large, menacing character named Vince, who wore a fedora hat and a fistful of rings. This whole adventure started for me when Steve Strange, in his high-pitched, studiously camp Welsh voice, invited me to the very first 'Bowie night' he was hosting there, with his mate Rusty Egan – the ebullient, flame-haired Rich Kids drummer from Kilburn playing the tunes.

The timing was perfect, a void was about to be filled. Little had happened in London since the punk pyrotechnic display had turned into a damp squib. Punk was a conflagration which raged with a furious luminescence, lighting up the sky, enabling us all to see new possibilities and propelling stars into the firmament. But within a year or so, it was all but burnt out. By 1978, it had faded to grey.

Many of us were bitterly disappointed by punk's rapid decline into mainstream culture and caricature. We'd believed in punk, invested in it and ultimately been let down by it. Sporting a mohican and begging for drug money on the King's Road was not my idea of a well-misspent youth.

After the exhilarating brouhaha of the Pistols and the Clash in their carefully staged and highly fashionable pomp, it was hard to get excited about bland new-wave bands or the lumpen ugliness of Oi! music and its knuckle-dragging Nazi followers. Alternatively, there were Gang of Four and the Fall and all the other militantly monotone post-punk groups, with their dour sound and grim indie image. Dreary was in, and I didn't do dreary, so when Steve proffered me a flyer for the opening of his club, an evening with some strutting clothes horses seemed worth a punt.

Steve Strange was the shop girl in PX, a radical new boutique that had recently opened in James Street in the Eliza Doolittle-less streets of Covent Garden. So quiet was that particular quarter in 1978 – its market long gone, its warehouses empty – that Covent Garden station closed at weekends due to lack of use. I'd been there to the Roxy, the seminal punk club in Neal Street. And I knew the area well because I was studying just round the corner at the LSE, where I was a bolshy politics student reading Gramsci and barracking visiting Tory politicians.

But I was also a hardened veteran of the style wars, a dedicated follower of street fashion, a dandy dilettante, having adopted just about every passing trouser tribe, from original skinhead through suedehead and soul boy to punk. From the age of ten – when I had first gone to Italian Tony for a number-one crop with a razor parting, and bought a Ben Sherman shirt, a pair of red braces and a Laurel Aitken ska single from Shepherd's Bush Market – I had defined myself by the threads I wore and the music I swore by. That's what we did.

So I was already a seasoned browser of overpriced boutiques on the day I walked into PX in 1978. It was the second time that pushing open the door of a clothes shop radically changed my life. The first was plucking up the courage to enter Malcolm McLaren and Vivienne Westwood's daunting emporia, Sex, on the King's Road in 1976. I hid in the phone box next door for ages before finally going in and joining this still relatively new, rebel-rebel, high-fashion cult.

Opting to man (or should that be 'boy'? I was only seventeen) the punk barricades had put me on a collision course with straight, deeply conservative, horribly judgemental 1970s mores. When I pierced my ears and dyed my hair, my mum took a bit of convincing and consoling. Now, two years later, with punk all but over, this new shop in Covent Garden appeared. It specialised in a kind of glam retro-futurism, a nostalgia for the new, designed by Helen Robinson, an old Chelsea face from Acme Attractions. I was about to enter a wild new Narnia.

I ventured into PX more out of curiosity than desire, believing that my dandy days were probably over. I was nineteen now and perhaps past it, ready to bow out of the teen caper. But I found myself investing some of my student grant in a dashing, royal-blue, rib-hugging, shoulder-padded top with a diagonal silver sash, which Steve Strange, who sold it to me, described as 'space Cossack style'. The PX silhouette was a pair of triangles, big wide shoulders with tight waist, voluminously pleated leather trousers, but narrowing to drainpipe bottoms. And Steve had it down to a tee.

He was wearing a sort of 'Thunderbirds are go-go' suit in pale blue, with a matching forage cap at a jaunty angle, a gaudy diamante brooch on his breast and eye make-up to match. As I was about to leave the shop with my new top, he handed me that fateful Xeroxed flyer. Steve told me it was going to be heroic; he wasn't wrong.

That Tuesday night, there were maybe forty or fifty people in this little once-whitewashed warren of damp subterranean rooms, the largest of which housed a rudimentary dancefloor, a bar and a sound system, and featured a rotating glitter ball so corny as to be ironically cool, even then. The winter of our disco-tent. But this weren't no normal disco. Those fifty or so people, sharing one toilet with a door that didn't lock and water which rarely ran, would go on to be the core of the Blitz club and its now-famous New Romantics. But on that first Tuesday night, we were just a bunch of wilfully overdressed kids in a dingy Soho basement looking for the next wave to ride.

Kraftwerk were playing as I first descended the stairs, past the till where Steve sat surveying the scene and taking the money, into this heavenly Hades. The sound was Teutonic and electronic, a motorik rhythm, pulsing round the room, insistent and robotic. The vocals cold and distant, the feel fiercely modern and yet somehow redolent of a sepia demi-monde of Sally Bowles and Tamara de Lempicka, with a touch of swinging London and Andy Warhol's Factory thrown in. In the murky corner, two boys, dressed as extras from some lost Jean Genet play, were performing a slow jive to this fast music, while a girl I knew from my council estate was wrapped around a bottle-blonde beauty in fishnet tights and little else. A massive smile spread across my face.

My companions were Graham Smith, Chris Sullivan and Melissa Caplan. Graham was my best friend from Orange Hill Grammar School, who was now an art student at Chelsea. Chris, a tough and brilliant Merthyr Tydfil-born mate of Steve Strange's, was studying fashion round the corner from Billy's at St Martin's and staying in my mum's spare bedroom on the Watling Estate in Burnt Oak. And, to this day, Melissa Caplan is just about the most fearless woman I've ever met, a Jewish north London individualist with a style so striking she was the most radically dressed fashion student of them all.

Graham was sporting a kind of neo-beat-boom look, all quiff, skinny tie, drainpipes and winklepicker shoes, the camera he carried everywhere around his neck. Chris was wearing fine 40s-style clobber, while Melissa had on her own fantastic monotone Bridget Riley-inspired creation, her hair in a crimson spike and a chain from her nose to her ear. I favoured my new PX top and a pair of voluminous baby-blue peg trousers, paired with kung fu slippers purchased from a supermarket in Chinatown, and with my barnet in an exaggerated, asymmetric wedge blocking out one eye. We looked a sight.

Through my other eye, I saw an even more flamboyant trio descend the stairs arm in arm as the music flowed into Bryan Ferry's

'Let's Stick Together'. In the middle was a man who looked ten years older than everybody else in the room: a theatrical Quentin Crisp tribute act wearing a wedding dress and a policeman's helmet, he stood out even in this extraordinary milieu. He was flanked by two scandalously skinny young boys: one in full Vivienne Westwood tartan bondage with his dark hair teased into huge stalagmite peaks, the other, no older than fourteen or fifteen at the most, in what appeared to be his school uniform, but topped with a battered stovepipe hat. They were Philip Sallon, George O'Dowd and Jeremy Healy. They were very Billy's. We were home.

I think I believed that this was it, that this was my future. The realisation was immediate and the memory intense. That night nearly half a century ago is still incredibly vivid in my mind because it felt instantly important, like we had wandered through a portal to a different, much more thrilling world full of possibilities. It was daring and decadent, but also sweetly DIY, more dressing-up box than haute couture. You had to decide almost on the spot if you really wanted to be part of this scene as it was clearly going to be a full-time job looking this preposterous. I also knew it was going to be dangerous.

London in 1978 was not an easy place to be noticeably different. Homophobic, bigoted, sexist, small-minded, racist, randomly violent, tribal, territorial, tough. The National Front stalked the streets and their neanderthal gangs were always looking for an excuse for a fight. The masses took umbrage at anything fancy. Most nights out ended up in a drunken punch-up of some kind, usually a performative rumble in the streets with lots of shouting and arm swinging and little harm done, but you had to be constantly aware. Trouble was everywhere.

I'd already been in plenty of scrapes. Being chased up the King's Road by irate Teddy boys with your legs tied together in bondage trousers was one thing, and receiving a hefty wallop from a sturdy steelworker at a QPR away game at Sheffield United for 'looking like a poof' was par for the course, but when I was spat at by an old lady at a bus stop for wearing eyeliner and a kilt, that was altogether more unsettling. This Billy's business, with its full on 'look at me' exhibitionist aesthetic, was bound to be grief, but it took me all of two beats to make my mind up. 'The Chase', Giorgio Moroder's pulsating, cinematic anthem, came on the sound system and I sucked in my cheeks and stepped forward to dance. The adventure had begun.

Billy's was a thrilling jolt of glamour in a glum time, an electro shock to the teenage system. It was new and now and not for the faint-hearted. It was the start of something very big, in a very small club, but it was not entirely without precedent. Nothing comes from nowhere. All roads lead back to Bowie.

Punk is perhaps the most dissected and least understood youthquake of them all. It has been portrayed – largely by male, middle-class rock writers who weren't there – as some sort of grungy, guttersnipe, back-to-basics rock'n'roll rebellion. Never mind that bollocks. Punk, at least in its earliest, most compelling incarnation, was a sartorial uprising, led by a swanky gathering of art students, hairdressers, fashionistas and wayward soul boys and soul girls high on Bowie. It was based around Westwood's incredibly expensive designer boutique in Chelsea, and its earliest gigs took place in art schools. It has also been taken for granted that 70s punk and the New Romantic scene which superseded it in the 80s were polar opposites, two ends of the teen cult spectrum. New Romantic was actually Punk Part Two.

Before punk, there had been the southern soul scene, where legendary clubs like Crackers, Global Village and Buzbys in London's not particularly glittering West End were full of hip kids in flash threads throwing dramatic shapes to imported American funk and jazz tunes. Young, working-class, black and white, male and female, the soul scene, unlike just about everywhere else at the time, was non-discriminatory and non-violent. If you could dance, if you could dress, you were in, and the tastiest, most up-to-the-minute kiddies, whatever their background or orientation, became famous faces on the scene, admired and emulated.

And the 'faces' – the most revered stylists – pushed things further and further out. In London, in the jazz funk clubs of the mid-70s, sartorial styles would change weekly, so it was vital to have the most up-to-date duds, as well as the latest obscure, imported tunes. Soho was the place to go to buy records, while the King's Road had the clothes shops. It became a ritual to pose and parade there on a Saturday afternoon, decked out in your most extravagant finery for all to ogle, a fabulous weekly display of teen peacockery.

It was also a soul scene thing to have the best, hippest nights, with the top DJs and the tastiest dancers, during the week, never on a Saturday night, which was far too febrile. Mondays at The Lyceum, Tuesdays at Global Village and the legendary Friday lunchtime session at Crackers meant you avoided the punch-drunk masses and the out-of-order out-of-towners.

The atmosphere in those funk clubs was ferociously competitive. The noted hoofers would try to blast each other off the dancefloor, while the style warriors would be sure to be seen in their latest creations, often personalised with a pin, a rip or a tear. And in among these soul city slickers was a subset of the most extravagantly dressed, whose primary allegiance was to our David from Bromley.

From 'Starman' onwards, Bowie's voice had been a kind of clarion – he was the prettiest pied piper, around whom the most daring and creative had gathered. His message was always to become who you want to be, then become someone else, in a process of perpetual reinvention. His sound, style and sexuality fluid and malleable, he was the supreme shapeshifter and every beautiful mutation led to a host of camp followers. By 1975, Bowie had transmogrified into a stick-thin soul balladeer making crystalline, cocaine-high dance records which fitted perfectly into the West End soul scene of the time.

So when Bowie's brittle 'Golden Years' or lush 'Young Americans' came on the sound system, the coolest kiddies slunk onto the dancefloor and performed. Boys and girls, the lines between them blurred, hair dyed postbox red or gunmetal blue, PVC and rubber, plastic sandals, peep-hole bras and piercings, 20s and 50s styling, a retro-modern melange. Some soul clubs actually had what was called a 'Bowie Room', where the more rarefied tastes of this soul subset were specifically catered for, with a constant round of Bowie, Roxy, Lou Reed and other assorted arty anthems mixed in with the funk.

It was the denizens of these Bowie Rooms, the outré outsiders, who made up the original punk in-crowd as they coalesced on the King's Road around Vivienne Westwood's designer shop or Don Letts' Acme Attractions. It is no coincidence that they were called the Bromley contingent. It is no coincidence that that first night at Billy's was described as a Bowie night.

This chic, ferociously cool, innately elitist group – Siouxsie Sioux, Steve Severin, Billy Idol, Jordan and Adam Ant, Catwoman, Little

Debbie, Berlin and a certain Philip Sallon, all of them noted, night-clubbing Bowie acolytes – went on to form bands and open shops, providing the initial impetus for the punk bandwagon. There was a slightly younger generation of us standing at the back of those early punk gigs, the sixteen- and seventeen-year-olds pogoing in the shadows and waiting for our turn in the limelight.

Once punk had gone mainstream and become seriously dull, the junior hipsters walked away, thinking they had missed the speed-boat. They were the people – we were the people – still almost all under twenty-one, primed by punk but also bored by it, who turned up at Billy's on a Tuesday night. It was the second-generation safety-pin kids.

Steve Strange had started his own briefly infamous punk band called the Moors Murderers when he was just seventeen. Rusty Egan was a teenage drummer who played with former Sex Pistol Glen Matlock in the Rich Kids. Gary Kemp and his manager mate Steve Dagger had seen the Sex Pistols at their local cinema The Screen on the Green in Islington and been inspired to start their own group. Midge Ure had been asked to join the Pistols by Malcolm McLaren. Siobhan Fahey, who formed Bananarama, had lived in the Pistols' rehearsal rooms on Denmark Street. I personally had been a Clash-obsessed seventeen-year-old, who had only recently hidden his white socks and his Lonnie Liston Smith albums to go hitching round the country in a Lewis Leathers biker jacket following the White Riot tour. We were all punks.

The life-changing catechism of punk was 'you can do it', which suggested, just like Bowie had done, that whatever your background or your education, wherever you came from, whoever you were, you could be whoever you wanted. It was the three-chord trick:

learn three chords and start a band, start a fanzine, a record label, a shop; become an artist, a designer, a director, an actor, a manager, a star. The Sex Pistols famously sang 'No Future', but ironically by doing so they created a potential future, a path to follow, for an entire generation of young people who grasped the liberating, you-can-do-it message of punk and ran with it. Punk turned us from consumers to potential creators. That's where Billy's, and subsequently the Blitz, came from.

The other revelation of punk was the fact that those up on stage were just spotty oiks like everyone else. Pre-punk, we had been sold the idea of the rock god and the guitar hero on a celestial pedestal, led to believe that those idols on *Top of the Pops* were somehow different to us – unattainable stars and distant celebrities. But Malcolm McLaren intentionally pulled back the curtain on fame, revealing and celebrating the ordinariness of those involved.

Following the Clash around, I had got to know them a little, been invited backstage or onto the smelly tour bus, and realised these were just eager young men a little older than but a lot like me. Mick Jones grew up in the council flats near my nan and supported the same football team as me. Strummer was an extraordinary Joe up on stage, but a proudly down-to-earth bloke living in a squat the rest of the time. Paul Simonon was great-looking, a star, but also a Ladbroke Grove lad. The Clash were us. What they did seemed perfectly possible. That was to be an invaluable lesson.

The Thin White Duke returned to London in the summer of 1978. David Bowie, in his coke-ravaged, ice-cold-from-Berlin persona, played at Earl's Court just a couple of months before Billy's started, and was a direct catalyst. I went with Graham Smith and Melissa and hated being in such a massive old hangar of a venue, so far away from the Starman. But I loved seeing Bowie. He looked fabulous in a billowing white shirt, leather trousers and matelot cap, and performed his whole "Heroes" schtick with aplomb. He was messianic.

I actually recall very little of the gig, mesmerised perhaps by his presence, and alienated by his distance, but I distinctly remember being really excited by the crowd. There were lots of little clusters of glamorous, splendidly attired teenagers who looked like us, many of them faces I recognised from funk and punk clubs. It felt like something was in the air; it was a gathering of the tribes and a portent of things to come. It felt like Bowie had come back to point the way, yet again. Steve Strange was there that night, seeing all those Bowie boys and girls gathered to pay homage to the main man. Billy's, and later the Blitz, was born in the presence and forged in the image of the great shaman, a new generation of shapeshifters about to be unleashed.

2

SOHO

NIGHTS

Just like fungus, youth culture thrives in dark, dank places, away from the blinding light of the public's gaze. Billy's – buried down an alley, secreted away on a Tuesday night beneath Soho's near-empty nocturnal streets, known only to a tiny, self-selected few –was the perfect spot for the spores of a new scene to germinate.

Central London in 1978 was far from the teeming, gleaming metropolis we know now, closer in time and feel to the Second World War than to today. There had been a brief West End revival when the 60s kicked in and Carnaby Street catapulted to fame on the back of a few groovy boutiques, but by the time I first started heading into town from my family council house on the far reaches of the Northern Line, it was monochrome, sombre and quiet. London had stopped swinging some time around 1969 and spent a decade in the dark, getting gloomier, emptier and sometimes scarier. It was a dysfunctional place with packs of feral youth prowling the night.

Urban theory in the UK at the time was based on American models of a suburban, car-owning city, where life was lived out in the verdant 'burbs and happy citizens whizzed around on freeways. The centre, which had taken a severe bashing in the war, was seen as antiquated, dirty and dated, so had been wilfully neglected, hollowed out and encouraged to decline. Much of it was marked for demolition.

Between the end of the war and the late 1970s, inner London had lost half its population, as people were displaced in a conscious attempt at slum clearance and town planning. And what the Luftwaffe hadn't destroyed, the Greater London Council tried to knock down. Families like mine were exiled from the supposed slums of Notting Hill and Islington, Paddington and King's Cross, to outlying estates in the leafy fringes, a mass working-class diaspora.

That explains why so many of the kids who gathered at the Blitz were from the outer suburbs, from Burnt Oak and Bromley, Ealing and Croydon, Ilford and Romford, or even Canvey and Clacton, a generation of Londoners exiled from their ancestral homelands but eager to get back to the centre of town. Soho was like a siren call to me. I'd grown up with the idea that the West End was where you went to be part of the scene, your stage for coming of age. Uptown was your birthright. My two elder brothers had bought their threads on Carnaby Street and worn their tonic suits and wing-tip brogues to watch Georgie Fame at the Flamingo jazz club. I expected nothing less and wanted my London to swing.

That was one of the main reasons why I chose to study at the LSE: it was in central London, which I saw as the centre of the universe. That was why I went all the way to Berwick Street and Hanway Place to buy records; they sounded better from there. That was why Soho was so perfect for Billy's; it was our fabled lost Shangri-La. So we sat on buses or Tube trains, did that long, sometimes risky schlep into town from the suburbs, exposed to the eyes of scornful others in all our extravagance, en route to the promised land. But, in 1978, there wasn't much there.

Soho had been London's cosmopolitan and bohemian enclave in the 50s and 60s, a notorious, shabbily glamorous haunt of artists, actors, poets and gangsters, as well as dancing girls and fancy boys. But by the time I first started seeking out the enticing 'old Soho' the Kinks sang about in 'Lola', it was much shabbier and considerably less glamorous. There were still a few famous gin-soaked artists and thespians, but these ageing bohos were confined to a handful of sweaty old pubs, bilious after-hours drinking clubs and a couple of moth-eaten restaurants.

In the 1970s, the area was so dominated by the sex trade that it was seedy and uninviting, peopled almost exclusively by men in dirty macs in search of dirty books and 'dirty' women, an almost hermetically sealed enclave of red lights and blue films. Pubs still shut in the middle of the day and at 10.30 at night. Clubs were mainly pick-up joints. Working girls still walked the streets. Piccadilly Circus was a notorious spot for male prostitution as wan young urchins lined up 'on the Dilly' waiting for clients, while Charing Cross Road was where the sad street junkies stood, anxiously fidgeting outside the toilets of Tottenham Court Road station, waiting for a fix. I loved it.

London, like New York City at the time, was edgy and dodgy, down on its luck and all but falling down. Corrugated iron was wrapped around abandoned buildings and whole crumbling blocks had been left to collapse, but it was also ripe with possibilities. Today, central London is swish and sophisticated, maxed out by developers, like a colouring book where every page has been filled, leaving no space for creativity. But back in the 1970s, whole areas were unused or underused, empty and dilapidated, just waiting.

Covent Garden was yet to find a function after the fruit and flower market closed in 1974, its grand piazza and maze of surrounding streets eerily tranquil. The whole historic and charismatic area was due to be razed to the ground in an extraordinary act of civic vandalism proposed by the GLC, flattening it all in favour of an elevated motorway and vast car park, until it was saved after a campaign led by its remaining, staunchly working-class residents. Paul Smith opened his first boutique in Floral Street in 1979, heralding a revival which eventually changed the area into a tourist magnet and Sir Paul into a fashion magnate. But that was still a good few years away. In 1978, PX, where Steve Strange worked, was pretty much on its own in a ghost town.

King's Cross, meanwhile, comprised rows and rows of old tenement squats and empty train sheds, plus grimy yards for storing coal and potatoes. Hoxton and Shoreditch, now so clamorous and fashionable, were literally wastelands, silent shells of warehouses and old factories, with bombsites, known colloquially as debris, everywhere. In 1979, Willie Brown – a denizen of Billy's and the man who designed Spandau Ballet's kilts and Russian constructivist suits – opened his first shop, Modern Classics, which was then the only business on the now-buzzing Rivington Street, EC2.

Soho, which smelt of semen and disinfectant from the numerous peep shows, strip clubs, brothels and clip joints, had scores of empty basements and garrets, many of which had late-night licences. The famed old discos like the Scene, the Whisky A' Go Go, Le Kilt and Le Discotheque, which had boomed when the 60s were swinging and the mods were dancing, were still there but struggling to find anyone to cut their beer-stained rugs. So when Steve Strange and Rusty Egan, friends and flatmates from their punk days, decided to put on a 'Bowie Night', Soho was the obvious choice. But it was not an obvious thing to do.

The idea that young promoters – Steve was just nineteen, Rusty was twenty – would take over a club for one night, invite their own crowd, play their own music and make their own money was, as far as I know, completely unheard of. They invented it. That kind of nocturnal entrepreneurialism became one of the tropes of the 1980s, when London exploded with specialist one-night clubs of every hue and cry, but it felt truly revolutionary when Steve Strange first did it.

Andy Czezowski, later of the Fridge in Brixton, had taken over Chaguaramas, a gay haunt in an old fruit-and-veg warehouse on the edge of Covent Garden, to turn it into the Roxy, London's premier punk club, but he had bought the lease and actually ran it as a seven-days-a-week venture. Steve Strange and Rusty Egan had a very different business plan, which wasn't really about business and didn't involve much of a plan.

They started the club to make enough to pay the rent on the flat they shared. Rusty had lost his job when the Rich Kids split up, and he was far from rich. But beyond that basic requirement, they were not originally motivated by money. Later, they went on to make rather a lot of it from Club for Heroes and Camden Palace, but at Billy's they charged 50p entry, which even then was not very much, the same as it cost to get there on the bus. If you didn't have the money one week, Steve would just wave you in.

Nor were they intending to create youth culture history. There was no grandiose scheme of any kind, more a desire to have a sanctuary for the odd and the excluded, somewhere safe and exciting for people like them to go. Rusty had a carrier bag full of records by Bowie and Iggy, but also some of the new synthesiser stuff coming out of Japan and Germany, while Steve had a photocopied flyer, high hair, a big mouth and a wide group of weird friends. They were both selectors, Rusty picking the tunes, Steve curating the crowd. Their brilliance was in recognising that there were enough people like them to start a club, and then a movement.

So they convinced Vince, the scary owner of Billy's, that they could fill his place on a Tuesday night: they would keep the door money, he'd take the earnings from the bar. Billy's was perfect because it was small and obscure, a place where their little group of bizarre-looking buddies could safely gather; Tuesday was perfect because it was traditionally the quietest night of the week, so the club would otherwise be empty. Importantly, so would central London, free from the gangs of marauding geezers who roamed the tenderloin on Fridays and Saturdays, which meant that this growing collection of extravagantly attired souls congregating from all corners of town could feel relatively safe getting there too.

And I got there every week. After that first eye-opening, life-changing night down in Steve and Rusty's mesmeric underworld, I became a regular Tuesday adventurer. There really was nowhere like it for both music and atmosphere, and that one night in Billy's with the in-crowd became the focus of my week. It was thrilling to feel like you were part of this tiny, unknown underground sect. We were on the inside with the outsiders and we felt special. Me and my little group got a proper ego boost from having been there from the very start: we were Billy's originals.

But no one yet talked about this being a scene or a movement. There was no buzz about it, no interest from outside, no press photographers or reporters, no prying eyes. We were just a few overdressed renegades huddling together in a basement, dancing to some strange futuristic music and using the past as a dressing-up box.

The crowd at Billy's was as yet unformed, and certainly not uniform. There was still a punky rock'n'roll tinge to some, slick soul-boy clobber on others, Hollywood glamour for the girls, some toy-soldier militaria, some gay-icon gear, fetish wear, a touch of retro-nostalgia. The only unifying factor was you didn't look like the lumpen masses out there. You had to make an effort, and I was soon raiding my mum's jewellery box for baubles and bangles, and trying on berets, bandanas and Sam Brown belts from army surplus stores. Anything to look different.

There was an inevitable split personality in being a student at a serious university during the day and then heading off into Soho at night dressed like Frank Sinatra or a gay Hussar. But then I'd been used to getting disapproving stares with every youth culture uniform I had donned over the years. It proved you were doing something right. Truth be told, vain and self-centred young soul that I was, I enjoyed the knowledge that people were staring at me as I went by; better to be looked over and all that.

It was great fun to watch the faces of all the censorious old LSE Trotskyist hippies, still in their flares and Dr Martens, as I wandered into a comparative political structures lecture dressed to the nines, ready to impress Steve Strange on the door later that evening. My mum's council house was too far away to go home and change to go out at night, so I went to college in my full garb and soon it became my everyday attire.

It was good to find out that I had a few confederates on campus. Graham Ball was already a firm friend and a fellow nocturnal traveller, a west London soul boy turned punk who also happened to be a brilliant social science and administration student. We'd first had words in the LSE library because he had the same Acme Attractions mohair jumper as me and I said we needed to work out a rota as we couldn't possibly both wear it at the same time. Being a natural proselytiser, I also told him about this great new Bowie night in Soho, and Graham was soon on the Billy's team. Naomi Gryn – now a noted writer and film-maker, but then a cool rabbi's daughter studying philosophy of science – would sometimes join us too and let us crash at her parents' West End pad.

One of the biggest misconceptions about the small crowd who gathered at Billy's and then moved on to the Blitz is that they were aloof and stand-offish, preening poseurs too arch and arty for any socialising. That could not be more wrong. These were indeed cool characters, but the atmosphere was anything but frosty. It was garrulous, scurrilous and gregarious, often hilarious, bursting with energy, a form of release perhaps for alienated souls who had finally found their tribe. Despite being full of some of the most self-aware and self-obsessed young people on the planet – ego was never in short supply – Billy's was wildly sociable, relentlessly hedonistic. It was electric with gossip, flirtation and desire; it was rollicking fun. If you had made it past Steve and descended those steps, you were in, and we were all in it together.

There were George and Jeremy, of course, and Julia, a colleague of Steve's at PX with a mountainous beehive, deadpan estuary accent and cackling laugh; Andy Polaris, a beautiful dual-heritage waif in an oversized demob suit who had the silkiest dance moves; Peter, who would morph into Marilyn, a peroxide motormouth spewing hilarious invective; Martin Degville, who looked like he came from outer space but sounded like Solihull; David Claridge, assistant DJ who would later become Roland Rat; Stephen Linard, the stick-thin fashion goddess from Canvey Island; Stephen Jones, the posh one with the hats; Michele with the shaved head; Siobhan with the hair; Jo Hargreaves, whose dad was on the telly; Stevie Stewart, Melissa's diminutive mate from St Martin's in stilettoes; Fiona Dealey, the statuesque fashion student; Ollie and Jimmy O'Donnell, the barbershop brothers; Simon Withers and Jo Strettell, a glamorous art-school couple; Midge Ure and Billy Idol, our own resident punky pop stars . . .

At this stage, Steve Strange did not have to work too hard on the door keeping people out. Apart from the occasional drunk who had wandered down the wrong alley, there were no clamouring crowds desperately trying to get down those stairs. Billy's was just a few weeks old and Steve was still trying to attract a big enough crowd to fill the place, but it was growing slightly busier week by week. It was solely word of mouth, so invariably the newcomers were friends of friends. A sort of in-the-know network developed as everybody there knew somebody else, and soon everybody got to know everybody. But there were still no more than maybe seventy or eighty of us; the venue couldn't hold much more than that.

At some point, I was introduced to Steve Dagger, another wedge-head London veteran of the punk campaign, who lived in his parents' council flat in Holborn, round the corner from the LSE, where he had just managed to wangle a place. It was not in college or in Billy's that we met, but at Rumours, a soul-boy cocktail bar in Covent Garden that served vivid pink drinks with umbrellas, which were briefly all the rage in 1978. He was a Spurs fan, I'm QPR and I think we originally bonded over football; it took us a while to realise that we were actually at the same university. Steve was also a student of pop culture and he would regale us with tales of freewheeling 60s rock impresarios Pete Meaden and Andrew Loog Oldham. All very prescient.

I saw Steve again a couple of weeks later, this time at Billy's, where he had come with his best mate from school, a guy called Gary. If I remember correctly, Gary was working on the print in Fleet Street at the time, a voluble Islington lad exactly the same age as me, with an accent and enthusiasm remarkably similar to my own. When I first met him, Gary Kemp was a prime, primary-colours soul boy with a curly quiff and a pair of bright crimson pegs, and we hit it off immediately. We were forming a clique.

The half a dozen or so of us guys and girls in my little group at Billy's, who would meet up to plan our outfits together, travel together, walk in together, were all straight – as in heterosexual – although nobody ever bothered to ask or tell. Clearly there were also groups of young gay or bisexual boys and girls, youths of every sexual persuasion. In Billy's, you could dance and snog with whoever you wanted, it didn't matter. Nobody cared. That was one of the most important things about the place: nobody gave a damn.

Because of the flamboyance of the crowd, Billy's (and later the Blitz) was often portrayed as a gay club, but it wasn't, any more than it was a straight club; it was truly, effortlessly epicene. And that was absolutely revolutionary. We'd all been to gay clubs and bars – there were plenty of them in London and they often had the best music and provided a safe haven for those whose style of dress would potentially provoke trouble in straight discos. I'd been to Chaguaramas and The Sombrero in Kensington, sat with the fashion punks at Louise's lesbian bar in Poland Street, and felt completely comfortable in such a milieu. But most people didn't.

There was a fairly strict apartheid between gay clubs – which would tolerate a few tolerant straight interlopers, but were aimed exclusively at a queer audience – and the straight-ahead, blokes-birds-and-beer discos where any signs of differentness would be dangerous. If two men or women were to dance together at a straight club, all hell would break loose. Billy's was not like that.

Perhaps it was because Steve Strange was gay and his business partner Rusty Egan was straight that the energy of the clubs they created and curated together was uniquely neither, or both, or it didn't matter. I would guess there was a roughly 60/40, maybe even 70/30 straight-to-gay split in terms of sexual orientation, although quite a few of the crowd were happy to try out various options and see what they enjoyed. Bisexual was not a word I ever heard, but there was a lot of it about. You could be whatever you wanted, and be with whoever you wanted that night, and then be something or someone else next week and nobody batted a painted eyelid. Nobody asked, nobody made an issue of it. We were perhaps the first generation of British teenagers in recent times to take multiple sexualities and possibilities, the idea of gender fluidity and a sexuality spectrum, as perfectly normal.

All of that is probably in retrospect. I cannot remember really thinking much about the sexuality of the people around me on a Tuesday night, except perhaps for a slightly gauche suburban schoolboy thrill at the apparent decadence of it all. I knew my friends and family back in Burnt Oak would be shocked if they walked into Billy's, which of course made it all the more seductive and compelling. It was like watching Bowie performing 'Starman' on *Top of the Pops* with his arm draped lasciviously around Mick Ronson and being part of it. Billy's was the Bowie night extraordinaire, the best disco in town. And then, just as suddenly as it had appeared, it stopped.

3

PARTY
PARTY

Nobody knows precisely when Billy's started and stopped, or how long it ran for. Steve Strange is dead, so I can't ask him – though I very much doubt he would have had the answer. Rusty, who can reel off playlists from forty years ago and instantly tell you the bpm of any record he ever put on a deck, just shrugged his shoulders and shook his head when I enquired of him. Nobody had phones to snap away and freeze-frame and date the action, of course, and although Graham Smith took a few black-and-white pictures that he developed in his mum's bathroom, there is no real record of what might have been the most important club of its era.

I never kept any sort of diary or aide-memoire, and nor, it seems, did anybody else. We were too busy living it to bother noting any-thing down. Besides, nobody at the time thought any of this was particularly noteworthy. Even the know-it-all internet has no idea. But I reckon Billy's was open for maybe three or four months in the autumn and winter of 1978.

By the end, it was rammed and word was certainly out; the crowd expanded exponentially to fill the space. Sweat would run down the walls, mascara would run down faces, and I recall some of the early adopters moaning a little that it had all got too big. But while it lasted, it was undeniably exciting to feel that we were part of the new big thing.

Bowie nights at Billy's came to an abrupt end because Vince in his fedora got greedy and decided to put up the price of drinks, which Steve and Rusty resisted because they knew their punters – students, apprentices, dole-claimers – were all basically skint and would not, could not, pay any more. We were deep in a recession, unemployment was at record levels and money was way too tight.

They were also fed up with Vince bringing down his bruiser mates, assorted Soho pimps and gangsters in camel coats, to gawp and ogle at the gathered weirdos, especially the girls in fetish gear. An argument ensued and, realising it was not a good idea to argue with Vince and his knuckles full of rings, the shop assistant and the ex-drummer walked away. And that might well have been that, a minor Soho footnote and a few disparate young clothes horses trotting off into the night.

What is obviously indisputable is that if it had all ended there and then, I would not be writing this book, as there would have been no Blitz club to chronicle. But I am also pretty certain that if it had all come to a halt after a few fabulous months at Billy's, I would probably not be a writer or broadcaster at all, that my life, and the lives of scores of people, would have been very different.

Steve went back to PX and Rusty went to Düsseldorf. Word was out that Vince was not best pleased and might be plotting revenge, so the young drummer considered it politic to jump on a plane and go seek out his synth heroes Kraftwerk. Apparently, he looked them up in the phone book and there they were. Quite what the famously taciturn Ralf and Florian made of this brash young Londoner, who talked as fast as a Donna Summer disco record, turning up at their studio, I have no idea, but I know he returned with a whole load of new synthesiser records and a plan to play them in a new venue.

There was something like a couple of months in early 1979 between the closure of Billy's and the opening of the Blitz, but it was not altogether without jollity. Although there were no Tuesday night gatherings to attend, this new tribe had found a way to gather. It was all about house – and I don't mean house music, I mean parties in people's houses, often unsuspecting people.

By now, it was a full-time business being part of this crowd and we would hang out almost exclusively with each other, always attired accordingly wherever we could. You could not be part of this scene by dressing up one night a week as if off to a fancy-dress do; it required complete commitment. Believe me, the likes of George, Marilyn and Steve Strange could spot a day-tripper a mile away and would tell them so in no uncertain terms. You were either part of it 24/7 or out of it. So we went all in and we all went out.

But it was hard to find safe spaces in a still randomly violent city. Because of the presence of myself, Graham Ball and Steve Dagger, The Three Tuns – the scruffy student bar at the LSE – became an unlikely but useful place to congregate. It was in central London, had subsidised beer and was safe. Despite the sneers of the Trots, and the handful of old fogey Young Tories with their new hero Margaret Thatcher, nobody was going to get aggressive with a load of ludicrously dressed art students and hairdressers.

There were also the Ralph West Halls of Residence in Battersea, where many of the St Martin's and Chelsea students lived, which provided a safe haven. The Covent Garden cocktail bar Rumours, with the slick soul boys, was OK. It had good music and we had our own little clique in the corner by the door, but we could never afford a Singapore sling. There was a bar in a hotel in Holborn which we descended upon, because Simon Withers liked the art deco styling and thought it somehow suited our clobber. Any glass of port in a storm.

Organising all this was very different back then. Obviously, there was no internet, no social media, no mobile phones – but there *was* Chris Sullivan. Nobody could work a payphone like the young Sullivan. Chris is an absolutely central figure in this whole story, indeed probably the main man in terms of London nightlife in the 1980s when he fronted Blue Rondo à la Turk and ran the now-legendary Wag Club in Wardour Street. He and Steve Strange were both young Welsh lads, part of a tough contingent of valley boys and girls who had been coming to London to go clubbing and shopping from the early funk and punk days. They were mates from way back, despite the fact that they were still teenagers.

Chris was a brilliant dancer and an arch dresser, who faced down the wrath of irate Presbyterians to see the Sex Pistols in Caerphilly in December 1976 aged sixteen. He was also a fine artist and secured a place at St Martin's, opting to do fashion rather than fine art, because it offered more of an opportunity to meet girls. I think we first met on the King's Road, parading in our pegs and plastic sandals – neither of us can quite remember – but soon after he moved to London and into the spare room in my mum's council house in Burnt Oak, arriving with a dozen bin bags full of assorted clobber from puttees to tuxedoes, jodhpurs to titfers. Burnt Oak had never quite seen the like.

The Watling Estate, one of the largest in London – full of rumbustious, mainly second-generation Irish families, slum-cleared from rundown inner London – was a rough, exuberant and wonderful place to grow up. It was notorious for the Burnt Oak boot boys, a large gang of first-generation skins who would take on all-comers in their Crombies, tonics and brogues, which I took to wearing as a ten-year-old in 1969. That's where the whole schmutter thing started for me.

As the youngest of three brothers, I was down by law, especially as Reggie and Barry were considered a bit tasty, which meant I could dress up and flounce about without any real problems, provided I stayed on the estate. Indeed, the Watling produced a number of recognised faces, from Debbie Juvenile, one of the Bromley contingent who worked at Sex, to Jean Ready, who had first taken me to Louise's with her girlfriend, and Steve Marshall, who was also there at Billy's and the Blitz all the way through. But when Chris arrived, he took it to a new level. And took me with him.

Walking along Watling Avenue to Burnt Oak station to bunk the Tube into town, or even into the Bald Faced Stag, our notorious rough-house local, with Chris dressed as Poirot or a gaucho – one night he went out swathed in robes à la Gandhi – was to run the gauntlet of open-mouthed stares and the occasional comment, but never any trouble. It was partly because I was there, of course, but also because Chris has the aura and demeanour of a man who can handle himself. He's a solid unit. Growing up in Merthyr, a rock-hard mining town, and dressing like the young Sullivan, you had to be pretty tough to survive. He always said Burnt Oak reminded him of Merthyr and the locals somehow recognised Chris as one of their own and treated him with nothing but respect.

One of the greatest misconceptions about the Blitz kids is that they were foppish and effete, a whole load of posh little Lord and Lady Fauntleroys in frills. Try telling Chris Sullivan that and see how you get on. But he wasn't the only tough nut in the club. Most of the regulars were working-class kids, often from rough parts of town.

There was a prominent group of lads from Hackney and Bethnal Green who were basically Tottenham Hotspur football lads in fancy gear. There were blokes off building sites and the print, a cab driver, a sex worker and a ducker and diver or two. There were street-smart and hardened young gay kids who had survived the rigours of life out there in an unforgiving town, a couple who had come from care homes, and others who had been fending for themselves for a long time. It was a gathering of misfits and miscreants coming together to ward off evil.

If you'd been an outsider, looked odd or queer all your life – looked like George O'Dowd, himself the scion of an Irish building-site family, or Melissa Caplan, a Jewish girl from a conservative community in Hendon – you had to toughen up, had to be able to defend yourself. Thick-skinned, quick-witted, bold as brass and twice as shiny, these were just about the bravest youngsters I have ever met. And we all met up to go out and have fun.

But it wasn't all jolly japes. Many's the time we had to fend off insults and worse, outright aggression and sometimes violence from ordinary Joes enraged by our appearance on the Tube into town or, especially, the night bus home. It was an almost daily occurrence to be called every politically incorrect 1970s name under the sun, but we stuck together and stood our ground.

As well as being tough, many of the crowd were also extremely lairy; confident, brazen and brash, I was never exactly a shrinking violet myself, pretty assured by nature and nurture, but when you start to hang with such a peacock crew, it rubs off. You bounce off each other, try to outdo each other, absorb the collective confidence, turn up the chutzpah. Walking down the street with George O'Dowd sharpens the reflexes. And living with Chris certainly pushed my boundaries, sartorially and socially. I found myself at the centre of an extraordinary web.

Somehow, despite having only lived in London for a couple of years, Chris knew everybody, from fellow art students to famous artists, pop stars to porn stars, drug dealers to street cleaners. London back then was totally tribal; there were Teddy boys and rockabillies, neo-mods and old-school rockers, the soul crowd, the arty crowd, the fashion crowd, the poshos and the squatters. But Chris, with his sartorial shapeshifting and talk-to-anybody egalitarianism, could fit in with any of them. And if any of them were having a party, we would go.

It wasn't just me and Chris. The group that had gathered at Billy's was scattered geographically across London; there were little cliques from different areas, with slightly different styles. The art and fashion students, originally from all over the country, many of them queer, mainly lived in the centre of town as they studied at St Martin's in Soho and the Central School of Art in Holborn (which would later merge to become Central Saint Martins) and had digs nearby.

My little crew were up in the north – Burnt Oak, Hendon – and we were allied to a gang from Barnet and Finchley. The west London lot, friends of Graham Ball from Ealing and Acton, were wild rocking boys and girls, anarchic and punky. The East End lads were old soulies often to be found in the rollicking music pubs of the Hackney Road. There was a bunch of Dagger's mates from Islington, a mix of working-class Arsenal lads and middle-class intellectuals, much like the rest of Islington. And then there were the mob from the deep south, perhaps the most outrageous of all, with George, Jeremy and Princess Julia as their standard bearers.

As soon as word was out that there was a shindig within possible reach, Chris would be on the phone, usually a payphone with a pile of ten-pence pieces. It was particularly important to find a party at the weekend because it still wasn't considered wise to be in a pub or a club with the drunken masses on a Saturday night, so we'd go to extreme lengths to get the address of a do to go to. Otherwise, we'd be all dressed up with nowhere to go. It might be a little terraced house in Chiswick or a mansion in Totteridge, a fifth-floor council flat in Hanwell or an arty loft in Docklands.

One night, we rendezvoused at Victoria station on our way to a party somewhere in Surrey, only to find the entire concourse awash with Regency courtiers, boy sailors, toy soldiers, riverboat gamblers, Chicago gangsters and their molls, all headed to a birthday party thrown by two sisters who might have invited a couple of those present, but not the seventy or eighty who turned up at their humble abode. I can only apologise now, but I believe everybody had a great night and those sisters are probably still dining out on it today.

Sometimes it all went awry: we'd travel a long way and not get in, or very occasionally we'd wish we hadn't. It all kicked off at a house party in leafy south-west London somewhere and I remember a dozen or so of us having to fight our way out of the house when the local rockabilly boys turned on us interlopers. Stumbling over Richmond Bridge, out of breath and almost out of luck, while being chased by a hoard of bequiffed and tattooed leather-clad rockers with deadly intent is not one of my favourite memories of that time. Another time, I took a right-hander at a shebeen in Bermondsey after a local thought he could try it on with one of the girls in our group because she was wearing a bustier. The ensuing black eye went wonderfully with a bit of pirate gear.

At the other end of the spectrum, we managed to gain entry to a fabulous soirée hosted by high-society sculptor Andrew Logan, the man behind the Alternative Miss World event, in his vast riverside studio in Butler's Wharf overlooking the Thames. Andrew was part of a group of glamorous, high-fashion and high-camp older artists that Peter York dubbed 'Them'. They were Andrew Logan, Duggie Fields, Kevin Whitney, Luciana Martinez, Derek Jarman and Zandra Rhodes, a clique of urbane 70s post-pop artists. 'Them' were from a different generation; they were Roxy Music and Andy Warhol, Biba and Tommy Nutter. We gave them a burst of youthful vitality and they bestowed upon us a certain credibility in more exalted circles. They kind of adopted us as their errant arty children.

At this party in Andrew's amazing loft, the older crowd seemed genuinely enthralled that a huge mob of exhibitionist kids even more outrageously attired than they were had suddenly arrived. We all got on famously and, at one point, both Chris and I were propositioned by a well-known female writer and a male jazz singer, but graciously declined their offer. We didn't turn down anything else, and it might have been the first time I ever tried champagne.

After that night, Andrew Logan and his chums became honorary members of the gang, often turning up on a Tuesday, hobnobbing with Steve Strange, raising the average age considerably, our older and more worldly and wealthy mentors. Luciana Martinez painted Princess Julia and Kevin Whitney produced a portrait of John Maybury. They were our link to the still-tiny London contemporary art world.

At some point, things turned around and rather than gatecrashing parties, we found ourselves being invited to them. Steve Strange was on every guest list and would drag us along as arm candy. It seemed to be all the rage to have those fascinating club kids at your do, particularly at posh bashes in Chelsea and Kensington with the louche young Sloane Ranger set. As a kid from a dodgy council estate, I was quite happy to be an interesting accessory for a free night with bubbles, nibbles and maybe a chance for a snog with a touch of class.

One week, we were due to go to a big, themed fashion event somewhere up in Barnet. Now it may seem odd, but I've always hated fancy-dress parties. We didn't consider what we did as fancy dress at all and sort of found it demeaning when others togged up for fun. We did that full time. In our pretentious young minds, we were sartorialists, students of style. Our look was a lifestyle, not a gimmick.

Anyway, somebody – I think it was Simon Withers – suggested we all go dressed as droogs from *A Clockwork Orange* and put the fear of God into them. I'd read the book, an absolute masterpiece, and could even talk a smattering of Nadsat, but I hadn't seen the film – nor had any of us, because it was banned in Britain. This was a problem because, obsessives that we were, we would need to get the gear absolutely spot on. Somebody else, probably Chris, suggested that we should go to Paris because Stanley Kubrick's ultraviolent masterpiece was showing there on a permanent loop in a cinema in Les Halles. I'd never been to Paris before; I don't suppose any of us had.

Four or five of us in full regalia boarded a coach at Victoria station and got off in Bastille, a selection of rather creased zoot suits, bell bottoms, stripy matelot tops and berets stalking the streets and metro tunnels of gay Paree, stopping traffic and causing genuine outrage and amazement among the locals as we looked for this picture house. We eventually found the cinema and saw the film, taking copious sartorial notes throughout. We also found a dirt-cheap hotel which doubled as a brothel, where the girls were absolutely fascinated by our presence. A week later, bowler hats, canes and cod pieces in place, we were the stars of the party.

I've got rather ahead of myself here. The Blitz was well and truly underway by the time we were swanning around Paris and posing at arty parties. We'd better head back there now.

4

'NO, I'M SORRY, BUT YOU CAN'T COME IN'

G reat Queen Street is only *just* Covent Garden. The nearest Tube is actually Holborn, over on the eastern side of WC2. Even today it feels cut off from the frantic throng of the piazza, separated by a warren of winding backstreets and anonymous red-brick blocks, which are still largely residential. There's a junior school just around the corner – where I once briefly worked for the Inner London Education Authority – a launderette and a corner shop, and a sense that this is still a local neighbourhood, albeit one dominated by a huge Masonic temple.

That brooding, foreboding building, known as the Grand Lodge, looms over Great Queen Street, its oversized neo-classical pillars and art deco adornments filling the southern side of the street. You often see groups of sepulchral middle-aged men in dark suits carrying monogrammed briefcases, walking towards the Brobdingnagian doors of the lodge before disappearing inside, presumably to roll up their trouser legs and don their ceremonial aprons and white gloves. Considerably odder regalia was once the order of the day on the other side of the road.

Over there, in the haunting shadow of the Grand Lodge, a row of handsome old Georgian houses has now been gentrified and there's a smattering of genteel boutiques and ever-changing coffee shops, bars and restaurants. Number 36 is a charmingly quirky atelier selling fantastical, theatrical hats and fascinators made by the famed society milliner Stephen Jones OBE, which might just give you a hint to the hidden history of this street. But you have to walk along to the shabbier end, hard by the roaring traffic of Kingsway, to find number 4.

This plain four-storey building is a nondescript concrete construction, lacking the handsome looks of its Georgian neighbours, and currently in a sorry state, locked and shuttered. A metal awning bears the name The Red Rooms, which was its last iteration as a dodgy 'gentleman's club', dancing pole and all. I visited once to do some filming inside and its tacky attempt at bordello chic – crimson walls and drapes and carefully positioned mirrors – had obliterated any trace whatsoever of its former glory, the ghosts of New Romantics past. But there is a small plaque outside, put up by the Performing Rights Society, celebrating the fact that Spandau Ballet first performed here on 5 December 1979 when it was the Blitz club. We all performed there every Tuesday night and Steve Strange was the ringmaster.

Before it was The Red Rooms, No. 4, Great Queen Street was predominantly brown. In 1979, the Blitz harked back to the smog-shrouded, bomb-damaged London of just thirty-odd years before. In this near-empty neighbourhood, with the 1970s coming to a sorry conclusion, it felt like little had changed in London since the Luftwaffe had it in their sights. We were once again knee-deep in shortages, gloom and austerity.

With its nicotine-stained ceiling and khaki-coloured walls adorned with enamel ads for Bovril, Woodbines and Digging for Victory, old newspaper reports on D-Day and VE day, ration books, framed portraits of Winston Churchill and General Montgomery, and cases containing gas masks and tin hats, it was a riot of dowdy nostalgia. This was not a cool, designer space.

A modern neon sign outside heralded your arrival, proclaiming 'Nightly Cabaret Club Restaurant Bar', but once you had entered the room, you were plunged into a drab recreation of the 1940s. As kids, many of us had played on real bombsites. Right up until the 1980s, London was still pockmarked with them, and we played football, British bulldog and run-outs amid the rubble. It was ironic that now, as teenagers, we were playing different games in a wine bar named after the Blitz. It was an adventure playground, no doubt.

The long, thin ground-floor room had old bare floorboards and a mahogany bar running most of the length of the right-hand side, with bar stools and a smattering of wooden chairs, and tables covered in cheap, plastic red-and-white gingham tablecloths. Halfway down the bar, on the opposite side of the room, were the steps down to the toilets. That became the main thoroughfare and trade route of the club.

Just beyond, there were steps up to a tiny, slightly raised dance-floor at the back where the erotic slow jive was studiously practised. Beyond that was an old-fashioned DJ booth with a door, a little like a phone box, where Rusty Egan played his records, and next to that was the cloakroom where George O'Dowd – when he hadn't fallen out with Steve Strange – was the light-fingered coat-check girl. Above all that, and up some stairs, was the top floor, a galleried mezzanine space for dining where nobody dined: people would stand and gaze at the goings-on below and gossip about who was doing what with whom.

A less suitable place for a transformative, modernist youth movement to call home would be hard to imagine. The irony of the future being so stridently invented amid the dusty detritus of the past was apparent even then. It was also proof positive that what makes a great nightclub is not the decor or the lighting, the sound system or the acoustics; it's the people in the room. Deciding who got inside the Blitz was entirely down to Steve Strange.

Steve and Julia (she wasn't yet a princess) had both frequented the Blitz for a post-work glass of wine while round the corner at PX on

James Street, and they got to know its manager, Brendan. He had recently taken over with the aim of attracting a younger audience, especially after dark when the area was deathly quiet. During the day and into the early evening, this was just a regular wine bar with a mixed crowd of locals, shoppers and shop workers sipping Sancerre and nibbling brie. Nobody stayed late, despite its 3 a.m. licence.

Brendan had tried different things. He put on a cabaret night with Biddie and Eve, a couple of splendidly camp cockney performers who attracted a mixed, theatrical gay crowd on a Thursday for a saucy evening of song and dance. On Sunday, there was a Motown night. On Fridays, he invited in the smooth West End soul set who gathered nearby in their expensive Woodhouse and Browns garms for cocktails at Rumours before coming on to the Blitz for a late-night boogie to the latest jazz-funk.

People who went to the Blitz earlier in the 70s, and those who came during the time the nightclub ran between 1979 and 1980 but did not come on a Tuesday, don't understand what all the fuss is about. The Blitz club that changed my world, and maybe *the* world, was only on one night a week, only on a Tuesday.

Without a venue since their argument with Vince at Billy's, and still in need of rent money, Steve and Rusty approached Brendan to ask if they could put their Bowie night on at his wine bar on this traditionally quiet evening, and it obviously seemed like a good idea for all involved. I'm not sure either side had any real idea of what they were about to unleash.

We need to talk in more detail at this point about Steve Strange: the Great Gatsby of Great Queen Street. Born Stephen John Harrington in Newbridge in May 1959, Steve was exactly two weeks older than me, although I always assumed he was much further my senior; he was so confident and competent, and carried himself with such stature. He had already done loads of stuff – been in bands, worked in fashion, moved in exalted social circles – and seemed to know everybody, while I was still a student living with my mum in a suburban council house.

He was the son of a soldier, so his family had moved around and he had latched on to a freewheeling group of Welsh lads, including Chris Sullivan, who became fixtures on the proto-punk scene. You would see them everywhere at gigs and clubs in London. Steve had already cultivated a minor degree of notoriety through his provocatively monikered band, The Moors Murderers, which he formed when he moved to London aged just seventeen.

One of the last generation of grammar-school kids (as was I and so many others on the Blitz scene), he spoke in a soft, slightly mannered Welsh accent and flirted mercilessly with all and sundry. He liked to kiss the boys. Steve was bright and sharp, but far from an intellectual: he didn't engage in the kind of theoretical or political debates I'd have with Steve Dagger or Gary Kemp, nor was he particularly arty, à la Simon Withers or Cerith Wyn Evans. He was a gossip and a good-time boy, but above all he was fearless, a relentless doer, a man who made things happen. Steve was a genius at geniality, and it has taken me a very long time to realise just how much we all owe him.

The entrepreneurial spirit he showed in starting Billy's and the Blitz was rare in the late 70s, when depression, decay and decline were the buzzwords of the time and unemployment its basic assumption. He was an individualist in an age of corporatism, an eccentric in a conformist age, a visionary of a kind, although one who was never able to explain or elucidate his vision; he just made it happen. He was almost supernaturally positive, and his will and elan in turning these two ludicrously unprepossessing spots, Billy's and the Blitz, into generationally significant places that people would write books about fifty years later was extraordinary. None of it would have happened without Steve. Then he became a bona fide pop star.

He had a steely sense of his own worth – that innate but hard-won toughness which so many of the queer gang possessed – and a raging vanity, certainly, though he was very good at laughing at himself and everybody else. But he also had a generosity, a camaraderie, an ability to put unlikely people together and act as the bond between them. He always called the Blitz 'our club', not his – it was our scene and he was fiercely protective of the inner circle who had supported him from the beginning.

Steve was magisterial on the door, never flustered or tetchy. He was cool and calm, enjoying his role as a benign dictator, that twinkling grin of his employed to lure in the ones he wanted and to repel everybody else. He could be catty but not cruel; he would fall out with everybody – especially George and Marilyn – and make up with them the following Tuesday.

His most extraordinary skill was to spot in an instant who would make the club a better place and who would not. He was a master human mixologist. He would let in Christos Tolera and Martin Kemp – two sixteen-year-old herberts arriving on the 38 bus from Islington in garish suits made from curtain material bought at Ridley Road Market, who most weeks didn't even have the one pound entry fee – but famously turned away Mick Jagger and other celebrities for not looking sufficiently fabulous.

When the Blitz became well known and rammed, Steve kept

out hordes of star-seekers and glory hunters, wannabes and prying paparazzi, but was always supportive and welcoming of his own, creating a place where those inside felt secure and valued. He would walk among us, dropping a tidbit of gossip or dispensing a salutation. He conducted that club like a maestro.

In later years, his life was marred by his addictions. Steve was a master of the night, but he became its slave, succumbing to its many dark temptations. The Blitz was remorselessly hedonistic and plenty of people fell into traps – unfortunately Steve never really climbed out of his. It was hard to spend time with him later on, the coke and heroin blunting his brilliance, dulling those shining eyes. But when I think of him now, it is an image of the arch arbiter, sitting on the door of No. 4, Great Queen Street in 1979, dressed as Robin Hood's immaculate gay mate, that huge, inverted pompadour bouncing before him, kissing his friends and cursing his enemies, stirring his mischievous cocktail of creative souls and creating just about the greatest nights of them all.

Bizarrely, despite such vivid memories, I have zero recollection of the very first night of the Blitz. I've asked others who were undoubtedly there alongside me on that opening night in February 1979 and no one has any specific recollections. I guess we just assumed it was Billy's part two – and, for the first couple of weeks, it probably was. The hundred or so souls who had transferred from Soho to Covent Garden picked up where we had left off, pulling on PX garms and posing to Bowie. But it soon became apparent that there were major distinctions between the two clubs, which would make a big difference.

Because the capacity at the Blitz was much larger, twice as many people could cram inside, about 200 in all, and this meant that there was more variety, a more diverse crowd. Billy's had been an almost old-fashioned Bowie night and appealed exclusively to a young, hardcore Soho nightclubbing crowd who didn't mind being in a cramped, smelly basement. Billy's was furtive and transgressive, where the Blitz was a 'posh' wine bar on a handsome street at ground level – more open, more comfortable, conducive to sitting and talking, socialising and flirting. Conducive to plotting to take over the world.

I loved Billy's precisely because it was secretive and seedy, a proper dodgy Soho joint, but the Blitz was undoubtedly an upgrade. Being in this new, relatively plush space gave us all a new-found stature, a confidence; it opened our eyes and widened our horizons. Once the Blitz was in its stride, the routine went something like this.

By Tuesday afternoon, you had already got your outfit together. It would take planning and sourcing, maybe ringing round to see if anybody had a cummerbund you could borrow or rummaging through your mum's drawers for a brooch. Chris and I would get ready together and he was both a font of sartorial knowledge and a veritable storehouse of bits and bobs, which he kept in black plastic bin bags. Need some jodhpurs or a kipper tie? Have a word with Chris.

Round about nine o'clock or so, our little gang would gather: Graham and Melissa, maybe Stevie Stewart, perhaps Steve Marshall. We'd always travel in a group if possible, mainly because it was safer, but also because seeing four or five of us together magnified the effect upon onlookers and we undeniably took pleasure in their startlement. It was a fine line: you wanted people to gasp and mutter, but not to be provoked to violence.

Once safely in town, we would often meet up with a larger group at the LSE bar, a five-minute walk away from the Blitz, or maybe at the Princess Louise, an elaborate old Victorian gin palace in Holborn, which had been a queer pub for the West End theatre community for generations, so felt like a safe haven.

We would have as many drinks as we could afford, pre-loading so as not to pay for the overpriced cans of Schlitz in the Blitz. Then, as the pubs closed at 10.30 p.m., we would walk together, maybe a dozen or more of us, by now emboldened by beer and the camaraderie and courage of the crowd, to parade in our finery, putting out and showing off. This was our territory and we lorded it, although there was not much of an audience as the streets were usually pretty deserted.

Just occasionally we might pop into The George, the pub next door to the Blitz, which usually had a smattering of funereal Masons, sombrely sipping away. We knew we were forging a kind of masonry, a secret society of our own, heading to our temple. There would also be a few of the local geezers present, residents of those old social-housing tenement blocks. They were Covent Garden lads who seemed to enjoy our presence, up for some teasing, but never aggressive; these were big city boys, fly pitchers or scene shifters in the West End, Fleet Street printers or Smithfield porters who had seen it all, unshockable. Then finally, nicely lubricated and primed, we would make our way to the front door of our holy place.

In the early days, we would just amble up to the door, which was right on the street, give Steve a kiss and a pound and enter the crazy world within. But once word was out and the Blitz was a roaring success, there would usually be a gaggle of hopefuls on the pavement outside by the time we arrived, which was our signal to perform. We became swans, puffing up our feathers to make as grandiose an entrance as possible. That kiss for Steve became a proper smacker for public consumption as we waltzed in, cocky and confident as veterans of Billy's that we would have no trouble getting past the gorgeous gorgon on the door and doing our best to make sure that we were seen doing so.

Those who didn't make it in might occasionally turn nasty; Steve regularly got abused and even spat on, but like most of the Blitz regulars he could handle himself – he was a tough lad. He never employed a security guard of any kind to assist him on the door. He dealt with the punters himself and knew that, if push came to shove, there was a club full of surprisingly handy lads and lasses to back him up, even if many of them were wearing more make-up than he was.

There were actual membership cards for the Blitz, small, wallet-sized xeroxed cards in black and white, which had something to do with the licensing regulations. It had to be a proper members' club to get a late licence, so they charged a pound for membership, but I don't remember ever having to show mine. If Steve knew you, or even just liked the look of you and wanted you in, you got in. If you had a membership but had fallen out with Mr Strange, forget it – no way were you getting in. It was all in his head. Steve knew everybody by name and knew exactly who he wanted and didn't want in the club.

Was it elitist? Of course, but we felt we had earned our place at the top table, worked hard to be part of London's nocturnal elite, just like the ace faces of the mods of yore, like the Swinging Sixties in-crowd we so wanted to emulate. The Blitz was a club in the true sense of the word, a group of like-minded souls with a common purpose, not a disco where anybody could pay to enter. Once inside, you could relax – you'd made it – then feel the energy, hear the pulse, survey the scene; scoping the room to see who was in, what was out, who was wearing what, who was consorting with whom. It was a kaleidoscope of colour and style, a shifting tableau of extraordinary creatures and it varied depending on exactly where in the club you positioned yourself.

Because it was a long rectangular room, it might be useful to think of the Blitz as if it were a swimming pool. The shallow end was at the front, often peopled by those just dipping their toes in the water, while the deep end, for the committed sartorialists and hedonists, was at the back by Rusty's DJ booth. Make it to the back and you had to be particularly buoyant to stay afloat in shark-infested waters.

The shallow end was usually where you would find the few vaguely famous older people, especially the celebrity punks: Siouxsie Sioux and Steve Severin, Marco Pirroni from Adam and the Ants, Midge Ure, Billy Idol, maybe Toyah Willcox. This was also the terrain of that established arty crowd from Andrew Logan's party: Jarman, Fields and Rhodes, augmented perhaps by Marie Helvin or Bianca Jagger, who would often be hovering around, relishing a new generation of exotic young things to mingle with. Steve Strange enjoyed a bit of glamour and could go in for a spot of social mountaineering; he liked the high life, but never forgot his roots or his mates.

As well as the regulars, as time went by and word was out, you would get the occasional pop star dropping in. One time Iggy Pop was there talking to Steve; another time Grace Jones appeared. They were acceptable because their music was Blitz music, and they passed the Steve Strange test, but they also served as a test for the rest of us. One of the unwritten rules of being in the Blitz was, whatever you do – and despite the fact that you are a starstruck nineteen-year-old from a council estate – do not acknowledge the presence of famous people: don't bug them, don't bother them. You have to stay cool, 'grace under pressure', even if it *is* Grace Jones standing next to you.

But then that wasn't too difficult; punk had taught us to mingle with the bands, to think of them as equals. And, besides, most of the people in the Blitz were already famous in their own heads. They thought of themselves as stars. So maybe if you could mingle with the famous, you could become just like them too.

The shallow end at the front was also where Steve Strange held court after midnight when everybody was safely inside, and just beyond there was the start of the bar and the first row of bar stools and gingham-cloth-covered tables. Because it was still quite quiet here, this zone would be taken up by the talkers and schemers, the would-be media, music and management types.

You'd find Steve Dagger plotting with Jon Baker, now a music-biz mogul and hotelier, or Perry Haines, who co-founded *i-D* magazine. Caryn Franklin, later of *The Clothes Show*, and Dylan Jones, editor-about-town, might be there with my LSE friend Graham Ball, who would go on to manage many of the Blitz bands. Record producer James Burgess would be discussing synth sounds with Gary Kemp, while Simon Withers talked about Eisenstein's lighting or Vivienne Westwood's trousers. Fashion journalist Iain R. Webb and film-maker John Maybury might be deep in debate about *Vogue*'s latest cover or fashion designer Stephen Linard's love life. It was a babble of sometimes brilliant, sometimes trivial, always engaging conversation.

It is important to remember that, at this stage in 1979, none of these young people are actually anything except hungry. It was a collection of students and schemers and unemployed wannabes whose sole qualification was that they were good in the room, and the room was crackling.

If the schemers and dreamers tended to congregate in one spot, the art school/fashion student crowd were all over the place, buzzing about in all directions so that everybody could ogle their outfits. They put on a perpetual fashion show, the entire club their catwalk. Most of them went to Central or St Martin's, both of which were within walking distance of the Blitz, and considered themselves the arty elite compared to the more commercial course at London College of Fashion, which they frowned upon.

They were walking, talking, dancing art pieces: Melissa with her hair in a crimson spike, part Jewish princess, part Hindu goddess draped in luxuriant jewellery; Stevie Stewart in her blonde periwig or ostrich feathers and tiny, pretty, terribly shy David Holah all in black, making up the duo who became the fashion label BodyMap; Stephen Linard, the wildest, funniest, perhaps most profusely talented of them all, like Charles Hawtrey meets Carmen Miranda; the ethereally beautiful Lee Sheldrick, who tragically died way too young, and Michele Clapton – who would go on to design the costumes for *Game of Thrones* – both with shaved heads and dramatic, liturgical accoutrements; Clare with the Hair, her barnet festooned in ribbons; Fiona Dealey, specialising in ruffles; Darla Jane Gilroy and Judith Frankland in nuns' habits. There was face paint and body paint, statement hats and headbands in all directions. The waft of cheap hairspray filled the room.

What they wore – most of it homemade, cobbled together, run up the night before, begged, borrowed and sometimes stolen – was often outrageous, extraordinary, provocative, yet always stylish, always somehow right. You couldn't just randomly put stuff together and hope it worked as an outfit; you had to endeavour to look fabulous, never ridiculous. Every ensemble had to have some sort of logic, integrity, intent. Movies were studied for historical details, books pored over, research done.

But you couldn't let it look like fancy dress; it had to have an individual touch, had to have the ring of truth. It was all about the way we wore. You had to sport every outfit like you meant it, like this was your natural attire and you knew you looked great. People in fancy dress appear self-conscious, like the clothes are wearing them rather than the other way round. Walk into the Blitz like that and everybody would instantly know. No matter how much effort you had put into your ensemble, you had to carry it with insouciance.

The care taken to make a statement, make an entrance, make an impression was staggering. These were the new generation of radical British designers, sartorial auteurs bringing their A game from the jumble sale, the charity shop and the cast-off box. Stephen Jones taking care of headgear, Lesley Chilkes supervising make-up, John Galliano looking on in awe, Grayson Perry taking notes.

There was something forward-looking and futuristic about it all, especially the music, even if this was combined with a big dollop of retro. Yellow Magic Orchestra or Cabaret Voltaire would be throbbing away, electronic, synthetic and symphonic – a rejection of sweaty rock music, a new form of entertainment – while a girl dressed as Maid Marian meets Marilyn Monroe and a boy done up as Rudolph Valentino's dashing doppelgänger danced the jive.

It was a self-consciously old-fashioned futurism. Alongside the electro music, a camp retro strand of *Cabaret* and Kurt Weill was part of the sonic and stylistic soundscape. Sartorially, the past was our dressing-up box; we could dip in and mix up. This was high-lighted when Willie Brown unveiled a wonderful line of angular Russian constructivist suits, as worn by Alexander Rodchenko, El Lissitzky and Martin Kemp. I wore mine with ballet pumps and a beret, and now I wish I knew where it ended up.

The fashion mob were straight A-students of style. Kim Bowen, one of the great beauties of the Blitz who went on to be the most in-demand Hollywood stylists, waltzed in one week as Elizabeth I, tiara, white face, bustier, beauty spots, ruffles and all. She was very tight with Steve Strange, often seen on his arm at events and match-ing his flair at every step, always immaculate despite living in a decaying squat with no hot water.

Chris Sullivan had an extraordinary array of looks hidden in those black plastic bin bags. One week, he would be a riverboat gambler; another a 1920s MGM cameraman, a member of the Maquis, an Argentinian gaucho or the Milk Tray man. Another great character, known as Miss Pinkie, defied the new-look-each-week rule, because she dressed every single day of her life as if she were Little Bo Peep – or maybe Marie Antoinette in the court of Versailles – always pedantically perfect in her eighteenth-century regalia. Where else but the Blitz could someone like Pinkietessa find a home?

My own outfits tended towards the cinematic – Sinatra in *Ocean's 11*, Rob Roy, Dan Dare. One week, I assembled a look I was especially proud of: hiking boots, thick polo-neck jumper, a khaki cagoule, beanie hat and Second World War backpack. I recall dancing enthusiastically, sweating profusely but feeling entirely vindicated having watched *The Heroes of Telemark* on the TV at Christmas. I'd always admired Kirk Douglas.

There was a tight-knit coterie of real extreme sartorialists, but not everybody at the Blitz went to quite such lengths. The hardcore inner circle of the club was the most theatrically and pedantically attired, but the rest were still well dressed, stylish, individual. Some of the punters, particularly those who came only occasionally, upped their game for the night and gambled on Steve spotting their effort. But, of course, it was the truly outré outfits which got noticed, and these came in waves – great minds clearly thought alike. One week it was pierrots and mime artists, the next maybe psychedelic hippy chic with a touch of pirate or troubadour. There was a period of a few weeks when religiosity abounded: crosses, capes, priests, nuns and vicars. Judith Frankland regularly dressed as a medieval papal emissary, while Melissa had a Hindu thing with golden nose chains and jangling bangles, and Stephen Linard came as an Ashkenazi rabbi. All faiths were catered for, nothing was sacred. Cultural appropriation was highly recommended.

Although nobody used the term, and not many knew the concept, this was post-modern bricolage in action, where there is just the past, the present and the possible. In the Blitz, anything was possible, as long as you did it with elan and wore it like you meant it. And then danced your arse off.

The small, square dancefloor was about halfway up the room, and it was another place to be seen. If you weren't dancing, you would be watching the show. Andy Polaris, lithe and liquid, a naturally graceful dancer who went on to front Animal Nightlife, would be jiving with some equally beautiful runaway urchin, while two girls in heels, frills, pillbox hats with veils and super-tight pencil skirts twirled and spun together. Two boys in britches might be entwined and exploring each other's bodies, while Christos Tolera made a gaggle of girls swoon by twirling his facial hair in a rhythmic fashion.

If a particularly popular tune came on, this small space would fill up, and you might even have seen Michael Clark, already at the Ballet Rambert and about to become the greatest contemporary dancer of his era, gyrating to 'Moskow Diskow' next to a plumber from Pimlico dressed as a buccaneer. Dancing next to Michael was like doing sums next to Alan Turing.

The house dance was known as the Blitz jive, which, despite Rusty's predilection for fast, electronic pulses, was a slow-motion, sensual jive performed on the half beat, hands interlocking, knees pumping into high kicks, the upper torso twisting, the head swishing from side to side. It was a touch Cossack, a hint of jitterbug, somewhere between swing, tango and vogueing before anybody had heard of it. It was simultaneously robotic yet erotic, performed by people wearing ski pants and ballet shoes or full crinolines and heels. It did not matter a jot what gender you or your partner were – you danced hand in hand, and cheek to cheek.

Beyond the dancefloor, at the very back of the club by Rusty's booth and the cloakroom, is where you would find the real arch fabulists. Jeremy Healy, still not yet eighteen, with a Dickensian ragamuffin look – all dreadlocks, ribbons and Kohl – studied the DJ's techniques for his future career. George, unless Steve had barred him that week, would be stationed there too, his big, booming voice cutting through the music, kimono and foundation on and chopsticks in his hair, or maybe wearing a Teddy boy's drape coat and blue face paint, his barnet touching the ceiling. He was a hulking stunner, taking coats and rifling pockets. George would curse you rotten, rob you dry and steal your heart.

George would usually be in tandem with Peter Robinson, aka Marilyn, the glamour twins at the back. Marilyn was DIY glam incarnate, her roots bursting through, her stockings torn, but still staggeringly beautiful, posing mercilessly, moaning constantly, waiting for Marilyn Monroe's 'Heat Wave' to play so she could take centre stage and outdo everybody, darling.

The terrible trio was completed by Philip Sallon, a practised scowl on his face, mixing Vivienne Westwood, fetish wear and Christmas tree baubles, bitching frantically and hilariously about George and Marilyn and everybody else. These three were perhaps the ultimate Blitz kids – though Philip, already in his late twenties, was too old for that title – and verbally sparring with them was a proper work-out with their well-honed, high-camp Polari, their barrage of insults and their killer kitten heels. If you could hold your own at the back of the Blitz, you could take on anybody.

★   ★   ★

George and Marilyn and Steve Strange and Martin Degville and all the heavily made-up, cross-dressing shock troops were certainly the most photographed Blitz kids on the block. They were the most exhibitionist, the most extreme. The 'gender benders' became the public face of the club and, to this day, most people's image of the Blitz involves boys in gowns or tights, theatrical slap and all. They were certainly there, but that is only half the story.

In many ways, what gave the Blitz its unique energy and creativity was the coming together for the first time of different factions: the white-faced, Widow Twanky fashion student crowd paired with the white socks and loafers of the flash working-class soul kids; the arty intellectuals with the punky rebels; the well-to-do sybarites with the dole-queue squatters. The Blitz was elitist until you were inside, then it was fiercely egalitarian.

Groups of friends arrived together in packs. The Kemp brothers came with their soul crew from Islington and were therefore known as the Angel Boys. Ollie and Jimmy O'Donnell, two north London Irish punk veterans – both brothers were wonderfully dressed and fiercely heterosexual hairdressers from the uber trendy Smile salon in Knightsbridge – led a little gang from Finchley and Barnet that included Lee Barrett, who later managed Sade, and the novelist-to-be J. J. Connolly.

They were all Arsenal fans, but a similar group of Spurs supporters hailed from Hackney and Bethnal Green. Mac, Kevin, Flid – nearly all Irish in heritage and republican in leaning – brought with them a terrace swagger and also a political edge: they were a left-wing, anti-fascist street-fighting group. Not most people's idea of Blitz types, but they were absolute stalwarts.

Another, slightly older crowd would come less regularly, maybe once a month, making a late entrance in their super-stylish, if more conventional, duds: Antony Price suits and Yves Saint Laurent dresses, Swanky Modes and Fiorucci, Manolo Blahnik shoes, very Ferry and Jerry. They were habitués of slick Mayfair clubs like The Embassy and Monkberry's; good-looking, free-spending and glamorous, these models and villains, actors and aristos were slumming it with the guttersnipes. They would go to the Zanzibar, a swish new members' club and restaurant that had just opened round the corner, and come on to the Blitz late for a nightcap. If Steve was in a good mood, he'd let them in, let them spend some money and invite us to their parties. Occasionally, they might take someone home for sex. They were widening our social horizons.

Rowdy and loud, the most joyously maniacal crew of the lot were the marauding west London mob. Still punk rockers at heart, they had taken to wearing leather motorbike gear, 50s rocker nostalgia and Marlon Brando glam. Dave Mahoney, later to be the lord of the illegal rave, was the recognised leader of this anarchic firm who came in on the Central Line from Ealing and beyond. He dished out nicknames for them: Sean the Boy, Swede, Plum, Dangerous Jane, Electric Barry, Rod Marsh, Don the Murderer, Boring Paul, Barry OD, Plug, Box, Carpet Head, Paranoid Pete . . . Real roughhouse punk lads and lasses, but proper into clothes; collectors of original Westwood Seditionaries gear and still harbouring seditious intentions. Steve Lewis, a Fulham-supporting, Marxist Vivienne Westwood obsessive, went on to become perhaps the best DJ of his age at Le Beat Route and the manager of Andy Polaris's band Animal Nightlife.

All these people, this fabulous mix and mismatch of young, uninhibited characters, could be seen in the perpetual queue to go up and down the stairs to the basement. Down the stairs were the toilets and the pharmacy. Down the stairs was the underworld. I laugh every time I hear about the current controversy over non-gendered toilets, and the shock and horror expressed at the idea that you might see somebody of the opposite or indeterminate sex when you go to take a pee. It's a good job those poor sensitive souls didn't go to the Blitz.

The basement was where the real hot action went on, the pot was stirred, the dirt was dished, the deed was done. It was where people went to re-do their make-up, study their reflection, adjust their outfits, row, fight, snog, occasionally have sex, sometimes take drugs, bitch about people upstairs and generally enjoy the myriad debauched pleasures of the night. Downstairs was a riot.

Whether you went to the boys' or the girls' toilets didn't matter – it was a party down there. There would always be someone powdering their nose in every possible sense of the term, while someone else might be spraying their hair or re-arranging their underwear. One time, someone discovered a secret stash of wine bottles stored down by the loos and free wine was handed out aplenty, though with no corkscrews it was tough getting the corks out without getting claret all over your outfit.

If you required something stronger than wine, this was the place. The primary pharmacologist was known as the Rat, though not because he would ever grass on anybody – God forbid. Rather, this tough but softly spoken trader in dubious delights got his nickname because his pet rodent went everywhere with him, including to the Blitz. It would be sitting on his shoulder or scurrying round his neck as he stood in his pitch just outside the gents, dressed in jodhpurs and a wing-collar shirt with collar studs and ruffles.

Speed had been the drug of choice in the punk scene, one of the reasons why there was so much frantic pogoing. As many of the Blitz crowd were former punks, they carried that habit over. Plus, it was dirt cheap and most of the people here were seriously skint, all their money going on the way they looked, so a line or two of sulphate or a little blue pill gave them the energy to get through a long night's posing, preening and jiving. This would also account for much of the club's animated chatter. But for many attendees, it was just a can of Schlitz – the overpriced American lager which was all the rage (and the only beer sold behind the bar) – and the abundant energy of desirous and excitable youth that kept them going.

5

THEY SHOOT CLOTHES HORSES, DON'T THEY?

Nobody became a clothes or style obsessive because they went to the Blitz. They went to the Blitz because they were already so wrapped up in what they wore that it felt natural – indeed, *necessary* – to seek out like-minded souls. But there's no doubt that going to No. 4, Great Queen Street once a week upped the stakes dramatically. It was like joining a high-altitude training camp for the British Olympic dressing-up squad.

If you've got Chris Sullivan planning his outfit in the next bedroom, Melissa Caplan meeting you at the station to journey together, Steve Strange casting his critical eye over you as you walk in and George O'Dowd loudly giving his opinion on your outfit when you drop off your coat, you had better look good. You had better put in the effort, be at the top of your game.

In retrospect, I had been in training for this from the moment that, as a ten-year-old in 1969, I had first pressured my mum into paying for a Ben Sherman shirt and a pair of red clip braces so that I could be a skinhead like my elder brothers. From that point on, schmutter and the music which accompanied it had been my conjoined twin passions. Fashion and music were indivisible, tribal.

I have always had obsessive tendencies, and so every time a new trouser tribe emerged, a new fashion cult, I went all out to get it right: the correct shoes on my feet, the correct record on my deck. That was how I defined myself, how I sought kudos and stature, hoped to impress boys and attract girls. I was always on the far end of the style spectrum, but I was not alone.

In the second half of the twentieth century, many young urban working-class British kids – particularly but not exclusively males – defined themselves primarily by the cult they called their own, the clothes they wore and the tunes they danced to. And it was always the gear which came first: define a style of dress, then find the music which fits your outfit. The first Teddy boys appeared in 1953, way before rock'n'roll, and there had been people looking like punks way before the Pistols. Although I went full-on punk, I used to go home and listen to Marvin Gaye and John Coltrane. Although I loved the Clash, it was everything that went with punk, the ethos and the outfits, the look denoting a lifestyle that I bought into; the music was secondary.

For working-class youth in particular, emboldened by the post-war welfare state but still marginalised by the rigid class system, street fashion was often their only outlet, their culture, their clan. So out there in the margins, on the estates, in the youth clubs, there was remarkable creativity. What they wore was all they had, so they used themselves and their appearance as a weapon in the style wars being fought out daily in the playground, on the football terraces and in the clubs. Find your style, find your gang.

From Teddy boys in their drapes, mods in their skinny suits, skinheads, suede-heads, soul boys and punks, one look evolved from and then superseded another in classic Darwinian style. It was a story of ragamuffin creativity, and urchin elan, created down in the gutter but aiming for the stars, and the kids who did it best, the faces, became stars of the streets. I can still name the most stylish, most hip kids on my estate – the streets never forget.

The history of British youth culture is one of restless, relentless sartorial brilliance, fuelled by high-grade teenage desire, always pushing on to the next new thing, pulling on the next new jacket. But by the time we got to 1979, that story had started to fracture. It was going post-modern.

Where once there had been a lineage of looks, with one style cult superseding the last, one fashion superseding another, there was now a panoply of stylistic subsets all co-existing simultaneously. There were numerous competing tribes in town. As the 80s drew nearer, the bizarrely attired misfits who just about fitted into the Blitz made up such a tiny group that we barely even registered. And nor did we have a name. But we did have a dedication to look like this all the time. Being part of this as-yet-unnamed tribe required complete commitment.

The soul and funk crowd were probably still the largest gang in town, though the least chronicled because their whole demeanour was subtle and slick, their music sophisticated and Black, their image non-confrontational. This was the time when the inky rock papers ruled and the soul scene was seen as far too bland for the bedsit rebels who wrote and read the *NME* et al. Those papers were penned almost exclusively by white middle-class men with grungy rock'n'roll fantasies, which meant they dismissed the most authentically working-class, multi-racial, mixed gender scene of all. They had no time for aspirational Cortina drivers with Fiorucci jeans and Maze albums.

Soon, another subset of the soul crowd would emerge, propelled by the same materialist zeitgeist. With their fascination with expensive designer sportswear labels and trainers – Fila, Tacchini, Ellesse, Diadora etc. – this group were wedge-head logo warriors. The 'casuals', as they were known, were largely shunned because of their association with football violence, but emerging from the backstreets and seething terraces of Liverpool and London, they were clothes obsessives, a genuine dandy outpouring, and harbingers of the label-obsessed era we still live in.

As the 80s approached, there were still plenty of punks and post-punks out there, plus their neanderthal cousins who followed the Oi! bands, the musical arm of the neo-Nazi skinhead movement, with their bleached jeans, shaved heads and tattooed torsos – probably the people you least wanted to meet on the pavement. Most of the violence between warring factions was performative and perfunctory, but there were serious, politically motivated clashes between these young fascists and their left-wing enemies. These were riven times.

Another offshoot of punk which gained ground at this time was goth – nice, geeky suburban kids sitting at bus stops sipping cider in purple and black while listening to the Banshees and Bauhaus, and fantasising about blood rituals. Goth often got confused or conflated with what was happening at the Blitz, but despite a shared love of make-up and drama, it was very different.

The Batcave was a Soho goth club, which appeared not long after the Blitz, and it appealed to those who cherish the dark: cartoonish, vampiric cosplay with strict rules and a conformity and uniformity among its adherents. I went a couple of times and felt desperately out of place. (I also felt smugly superior, but then I was a very superior young man at this stage.) Gloomy music, Camden Lock costumes, badly dyed hair and an air of teen ennui. It wasn't for me.

Some of the people at the Blitz could and did do goth with great panache, but then they would do something else next week. There were crucifixes and capes occasionally, but for every person who looked like the Prince of Darkness on a Tuesday night in Covent Garden, there was one who looked like Princess Grace Kelly. Or even Gene Kelly.

The essence of the Blitz was that it encouraged individuality and creativity and shunned the uniformity of all the previous youth cults. With Bowie the arch shapeshifter as its inspiration, change was the only constant. You could be any hero you wanted, but just for one day. It was against the grain of everything that had gone before and, as soon as a look caught on, it was jettisoned. We rejected having a name for the same reason. Indeed, when I first started writing about this scene, I came up with the clumsy epithet 'the cult with no name'. Really, it was the cult with no limits.

Another youth faction which emerged at roughly the same time as us was Two-Tone and its subset of neo-mod. Two-Tone was technically a Coventry thing, before it exploded and went nationwide, but here in London, bands like Madness and the Bodysnatchers were appealing to a similar retro-ska sensibility: Crombies, sta-press and pork pie hats. It was marvellous music, honourable politics and a style which still looks good today. But I had been there and done that as a small boy. I remembered it fondly yet had consigned it to the past. We thought we were avant-garde, cutting edge, intellectual . . . Pretentious, nous? We certainly were, and we definitely considered ourselves the future.

Steve Dagger suggested we ought to go and check out the opposition, however, because a band called Secret Affair were playing at a place called Conway Hall in Holborn, a few minutes from the LSE and directly opposite his mum and dad's flat. It seemed like fun. They were part of a mini mod revival, dressed in a similar sartorial vein to the Jam, who I had seen many times and rather dismissed because they were too reactionary and backward-looking for my absolutist idea of punk.

I can't recall exactly what I wore, but it was clearly provocative. We caused a huge stir among the ranks of nice, neat scooter boys in their parkas and bowling shoes, who had clearly never seen the like, and we had to leave before it all got messy. It was apparent we were still a tiny, as-yet-unnamed, unrecognised, unenvied sub-species.

It was a myth that we Blitz kids were all loaded, spending fortunes on fancy duds. The truth was exactly the opposite: ours was largely giro-cheque chic. We spent more time than money, more effort than cash. Steve Strange, working in the hippest boutique in town and actually making dosh from the club, usually wore fairly slick outfits. He looked polished by comparison with most of us, while the fashion students could make stuff for themselves and each other. But, for the majority, it was about trawling the bargain bins, charity shops and army surplus suppliers.

Both Steve Dagger and I had part-time jobs as playleaders for the Inner London Education Authority, looking after impoverished city kids after school, which augmented our student grants until Margaret Thatcher's government attacked the ILEA and these jobs were cut. In the summer holidays, Chris Sullivan and I cut the grass at the Welsh Harp reservoir for Brent council. Gary Kemp and his Islington mates all earned a few bob handing out freebie magazines at Tube stations, sometimes going straight from the Blitz to do so. We had part-time jobs to earn money, but it was a full-time job looking like we did. Most of us managed to get together enough wedge to make sure we could at least go to Laurence Corner once a week.

Now a chemist's on the rundown corner of a main road near Euston station, Laurence Corner was a veritable institution back in the late 70s and arguably the main outfitters for the whole Blitz craze. Because the war was still within living memory, there was a slew of places selling old military stock, from hobnail boots to two-way radios, and just about everything in between, but none were as good as Laurence Corner.

Sprawling, chaotic, exhausting but cheap, and also seriously authentic, this place was legendary. I'd first gone there in my soul-boy guise to buy what we called 'jungle greens', big baggy cargo pants as worn by sweaty commandos in tropical lands, paired with plastic sandals or jellys, as worn by sweaty nightclubbers in Crackers, both of which were hard to get in mainstream shops.

Next, I went for the full Bryan Ferry GI Joe, 'overpaid, over-sexed and over here' look: pleated chinos, khaki shirt with epaulettes, tie tucked in, forage cap. As a rather insipid-looking, ginger-haired seventeen-year-old, I'm not convinced I ever appeared quite as dev-ilishly dashing as the Roxy Music main man, but I loved that outfit and revived it very successfully for the Blitz.

Every time you went to Laurence Corner, you came out with something. There were Jolly Jack Tar bell bottoms, Grenadier great coats, Sam Brown belts, RAF flight bags, even US and Russian kit, all lumped together, in piles, in disarray, everything smelling of mothballs and the NAAFI, heavy woollen materials, itchy and rough. They also had a kind of costume section where you could buy theatrical off-cuts and cast-offs, presumably from the West End. It was an Aladdin's cave, with Aladdin's original harem pants in there somewhere.

This was also before the term 'vintage' was invented to inflate the price of second-hand clothing, and so used and old dead stock was everywhere in London. Wonderful stuff dating from the 30s to the 70s was almost given away if you knew where to look – and we made it our business to know. Just up the road from Laurence Corner, in Camden Town, was a place called Alfred Kemp's, an ancient gentleman's outfitters specialising in second-hand, usually deceased men's clobber. Their slogan was 'We Fit Anybody', and indeed they did, even myself and Gary Kemp, a pair of skinny, pallid nocturnalites. I quietly hoped we might get a discount because of some family connection of Gary's. We went there in search of demob suits and trilbies, and got suitably suited and booted in dead men's duds.

It was the other Kemp brother, Martin, who accompanied me to Covent Garden to Moss Bros, the hire company who was flogging off a load of old ex-hire tuxedoes, top hats et al. We gorged ourselves on cummerbunds, bow ties and wing collars, all of which had seen service at many a wedding. You never know when that stuff is going to come in handy; Martin would still look good in it today.

The East End was particularly sartorially fecund. Although the Bengali community were rapidly displacing the Ashkenazi Jews, who had lived and sewed there for generations, Brick Lane still had old Jewish tailors, cloth merchants and outfitters who had stock stretching back through the ages. There were also still a few old bespoke tailors, and I must have just got a grant cheque at some point, because I remember going with Chris Sullivan to get a whistle made by a wonderful old Hebraic chap in a Dickensian workshop round the back of what is now Altab Ali Park in Whitechapel.

I'd done my homework and said I wanted a high-breaking, tight-fitting two-piece in a houndstooth check, with what's called a Max Baer back – a pleated, half-belted style named after the world heavyweight boxing champ and noted dandy from the 1930s. Immediately, this old bloke with pins in his mouth knew exactly what I meant and produced the perfect suit and still allowed me to keep enough money to buy a Schlitz in the Blitz. That suit was a huge success and made me feel like a real stylistic heavyweight when I wore it with a pair of highly polished (second-hand) Anello and Davide dancing shoes on a Tuesday night. I danced with an extra spring in my step that night and broke the sacred Blitz rule by wearing that suit numerous times.

The fashion students had their own particular look, and would make clothes not just for themselves but also for their own little clique. When Melissa produced a collection, Steve Strange and half a dozen of the inner sanctum would suddenly all be wearing her complex geometric tabards, which were difficult to get on and almost impossible to get off, as evidenced by the chaos and the shrieking down in the toilets when any of them needed a pee. Stephen Linard's look was based on the austere black-and-white clothes of the Hassidic Jews. It was as if the club had suddenly been invaded by devout, Torah-reading rabbis from Stamford Hill.

The St Martin's crowd in particular was fiercely competitive with each other, always trying to outdo, outshine, outrage. Princess Julia tells a brilliant story of seeing two of them literally rolling around on the floor fighting over a scrap of material from the off-cuts bin outside Borovick Fabrics, the haberdashers in Berwick Street in Soho: 'It was like Danny La Rue versus Charles Hawtrey.'

But the biggest sartorial bunfight came when Charles H. Fox & Co., a venerable theatrical costumiers and wig makers in Covent Garden, decided to sell off a warehouse full of their old stock, all originally made for West End productions. The highly theatrical Blitz darlings descended upon the sale with the most sharpened elbows and lightning reflexes, battling it out to buy that Regency gown or Victorian frock coat, that Hussars jacket or Mississippi riverboat gambler's hat. The quality of schmutter at the club definitely peaked for a few weeks after that.

Willie Brown, a charming, self-effacing and rather studious young designer from the same part of north London as myself, was the first of the Blitz crowd to get his own brand and shop, Modern Classics, out in what was then proper bandit country: Rivington Street in Hoxton. His girlfriend was the beautiful Vivienne Lynn, one of the leading fashion models of the age, who lent a catwalk glamour to the club, often standing looking striking with Steve at the front by the till.

The very name Modern Classics hinted at our collective post-modernist blending of old and new, and its silhouette drew heavily on the revolutionary designs of 1920s Russian constructivism. Its location put the fear of God into us, however. I went with Gary to see the shop a week or two after it opened and we were both quietly anxious about heading to such a barren and brutal land. Gary came from Essex Road, not much more than a mile away, but even he was wary. Back then, Hoxton and Shoreditch – now so fashionable and lively – were famous for dereliction, villainy and fascism. All but abandoned, this was one of the strongholds of the National Front and, even on a weekday afternoon, we had to be really vigilant getting the bus out to EC2.

Willie was a proper pioneer in that part of London, the very first to see the potential of all those empty warehouses, shuttered shops and desolate streets. Our clubs were in Soho and Covent Garden, our haunts in the West End, our shops in and around the centre of town. There was a tenacious urbanism about the Blitz crowd, a determination to make this town swing again and a love of the inner city that went against the still-pervasive suburbanism of the time. A little later, I bought a beautiful, plain, grey, woollen kilt from Willie and wore it home on the Tube. It was the first time I had ever felt my inner thighs rubbing together on public transport, a memorable experience.

Our focus was on rundown inner London, but there is one other unlikely location which played a surprising part in the story of the Blitz: Bournemouth, the sleepy, south-coast resort much favoured by retirees and old football managers. Before Ibiza, there was Bournemouth.

Back in the 1960s, the mods had famously revved up their scooters and descended upon the seaside every bank holiday for a tear-up with the rockers at Brighton and Clacton, and this tradition of mass bank-holiday beanos at the seaside had continued into the 70s. For some reason, the hipper end of the soul scene had made Bournemouth their chosen destination, taking over the town's nightspots, installing good DJs and generally having a funky good time. Chris Sullivan, who had been there in his soul days, was full of enthusiastic tales of dancing, drunken debauchery and sticky rock down Dorset way. So a group of us decided that we should join in.

It was May bank holiday 1979 and the rowdier elements of the Blitz crowd assembled at Waterloo station in all their slightly bedraggled holiday finery to head down to the south coast. My little group was all there, as were Dagger and some of the Islington crowd, the O'Donnell brothers and their crew, the wild west London lot and a glam rockabilly mob from St Albans – maybe fifty or so overdressed herberts, intent on jollity at the seaside. Ollie O'Donnell wore five types of tartan, Christos Tolera wore an Italian-cut mohair suit.

Almost nobody had bothered to book accommodation – sleeping was not high on the agenda – so lots of improvising had to be done. None of us knew quite how we would be received by the locals, or by the young soul revellers who headed there from all corners of the land. In those days, things could easily turn nasty. But that bank holiday, they turned interesting.

Our arrival in town caused an instant frisson among the many hundreds of party people already there, but it was a buzz of an entirely positive kind. Everywhere we went, we were welcomed into pubs and clubs, treated almost as celebrities, the centre of just about every party. And there were plenty of parties – starting at lunchtime in the Vaults, the Fox or the Badger, continuing at the beach itself with boom boxes and bikinis, then as far into the night as you could stretch in one of the many late venues.

There were groups of young revellers from all over the country, many of them fascinated – some sexually so – by the pretty poseurs down from London. We were very popular, which solved the accommodation problem for some. As one uncouth youth put it, 'we were welcomed with open legs'. It also became clear that, in among the party people, there were some like-minded, similarly attired souls, kindred spirits. We saw people who looked a bit like us, the first sign that this thing was expanding.

Chris knew a big group of ex-punks from Wales who were now very much in the groove; they spoke of a club in Cardiff with a similar vibe. We also met a small, brilliant cohort down from the Midlands – lots of leather trousers, big back-combed hair and shoulder pads. Birmingham Eddie and Valentine were two of the most prominent Brummies, terrific raconteurs who told tales of a club in their hometown called the Rum Runner, which sounded a lot like the Blitz with a Black Country accent. We all swapped contact details and handed out invitations. The DJs even started responding by dropping some electro tracks in with the funk as we took over the night.

I remember Steve Dagger, a bandana round his neck and a gleam in his always inquisitive eyes, saying to me at four in the morning, somewhere on the Bournemouth promenade: 'This thing is catching on. It's gonna be big.'

6
ELECTRO
DISCO

Rusty Egan is irrepressible, a force of nature, a whirlwind of rhythm. If Steve Strange's vigilant bonhomie set the high bar for the characters who made it into the Blitz, Rusty's music set the tone and defined the mood. It was upbeat, modern, positive, progressive, but also exotic, dramatic, cinematic; the glamorous soundtrack to the movie we were starring in, propelling us all to fame, fame, fame.

Rusty, the son of a musician – his dad ran the Bernie Egan Trio – is every inch a drummer. He talks in a rapid staccato patter, paradiddle sentences ricocheting around and sudden rimshot stops while he draws brief breath and unleashes the next volley of sometimes-indecipherable stream of consciousness. When talking about music – and he's always talking about music – he uses his hands to tap out bpm tattoos on his body and his mouth to provide a beatbox illustration. He smiles a lot, he talks even more, he misses his buddy.

Steve Strange and Rusty Egan were a wonderful double act, ying and his mate yang, the classic odd couple who complemented each other perfectly and rowed perpetually. Where Steve was flamboyant, Rusty was sober and dapper, DJing in a suit and tie and formal shirt with cuff-links. Where Steve was high camp and theatrical Welsh, Rusty was straight-ahead, no-nonsense London Irish. Steve was softly spoken, Rusty was loud. Steve was queer, Rusty straight. Steve was wildly hedonistic, Rusty too obsessed with his records to do drugs or even drink. They both wanted to make enough to pay the rent on the flat they shared in Chelsea. Steve Strange wanted to be famous, Rusty Egan wanted to make music.

And the music he made us listen and dance to was, in its way, every bit as radical and transformational as punk ever was. Rusty

Egan created the soundscape of an era and provoked and propelled a generation of musical talent. He also became one of the first celebrity nightclub DJs.

At Billy's, he didn't have much to work with: it was a Bowie night, so every third record was by the master himself, or Roxy, Iggy or Lou Reed, the classic glam staples. There was also the arty end of punk: the Banshees, the Cure, Magazine and the occasional novelty record – the theme from *Stingray* anybody? But it was the instrumental synthesiser-driven stuff by Kraftwerk, Giorgio Moroder and Yellow Magic Orchestra which really stood out and made you stand still for a second before hitting the dancefloor. You didn't hear that anywhere else. That was different, that was new. And it would become the distinctive soundtrack of the Blitz.

It was also a break with tradition that Billy's and the Blitz did not feature live bands. For all its revolutionary rhetoric, punk – with its emphasis on sweaty blokes with guitars and drums bashing away in the room – was musically quite reactionary. It was old time rock'n'roll with a slightly different snarl. The lumpen punks hated disco, whereas most of the crowd in Steve and Rusty's clubs, despite a punk dalliance, had come through the soul scene or the gay scene. They'd been clubbers, they grew up on dance music, they loved disco. That gave them a different perspective.

When you go to see a live band, the musicians up on stage are the centre of attention and you are the audience, but when you go to a nightclub where they just play records, you are the centre of attention, you are the star of your own show. What you wear, how you move, who you socialise with, dance with, flirt with, is the essence of the evening. Music in a nightclub is a social and sexual lubricant, a rhythmic backbeat for everything which goes on.

Rusty, a drummer always obsessed with rhythm, played music for would-be stars to perform and parade to. It was a catwalk serenade · in 4/4 time.

His constant search for new and unheard sounds was part of a rapidly changing contemporary soundscape which he cottoned on to very early on. Central to all this was a technological shift whereby synthesisers went from being huge, refrigerator-sized machines with a million knobs on, like something out of NASA operated by proper boffins in lab coats, to small, affordable, portable keyboards that pretty much anybody could buy and play. This first manifested itself in the UK with dark and arty acts like Throbbing Gristle, The Normal and Sheffield's Human League making hard-edged, industrial-sounding records. They found a place on Rusty's decks, especially 'Being Boiled' by the Human League, which become one of the anthems of the night.

When the Human League played in London at the Marquee in 1979, there was a big buzz and a massive turnout, especially from the Blitz crowd who went to see what the fuss was all about. There was something brewing, a new zeitgeist perhaps. That tiny room was heaving, so crowded that apparently Iggy Pop and Bowie, who arrived late on their own spying mission, could not get in. I did and was impressed with Phil Oakey's hair; we shared the same exaggerated asymmetric wedge. They were very good with a few memorable tunes, but in terms of presentation, the whole thing felt slightly old-fashioned. They were still a band in a rock venue, after all. By that stage, we had moved on, jettisoned rock'n'roll. We were turning Romantic.

Rusty had used his post-Billy's sojourn in Germany to good effect by collecting a whole new set of discs, and he made it his mission to make sure that there were always cutting-edge tunes every Tuesday at the Blitz. He spent most of his week hunting down vinyl and if you went into a record shop in London, Rusty would be there, demanding to hear anything with a synth or a syncopated drum pattern. He was now playing more and more electronic music, matching and mixing beats, often big, lush space-age anthems like 'Underwater' by Harry Thumann or 'Supernature' by Cerrone, which were just a wafer away from being disco and a few years ahead of house, EDM and the whole four-to-the-floor rave scene. Rusty got there first.

But he could also throw a good curveball, mixing the out-and-out dance stuff with Marilyn Monroe or the Walker Brothers or Grace Jones doing Piaf or Bowie singing "Heroes" in German. Operatic, romantic, decadent, the influence of the movie *Cabaret* was writ large but it never became pastiche. Just as the clothes horses in the Blitz picked from the past to create the future, so did the DJ. He was inventing a whole new style as he went along. It was cosmopolitan, eclectic yet focused, pretentious but never po-faced. It was great fun: jiving to Sylvester's 'You Make Me Feel (Mighty Real)' with a they/them in suspenders and a veil or a bloke in a biker's jacket is undoubtedly a good time.

And Rusty never played too loud. The music at the Blitz was always an accompaniment, never the absolute focus, so you could talk, you could argue, you could hear exactly what George thought about Marilyn or Simon Withers thought about the Neue Sachlichkeit movement. This was not a rave. This was a soirée with the most pretty and bolshy young things in town. And Rusty never played the star DJ game either – there was no spurious knob-twiddling or fader-shifting. Nobody ever stood and watched Rusty do his job. He knew he wasn't the show, but rather the musical director of our collective show, that phantom film we were all making.

The music at the Blitz, indeed the whole ethos of the club, was anything but rock'n'roll. It was anti-rock'n'roll. Punk had been rock's last hurrah and yet, for the kind of people who went to the Blitz, it had turned quickly sour, commercialised and commodified, watered down to new wave. So we turned our backs on noisy boys with guitars. There really was no Elvis, Beatles or the Rolling Stones for us – those were the old days. Peter York put it brilliantly when he said we were 'kids who'd grown out of the twentieth century'.

There was every reason to want to leave 1979 behind. Britain was dubbed the sick man of Europe, a failed state in hock to the International Monetary Fund, in perpetual turmoil, economically depressed, politically riven. In May of that year, just as the Blitz was really starting to swing, Margaret Thatcher arrived, promising to bring harmony where there was discord. Yeah right. Rather, one of the most bitter and tumultuous periods of our history was about to be unleashed: strap yourselves in, there's turbulence ahead. A battle for the soul of the nation was fought out on the unemployment and picket lines, in the coalfields and the gay bookshops. In the Blitz, we were having a party.

Certainly, there was an element of escapism – there was a lot of shit to escape from; we were living in a wasteland – but it was much more than that. We were well aware that you're only young once and we were young at a tough time, but despite that intended to make the most of it, make the most of ourselves. Because prospects were so bleak, because the situation was so bad, especially for people emerging into adult life at a time of record unemployment with a nation seemingly mired in decline, nobody could rely on the conventional routes to success: safe jobs and straight careers, which seemed extremely unlikely. So we started creating our own paths, relying on our own support systems, using all we had, which was ourselves and the clothes we stood up in. Money was rarely mentioned because nobody had any or really expected to get any. Our currency was style.

Nobody sitting on those bar stools at the front of the Blitz at 2 a.m. talked about getting a proper job. Not one, not once. It just wasn't an option. These were shining bright girls and boys, about to emerge from top educational establishments, or out there already successfully ducking and diving, quick and clever, creative and courageous. We spent many hours talking loudly over Rusty's records, discussing and arguing and planning and plotting.

We talked about art and music, fashion and style, starting bands or shops or magazines or clubs of our own, putting on shows and exhibitions, making movies, taking photos, doing whatever we could. None of us had actually achieved anything yet, but we felt like we could, we would. It was the punk, three-chord, do-it-yourself ethic made manifest. It was the arrogance of ignorance. All we knew was we felt special. After all, we were here in this special place: the chosen ones.

★   ★   ★

A plot was hatched at the Blitz one Tuesday that we should make a trip to Berlin. Berlin at this stage – the Cold War raging, the wall standing, the city brutally but romantically divided – was the most darkly glamorous place in our collective imagination. There was the Bowie link, of course, all those magnificent albums recorded there. If David loved it, so surely would we.

In our imaginations, Berlin was all spies and soldiers, Soviet agents and red guards. It was a movie set with good gear. There was a Teutonic, electronic thing already going on within our scene, with Rusty virtually making Kraftwerk the house band of the Blitz. Plus, Berlin had the whole 30s *Cabaret* chic, Sally Bowles in a bowler, great coats and great Soviet iconography. We had to get there. So obviously we organised a football tour.

You can fly to Berlin now on a budget airline in a couple of hours for a few quid and go raving to your heart's content, but in 1979 it was a very different, much more complex and costly prospect. But somebody, probably Graham Ball, had discovered that we could get a grant from the LSE to help fund a football trip. Myself, Graham and a few other friends – including Iain Hill, who went on to become one of Europe's leading music promoters – already played for our own ad-hoc LSE team called the Cosmos. So we contacted a Berlin university to organise some matches and some accommodation and let it be known that if anybody fancied joining us, the trip was on.

Chris Sullivan, Simon Withers, Graham Smith, Ollie and Jimmy O'Donnell, Steve Lewis and the wonderful Jo Strettell – at that stage Simon's girlfriend – all signed up to be part of the squad. I bought a red CCCP hammer-and-sickle football shirt, packed a bag with my best Vivienne Westwood bondage in it and headed for Victoria station, where we were all going to rendezvous to get the train to Berlin. The train to West Berlin, with a few left-wing student footballers and a crowd of Blitz regulars: now there's an adventure.

Given that this was way before the Channel Tunnel and that we were heading in the cheapest seats possible for a besieged enclave on the eastern periphery of the known world, it was a long and arduous journey of trains and boats and trains and trains. I remember very little of the detail, but I can still distinctly recall the sounds and smells of an old-fashioned corridor and carriage locomotive rattling noisily across Mitteleuropa for hours and hours and hours. There were stops in drab towns the colour of putty to buy bread, sausage and beer, which just added to the aroma, and many hours spent gazing out the window pretending to read Marx as some sort of research. One section of the epic schlep is still absolutely vivid in my mind, however.

Like a scene out of a James Bond novel, when we reached the border with communist East Germany, the train stopped and we waited with some trepidation. We were about to make the last leg of our journey in occupied territory through a barbed-wire corridor to the completely surrounded bastion of West Berlin. Soviet guards in all their stern communist regalia boarded the train and inspected everybody's papers to ensure that no ne'er-do-wells were entering their workers' paradise. The looks on their faces when they came to our carriage, only to be confronted with a first eleven of London's nocturnal finest, attired in a bizarre concoction of theatrical garb made more than a little crumpled by the rigours of the journey, were priceless.

Chris was wearing his all-black 'Milk Tray man' outfit, I was in leather trousers and spiky Westwood bondage boots, Simon was in Willie Brown constructivist kit and the O'Donnell brothers, both with huge bouffant quiffs, were sporting quadruple denim and biker boots. When we tried to explain that we were a university football team heading for a tournament in West Berlin, they seemed to realise that everything they had ever been told about the decadence of the capitalist West was undoubtedly true. After much inspection of bags and passports, they finally – and reluctantly – let us proceed when we showed them our football boots and our lairy yellow and green Brazil-inspired kit. But it was touch and go for a while.

Once in West Berlin, we were met by a delegation of local anarchists who had been told we were a well-known and highly respected far-left football team here to play some matches and show solidarity with the Red Army Faction and the like. They took us all to their squats in Kreuzberg, where we were going to be staying. Clearly a few porkies had been told in the organisation of this trip.

All our lurid fantasies about Berlin were true. Surreal, dramatic, exciting, it was a bizarre place, cultured but claustrophobic. Hemmed in by that wall, everything was exaggerated and intensified, hedonistic and yet deeply Germanic. Those anarchists, who so kindly let us crash in their vast, squatted old factory building hard by the river that marked the border with the east, were seasoned revolutionaries constantly talking about violently overthrowing capitalism, yet were appalled when we crossed the road at night without waiting for a green light.

They were also amazed at our outfits and our chutzpah. Within a couple of days, we had taken over a local nightspot and turned it into an outpost of the Blitz. We talked the management into letting us run the night, select the music and invite the guests. Somebody discovered that you could buy slimming tablets over the counter in German chemists which, if taken in handfuls, would provoke much dancing. We would invite the best-looking people we saw on the street to come and join us – and they did, in large numbers.

I don't think there are many similarities between Berlin and Bournemouth, but like our trip to the latter, we were welcomed enthusiastically by the local hipsters of the German city and became part of the best party in town. There was a fabulous group of women a couple of years older than us – Bettina and Gudrun are the two I remember – who were part of a band called Malaria!, a little like the Slits back in England. They adopted us and introduced us to their studiously arty crowd. Later, Gudrun would go on to form Einstürzende Neubauten, the leading German industrial band. Every night, we found ourselves in this wild whirl of clubs which, because of the unique laws in West Berlin, were open all night. So we stayed up all night and then had to play football. Or some of us did.

Only two games were actually completed and, of course, we lost both heavily. One of those was in a proper stadium with supporters; the captain of the opposition team handed us a commemorative pennant and made a speech in flawless English about what an honour it was to play such an esteemed team from London. Little did he know that half of our starting eleven had spent the night in a subterranean S&M club and been asleep on the floor of Alexanderplatz station just half an hour before the game.

The highlight of the trip for me was a foray into East Berlin, which really was like something out of *The Third Man*. Still pockmarked and scarred from the Second World War, dimly lit and eerily quiet, oppressive but impressive, it was deeply, darkly glamorous and a bit scary. There was genuine fear crossing over to the communist side, particularly because we had pulled some dodgy currency trick which meant that we were laden with illicit East German currency secreted about our bodies, which had to be smuggled over the border at the famed Checkpoint Charlie.

It was hard for us to look anonymous as we filed past the grey-faced guards, who studied us as much as they did our papers. One of our lot got stopped, questioned and then taken into a menacing-looking room to be interrogated by the higher-ups. We all waited nervously to see if he'd been arrested for currency smuggling, but after a few minutes, he walked free with a smile on his face. It turned out they were fascinated by his footwear, which they had taken off and inspected, handing them around because they had never seen a pair of winklepickers before. If they had looked closer, they would have found a fortune in his socks.

We all headed to the most expensive restaurant in East Berlin, which was in the communications tower where they spied on the West, a bit like the revolving restaurant atop the BT Tower in London. We emptied our pockets and hosiery of all that cash and ordered the best vodka and bowls full of prime Russian caviar, which none of us had ever eaten before. The waiters were perhaps understandably miffed by our apparent opulence and extravagance when, after we'd finished this feast, Chris pulled out another vast wad of notes from his pink zoot suit and ordered another round. But we tipped them at least a month's pay as we had to get rid of it all before heading back over the border before the curfew.

Berlin was great, but it wasn't London. To our minds, they had nothing to equal the scene we were part of back home; in the couple of weeks we spent in their city, we certainly did the research. One night, while we were out partying, Chris Sullivan and I found ourselves in the toilets of a particularly arty but grotty Berlin bar. As was the way in those days, there was a mess of graffiti scrawled all over the walls, doors and cisterns. Amid this jumble of Germanic hieroglyphics, somebody had written the words Spandau Ballet. One of us, and to this day neither of us can remember which, said, 'That would be a good name for a band.'

7

TRIBAL
BRITAIN

Britain was a hundred years behind, but ten years ahead. In the late 1970s and early 80s, the British Isles were an untamed, dysfunctional yet fiercely creative place. Nothing worked, including large sections of the population. We had none of the urbane sophistication of our continental neighbours, food was terrible, restaurants abysmal, high-street fashion horrible, the film industry was moribund, intellectualism was derided, modern art was dismissed and design was something poncy that the French and Italians did. We were still obsessed with chintz, while the chinless, posh Sloane Rangers were all the rage. And yet we excelled at certain things. The French did cuisine, the Italians did furniture, the Germans did cars and we did football hooliganism and youth culture.

Football hooliganism, punk rock, mod and this new dandy cult awaiting a name all stemmed from the same tribal roots. I was far from the only Blitz regular who went to watch my team every other Saturday; Dagger and Graham Smith were part of a large Spurs contingent, the Kemps were Arsenal, Graham Ball, Brentford. I had to tone down my outfits a little when going to a game, especially after receiving that clump round the head at Sheffield United away, but back then the terraces were a fecund place in terms of fashion as well as fighting. From the late 60s onwards, when I first started going to QPR, I was aware that football crowds were joyous, lawless and dangerous, but they were also incredibly creative.

Football was still strictly a working-class sport: the middle classes had rugby and cricket and Sky was yet to commercialise and commodify it. Going to games was cheap, the grounds were decaying and the fans were pretty much allowed to get on with it. There was little policing and little reporting of what occurred. Middle- and upper-class British society didn't care if oiks in designer labels kicked lumps out of each other on crumbling terraces. A whole subculture grew up around the sport. The fighting was the dark side of the coin, but there was also fashion, fanzines, singing, chanting . . . A way-ward, anarchic tribalism fed by the bravura brilliance of the excluded and ignored. And that's exactly what youth culture was, too.

Our propensity to produce these amazing collective manifesta-tions of outsider style and creativity is what made Britain ten years ahead of everybody else when it came to popular culture in all its forms. Can you imagine the French or the Italians producing punk? We were mired in the Dark Ages when it came to bourgeoise ni-ceties, but leagues ahead in trousers and tunes. It's what we became internationally famous for. In fact, it's almost the only thing we exported, as both football hooliganism and punk rock and Two-Tone and later New Romantic found adherents in many countries. Two examples of a uniquely wayward British street genius: bovver boys and bands.

The same energy and creativity, the same devil-may-care, risk-taking, group-identifying, live-for-the-moment passion, fed both. It led Liverpudlian casuals to rob Europe dry of designer sportswear whenever they played abroad. It led Two-Tone kids in Coventry to go fighting in the dancehalls while skanking to great tunes, and punks and skins to battle it out on the streets over political news-paper pitches. This rebellious spirit led rastas and rude boys to stage a resistance on the streets of Brixton, Bristol and Liverpool; it led to every subcultural development out there, including, believe it or not, to New Romantics prancing about in Covent Garden.

The young people who went to the Blitz might have been more extravagant, more flamboyant, more arty, more educated than some of the other youth tribes, but they were every bit as feral. These were piratical times. The queer lads in particular were not just outsiders, they were outlaws. The age of consent for male homosexual sex was twenty-one, so most of them had been criminals for years and were used to flouting the law. Illegal drugs were commonplace, another way in which many of the Blitz crowd were beyond the pale. Many lived in squats, entering and taking over properties in decaying central London, changing the locks, stealing the electricity and surviving off the grid and outside the mainstream. Everybody who went to the Blitz was flouting normality; just dressing the way they did in the face of open hostility was both transgressive and dangerous. Going to the Blitz meant being a risk-taker, which would pay dividends later on.

One particularly wild Tuesday night has gone down in London lore. It was shortly after we arrived back from Berlin, by which time the Blitz was a raving hit with lines of people forming early outside, desperate to get in.

Inevitably, a couple of alternative one-night clubs had opened to challenge this nocturnal hegemony – and to cater for those who Steve Strange deemed unworthy. One of these was the Batcave, which, as previously mentioned, was aimed squarely at the always rather square but quite charming goth mob. It was much less a rival than a theatrical adjunct for those who favoured mauve.

Another was called Studio 21 at 21 Oxford Street, up by the scuzzy Tottenham Court Road end. Held on Thursday evenings, it was run by a bloke called Jock McDonald who, although Scottish, was part of a rough-house north London, Arsenal-supporting crew with links to Johnny Lydon and his brothers and their pals. This was a more blokey post-punk place where a geezerish gang of spiky-haired Pistols fans had a house band called the Bollock Brothers. Lacking any of the panache of the Blitz, it was nonetheless on the nocturnal circuit.

Occasionally some of the Blitz crowd would find themselves mixing uneasily with the Studio 21ers, including one night when Chris Sullivan and Jock McDonald ended up in an argument and then a fight, supposedly prompted when Chris accused Mr McDonald of being less than chivalrous. Fists flew but no serious harm was done. Not an unusual event in 1979, and that should have been the end of the affair, except it wasn't.

The following Tuesday, we were all in the Blitz and the usual stuff was going down. Rusty was raving to anybody who wouldn't listen about some new electro tune he'd discovered, Melissa was damaging the ozone with hairspray, Marilyn was bitching, Steve Dagger was trying to persuade me that Gary Kemp would one day be a great songwriter and Christos had found a new girl to snog on the stairs while maintaining his carefully waxed moustache.

Sartorially, it was in that period when there was lots of ecumenical religious gear going on, and a fair bit of body paint. I can't recall exactly what I was sporting but it might have been my Max Baer-back whistle, as some of us had started rebelling against the theatrical extremes and were dressing as 'straight' as possible. Chris interpreted this as wearing an Edwardian suit, cravat, spats and a monocle.

It was quite late in the night, certainly way past midnight, when we heard a kerfuffle at the door. Usually by now Steve had seen off any wannabes and everything had settled down, but a sudden bout of shouting and banging alerted us all to the fact that something was going down at the shallow end. Jock McDonald and a group of maybe half a dozen or so of his Gooner cronies had barged past Steve and were heading straight for Chris armed with the bar stools they had picked up on the way. What came next was an almighty, no-holds-barred, bar-room brawl in a fancy-dress shop.

I was actually on the dancefloor as it kicked off, which thankfully meant there was quite a crowd between me and the action, but I had a perfect view of what was going on as I tried – without too much conviction – to get to the frontline. I saw a stool bounce off Chris's bonce, dislodging his monocle, but seemingly doing no other damage as he used his noggin to head-butt McDonald. At the same time, one of the many religious converts present, a nun if I remember correctly, started aiming beer glasses at the heads of the invaders. The whole crowd leapt into the fray, including some of the beehived girls. Rudolph Valentino threw a punch or two, Bonnie Prince Charlie took a right hander, Dan Dare was right in there. John Wayne would have been proud.

For a second or two, it was touch and go, with the punky interlopers and the glamorous denizens going at it hammer and tongs. But then the wild west London rocking lot, who had been up to no good down by the toilets, came running up the stairs to join the action. They quickly routed the ne'er-do-well Studio 21ers, who were last seen running down Great Queen Street, their spiky blonde barnets gleaming in the lamplight. A cheer went round the room, a couple of black eyes were proudly paraded and we went back to posing the night away. It was just one of those nights.

I have no recollection of the night that Steve Strange denied Mick Jagger entry. I was undoubtedly there, but nowhere near the front door when the Rolling Stone and his retinue got turned away. I only read about it in the press later. I'm sure that Mr Strange knew exactly what he was doing. It was a perfect statement and wonderful publicity; by that stage, he had an eye for exposure and his own mythology as the great arbiter. A twenty-year-old boy telling the most famous rock star in the world that he was insufficiently fabulous to enter his club is just about the most punk rock thing you can possibly do. No Elvis, Beatles or Rolling Stones in here. And Steve told everybody else for weeks afterwards exactly what he had done.

Even by the extravagant standards of the Blitz, one of the more memorable nights was when a bunch of the young art students, who went by the collective name of the Neo Naturists, performed some sort of tableau. Led by the splendid Miss Binnie, who always seemed to be taking her clothes off at every available opportunity, this involved running round the club bollock- and fanny-naked applying body paint and incanting, while Iain R. Webb (now Professor Webb, a leading writer, curator and educator), dressed only in a loin cloth, was suspended on a giant crucifix on the dance-floor in decoratively dolorous style. I have no idea what it was all about. Perhaps it was Easter. It was only years later I discovered that one of those naked naturists was none other than Grayson Perry.

It was, of course, splendidly silly and crushingly pretentious, but surely you should allow yourself to be pretentious when you're a teenage artist? Not being scared of being labelled pretentious or a poseur was one of the great liberating qualities of being part of the Blitz scene. Be whoever you want to be, do whatever you want to do; just make sure you do it with style. It meant we were free of the debilitating British fear and dismissal of anything arty or outré, that we could do stuff and try stuff and not worry about being mocked or laughed at.

Nobody in the Blitz was going to diss you for going too far. They had no concept of over-the-top, and everybody outside was laughing at us anyway. When you've been derided daily in the streets for the way you look, it makes you pretty thick-skinned and immune to criticism. When the time came for me to stand on stage under a spotlight and recite my preposterous poetry before Spandau Ballet gigs, I had no shame or shyness whatsoever in doing so.

Perhaps the most famous night at the Blitz was the one when the messiah arrived. Steve certainly let *him* in. It is hard to exaggerate how important David Bowie is in this story: he was our raison d'etre, our inspiration, our catalyst, our hero who assured us we too could be heroes, just for one day, which was pretty much the motto of the Blitz. Even if you weren't a massive fan, he was a huge influence on every one of us, whether individually or collectively. As George O'Dowd put it, 'It was all Bowie's fault.'

The night the Thin White Duke turned up at the Blitz, it was as if Jesus had nonchalantly walked into our local church and sat down on a pew. The internet tells me it was Tuesday, 1 July 1980, so the Blitz was well into its stride. In retrospect, it's a surprise it took the great chameleon so long to get there.

As well as being a perpetual innovator and shapeshifter, David Bowie (née Jones) was also a compulsive jackdaw. Throughout his life, through every one of his incarnations – from the ingénue mod, through the hippy troubadour, the glam titan, the plastic soul man, the Man Who Fell to Earth, the Thin White Duke and the Berlin aesthete – he had researched and read, borrowed and stolen, adapted and adopted and made things his own, as all the greats do. Bowie was the ultimate artful dodger, a creative picker of intellectual, musical and stylistic pockets, so that he was always up with the latest trend and down with the hippest kids.

By 1980, he must have heard that there was a club full of Bowie acolytes forging a dramatic new sartorial and musical path, though his own career was somewhat in the doldrums. After the triumphs of *Low* and *"Heroes"*, the third part of the Berlin triumvirate, 1979's *Lodger*, felt a bit flat and, 'Boys Keep Swinging' aside, had not been a big hit. So eventually he made his way to No. 4, Great Queen Street to scope the scene and co-opt his offspring in order to give his own career a boost.

No prior warning was given. He just arrived at the door with a couple of assistants (one of them Des O'Connor's daughter Karen) and, upon spotting him in the queue, Steve Strange immediately decided that the great man could not be forced to make his way through the melee and so whisked them round the back and in through a fire escape, somewhere by George's cloakroom.

He was then ushered to a table upstairs where Steve sat with him and his clique deep in some kind of conference. Bowie very sensibly did not try to compete with the overdressed denizens. He was attired in a well-cut, rather straight grey suit and white shirt, and appeared smaller, slighter but even prettier than I had imagined, a beatific smile upon his face.

Word flew round the club that the maestro was present, but there was a kind of muted frenzy, a hushed hysteria as everybody tried to appear cool while hoping not to wet themselves with excitement. I recall nodding in agreement when someone declared David Bowie to be yesterday's man, though we both knew he didn't mean it. After a while, Bowie got up and mingled and most of the crowd maintained an admirable sangfroid as this charming man introduced himself, smiled a lot and asked a few questions, a little like royalty does. Nobody asked for an autograph or took pictures, nobody took liberties. Everybody hoped he'd grace them with a wonky-eyed gaze.

He was there, of course, not just to spy on the scene and cast a glance at his supplicants, but to recruit some little helpers to appear in the video for 'Ashes to Ashes', the lead track from his new album *Scary Monsters (and Super Creeps)*. Steve made sure he was involved and pulled in a few potential candidates. Some were furious when they didn't get a part; others were adamant that they never wanted the gig anyway.

Personally, I had no desire to be in a pop video. I'd already started calling myself a writer, though there was no evidence to support that claim. Besides, I knew they were going to be looking for the more theatrically attired and made-up characters. Eventually, Steve roped in a couple of the most striking women, Judith Frankland and Darla Jane Gilroy, who were both at the heart of the whole nuns-in-space, flowing robes and white faces look. The deal was that they would get fifty quid for accompanying David dressed as a pierrot as they trudged across an East Sussex beach, miming to words about dear old Major Tom.

When it came out, the video was a major pop culture moment, one of the defining images of the new decade. It was Bowie's first number one for years and his fastest-ever-selling single; the start of the most commercially successful period of his life. The Starman had done it again: co-opted the zeitgeist, captured the times and sent out a message that this scene was really about to go stellar.

The night that Jackie Charlton – yes, *that* Jackie Charlton, the gangly, Geordie Leeds and England centre-half – made an appearance and stood in the shallow end, benignly surveying the scene, has not quite gone down in history. Nor has it ever been explained what he was doing there or how he got in, but it definitely happened. Odd things happening at the Blitz was not unusual. We were used to it. Most nights at the Blitz were special in one way or another, and even as we were living it, thoroughly immersed in its choppy waters, I think we all sensed we were part of something which would be remembered long after the night was over.

The other big event to recall is the one which resulted in the plaque that still stands outside No. 4, Great Queen Street today. It marks Spandau Ballet's first gig on that spot, on 5 December 1979. Unlike regular Blitz nights, it was a Wednesday.

Steve Strange had put on an extra night for the Blitz club Christmas party and was recognising that fact by putting on the first ever live musical performance by a five-piece band who were themselves all regulars at the club. This marked a major turning point in the story, not just of that bunch of boys from the Angel who became a band, not just of the Blitz club itself, but of the fortunes and futures of so many of the crowd who gathered there. It was the point where we began to break out and force our way in.

8
LET'S
GO
TO
WARREN
STREET

I was still living at home with my mum and Chris Sullivan, an odd triumvirate if ever there were one. She was a proper old London girl, a former clippie* with a sweet gorblimey accent, a big-city tolerance and a fiercely protective attitude towards her boys. If any of the neighbours asked why we dressed in such a bizarre fashion, she would tell them we went to lots of fancy-dress parties. If they persisted, she would tell them where to go. She was a firm believer in 'each to their own' and 'live and let live', my mum.

Melissa and Graham Smith would often pop round and, very occasionally, if we went to a party in outer north London, a gang might end up kipping on our floor. The sight of half a dozen make-up-splattered youths, their spikes and pompadours collapsed, their outré outfits dishevelled, scattered all over her living-room floor never phased her. 'What would you like for breakfast?' was her response to such a scene.

By now we were going out four or five nights a week. Tuesday was still the focus, and we would still be planning our outfits a week in advance, but there were a plethora of parties and events and clubs to which we were increasingly invited – or, at least, where we were tolerated. We were at the centre of a social whirl which was the opposite of centrifugal, and we were continually finding ourselves in the centre of town at three or four o'clock in the morning. There were no night buses to Burnt Oak, no night Tubes to anywhere, so there was the perpetual question of where we were going to crash.

The art school hall of residence would often find its population doubled at dawn. If it was just me, there was a small, plush room at the top of the LSE called the Founders' Library, which had panelled

---

* An affectionate name for a female conductor on the London buses.

walls, self-important portraits of Sidney Webb and George Bernard Shaw, and a comfy sofa to kip on. I discovered that it wasn't locked at night and so would sometimes sneak in there, especially on a Tuesday as it was just around the corner from the Blitz and I had a class on Wednesday morning. But it did mean being rudely awakened by the porters at 8 a.m., still attired in my outfit from the night before.

Often the aim was just to stay awake until the Tube started again at about 5.30 a.m., but London back then was not a 24-hour city. If we had any money left to buy food or drink, we could head to one of the few all-night spots in town. There was Fred's diner in Kingly Court just off Carnaby Street, which stayed perpetually open. You would often see bedraggled post-Blitz kids sharing a burger and a shake in the company of the local sex workers from the Dilly. One of the Chinese restaurants on Gerrard Street stayed open late and served beer in teapots, or else we could try the pubs of Smithfield, where you could buy a pint at 5 a.m. but had to pretend to be a blood-splattered bummaree.*

Or we could go to Warren Street – 65 Warren Street, to be precise, though I'm not sure it had a number on the door. In fact, I'm not entirely sure it had a door. This was a vast Georgian townhouse of the grandest type, an entire block deep, four storeys high, three sash windows across, with a huge sweeping central staircase and large, high-ceilinged rooms radiating in all directions. Today it would be worth many, many millions, but back in 1979, it was just left dilapidated, seemingly abandoned, a perfect metaphor for London at that time.

---

* A bummaree is a meat-market porter.

This place had been empty and neglected for years until late one Sunday night when Stephen Linard, Kim Bowen, Barry Bryant and Lee Sheldrick, four of the most hardcore Blitz denizens, were heading home, walking down Warren Street from the Embassy Club. Sunday at the ever-so-glam Embassy on Old Burlington Street in Mayfair had become one of the fixtures in our weekly calendar. It's when we all got to eat.

The Embassy was a flash, New York-style disco – all full-length mirrors and marble pillars and city boys, villains and models dancing badly in high heels to Chic. But on Sundays they had a special deal which we took advantage of. You had to be signed in by a member and pay £10 per head, which was a fortune, but once inside it was all you could eat and drink all night – champagne and steak in this ritzy disco. So we would put aside any aesthetic considerations and be there all night doing both. For some of our crowd, this would be their only proper meal of the week.

On that particular Sunday night in 1979, this foursome, all their money spent, were walking home in the early hours to Wood Green in far north London, where they lived in a series of semi-legal squats alongside a certain Helen Folasade Adu, a fellow St Martin's fashion student. But like most of us, they hankered after a central London pad and somebody noticed that this veritable mansion just off Tottenham Court Road seemed to be unoccupied.

A quick recce revealed an open window and they all clambered in to discover this extraordinary house, worthy of Miss Havisham. It was covered in cobwebs, with cracked windows, bare plaster and floorboards, treads and banisters of its grand stairwell missing, doors hanging off hinges, holes in floors and walls, but impossibly glamorous in a decaying Dickensian fashion. Bingo.

That night they huddled together in one room for warmth and the next day set about making this their home. Rooms were divvied up, furniture moved in, electricity was connected, though there was never hot water – the plumbing was medieval and the cooking facilities consisted of a single gas hob and a kettle. Amazingly, there was a functioning telephone line, so word was put out that they had a new base. It became what must surely have been the craziest, most inspirational house in Britain. It became the famed Warren Street squat: this was where the Blitz kids lived.

There was something of a shifting roster of residents, but the four original finders nabbed the best rooms and stayed throughout, Warren Street royalty. They were joined by the lovely sisters Jayne and Lesley Chilkes. Lesley was the house make-up artist and went from room to room applying slap. Film-maker John Maybury and David Holah of BodyMap, who were a couple, took a room; Melissa Caplan had the garret at the top; Jeremy Healy shacked up with Kim Bowen; Princess Julia lived there; Stephen Jones made his hats there; Christos was forever making passes; Cerith Wyn Evans was making art; Graham Smith used it as his photographic studio and dark room. And just about everybody who was anybody on that scene would turn up, join in and crash out. It was communal, chaotic and incredibly creative.

Warren Street, which on the one hand was a squalid, dangerous, cold-water squat with living conditions which would be rightly condemned in any decent society, was also the most fantastic, fascinating and thrilling house I have ever entered. Everybody was busy making art or craft of some kind – there were mannequins and sewing machines, sketches and patterns, easels, cameras, hats, kilts, costume jewellery and scraps of fabric scattered everywhere. But, most of all, they were busy making art pieces of themselves. It was a laboratory of style.

Any time of night or day, the residents and the visitors would be experimenting with looks and themes, trying on wigs, shortening hems, pooling resources, borrowing accessories, dyeing hair, painting nails, stealing food from each other. In many ways, Warren Street was almost as central to the whole Blitz story as the Blitz itself.

George O'Dowd never lived in Warren Street, but he soon found himself another squat just round the corner in Great Titchfield Street, which he shared with Andy Polaris. The pair of them and Marilyn seemed to always be around cadging hairspray. After that, they moved to yet another even more rickety and perilous squat in nearby Carburton Street. (At that time, you could pretty much just decide where in central London you wanted to live, pick an empty building and move in.) That house in Fitzrovia became the centre of a broader community of freaks and artists, a magnet for the wild, weird and wonderful. And if you had nowhere else to go after a night at the Blitz, or anywhere else in town, there was always the option of 'Let's go to Warren Street.'

The place was riotously incestuous and you'd never know who would wake up in which room. Many a fleeting liaison of every configuration was formed and just as soon forgotten, especially after the parties held there, which were legendary and perilous. A party night in Warren Street was like *Withnail and I* in drag times ten, with a script in Polari. Many of the love affairs, alliances, dalliances, friendships and enmities, the bands and the brands that came out of the scene were forged in the bedrooms of Warren Street.

The squat would come to a tragic and tawdry end when a Japanese girl known as Mitsu, who was on the fringes of the scene, was found dead of a heroin overdose in one of the rooms. The stench of despair descended upon the place, as did the Metropolitan Police. All the fabulous creatures moved out and a gang of hardcore drug users moved in, a sorry final episode to a briefly brilliant tale. Prior to that, though, Warren Street was the venue for Spandau Ballet's first-ever photoshoot.

Spandau was not the first Blitz-inspired music project: the first demos were made in mid-79 by the established musos in the club. Rusty Egan was a drummer, after all, and Midge Ure had been in numerous bands, including the Rich Kids with Rusty, so they began working on various incarnations of an electro-music project dubbed Visage. Steve Strange had always believed he should be the frontman of a band, rather than just front of house in a night-club, so he stepped forward to sing and they were demoing tunes together from early on.

But the boys who would become known as the house band of the Blitz, the first ones to break out of the scene and onto *Top of the Pops*, did not even let anybody know that they were musicians until pretty late in the game.

Gary and Martin Kemp were the two brothers at the centre of a small coterie of lads from the working-class side of Islington, maybe ten or so in total, known collectively as the Angel Boys. The youngest and most charismatic was Christos Tolera, now a highly respected artist, but then still at Central Foundation School in Old Street with Martin, who was the baby dreamboat of the Blitz, according to many of the gay guys and straight girls.

The rest included Steve Norman, who was a good-looking, easy-going blond boy from the rough Bourne Estate in Clerkenwell, with a floppy fringe and a cab-driver dad; John Keeble, who was the quiet one from far-off Kentish Town; and Tony Hadley, tall, dark and statuesque, with a passion for Frank Sinatra. They'd all been to Owen's Grammar School where they met Steve Dagger and Stephen Woolley (he of Scala Cinema and Palace Pictures fame), both in the year above.

This Islington clique formed one of the many little subsects at the club and, from the moment we first met back at Billy's, I hit it off immediately with Gary. He didn't tell me he was a musician – or maybe he did, in the way that I told people I was a writer without actually doing any writing. Much of what people said they 'did' at the Blitz was theoretical, in that what we actually did full-time was dress up and go out. Anyway, I didn't know that Gary and some of his gang had been in a series of power-pop bands called, variously, the Roots, the Cut, the Makers and the Gentry. No wonder they kept changing names.

It was actually Steve Dagger who first informed me that Gary and his handsome brother Martin, Steve Norman, John Keeble and Tony Hadley were in a band and, what's more, that he was their manager. All those stories of Pete Meaden and Andrew Loog Oldham, quintessential swinging London Svengalis of the Who and the Stones were his inspiration and told me that he was going to do something similar with Gary's band – and, seeing as I was a writer, I had a part to play too. All this was during a lecture in comparative political structures or in the library over a Hegelian tome or two, on one of the days that we had actually made it into the LSE.

Steve, although theoretically studying politics and economics, was really an A-grade student of London's pop culture history. He was obsessed. He'd grown up in the West End, his family originally from Soho – his dad was a father of the chapel (a trade union leader) on Fleet Street – and he saw the whole music and fashion world as both his birthright and his career path. He would rant and ramble on about the 2i's, the Old Compton Street coffee house where the British music scene first percolated; about Larry Parnes and Adam Faith, David Bailey and Twiggy, Justine de Villeneuve and Jon Stephen; about 60s venues such as the Scene, the Whisky and the Scotch of St James. He knew his stuff and decided that we needed to do something similar for our era.

From the moment he first walked into Billy's and saw this nascent scene emerging, Steve had been plotting how to make sure that he and his boys were part of it and could somehow use it to become famous. Gary and Steve had both seen the Sex Pistols at the Screen on the Green, their local flea-pit cinema – a gig which had been put on by their schoolmate Steve Woolley – and Dagger was more than au-fait with Malcolm McLaren's music-biz machinations. He spent all his time working out how to do something equivalent with the thrilling milieu we found ourselves in.

One step towards fame came courtesy of myself and Chris Sullivan, when on 10 March 1979, we organised and promoted what I believe was the first ever warehouse party in London. It was literally in a warehouse in Battersea, an old railway store under the arches, hard by the river, owned by Toyah Willcox – who was herself an occasional Blitz kid, usually in the company of Derek Jarman and often dressed by Melissa Caplan. On the proceeds of her burgeoning career in film and music, she had acquired this crumbling edifice near Battersea Dogs Home – which looked like something from the set of *Popeye*, all rickety wrought-iron stairs, pulleys, cranes and wonky wooden floors and walls – and lived in a tiny part at the top, sleeping in an old coffin. You could do stuff like that back then.

Chris, who got on with just about everyone, knew Toyah well and convinced her to let us use her large, ramshackle space to put on what was effectively a rave. She had dubbed her gaff 'Mayhem Studios', and we set about adding to the mayhem by inviting every cool hothead in town to come and party there. Graham Smith designed the invite using an old Diane Arbus image, Simon Withers did the lighting and projected vintage porn films onto the ceiling and Steve Marshall took care of the sound rig. I was going to DJ and Chris would do the door. We all chipped in a few quid to cover costs and didn't even think of charging people to come in; we just wanted to have a good night. We had a great night.

That was my first experience manning the wheels of steel. I'd seen Rusty do it enough times; I had a pretty good record collection and just had the attitude that *It can't be hard, can it?* Actually, it is considerably harder than it looks and, despite being a pretty decent selector, if I say so myself, I never really mastered the technical side. My speciality was playing the wrong side of the record at the wrong speed, but on a night as tumultuous as that first Mayhem gig, nobody seemed to care. 'Give it a go and learn on the job' became part of the credo of being at the Blitz, a blithe assumption that you can do anything if you just try. What we did between us was put on a truly great event.

The first Mayhem party became instantly legendary, with seemingly every face, rascal, trendsetter and mind-bender in town present. The police inevitably came, but faced with this extraordinary scene, which looked like somewhere between a 60s freak happening and a futuristic sci-fi cosplay party, they gave up and let us be. For weeks after, nobody talked of anything else but that event at Mayhem and everybody bragged about being there whether they had been or not. Steve Dagger noted this and put it in his playbook for the moment his protégés were unleashed.

That moment came, as unlikely as it sounds, on a wet, autumnal morning on the Holloway Road on Saturday, 17 November 1979. I say unlikely for two reasons: firstly, the Holloway Road – a grotty, traffic-choked north London thoroughfare – is about as unglamorous a setting as you can get, and, secondly, because this was not a group of people who did mornings. But somehow Steve Dagger persuaded Steve Strange, Rusty Egan, myself, Chris, Simon Withers, Graham Smith, Melissa, Jo Strettell, Julia and a couple of others to come along to Halligan's rehearsal rooms, a dank and distinctly smelly warren of dark cave-like spaces on this grim street, to see his boys play. Most of us had not yet been to bed. Hangovers were being nursed and expectations were not particularly high.

Gary has since described the performance on that Saturday morning as the most important gig they ever played (an audience of a dozen or so sleep-deprived London trendies vs 1.5 billion worldwide viewers for Live Aid a few years later, and he chose this one). In retrospect, it was important even for people who weren't there, because the success Spandau achieved almost overnight opened up doors and possibilities for everybody, myself very definitely included. And it all relied on Gary's band being well received by a bunch of hungover Blitz kids on the Holloway Road.

If the handful of carefully selected 'influencers' (that term had, of course, not been invented, but it is very apt) hadn't been impressed, it's hard to see exactly where Steve Dagger would have gone from there. His whole strategy was to use the connections, the contacts and the clout forged within the confines of the Blitz club – the glamour by association, the momentum of the moment and the movement – to propel his band forward. We were the wave and Gary, Martin and the boys were going to ride upon it. Or, as somebody else put it, we made the mould and Dagger poured the band into it.

First, and perhaps most importantly, they looked the part, albeit in a rather do-it-yourself, buttoned-up, dark and arty way. It was cold in Halligan's and overcoats were worn. Given that they were by now all regulars at the Blitz, it is not a great surprise that they looked good, but to be honest it was really only Gary, Martin and Steve Norman who were genuinely into the fashion aspect; Tony and John went along with it. Martin in particular, with his chiselled chin and natural pizazz, had become a proper Blitz face and had a perfect eye for the visuals. Gary wrote the songs, Martin orchestrated the look, the others were the musicians. It is often said that, back in the 60s, the Small Faces were mods who became a band, while the Who were a band who became mods. Half of Spandau Ballet were Blitz kids who became a band, and the other half were a band who became Blitz kids.

By this stage, they were going all out to be the embodiment of this as yet unsung, unnamed and still underground scene. Steve Dagger knew that it was only a matter of time before this whole Blitz thing blew up into something very big and he was desperate to make sure his wards were right at the front of the charge. This meant they had to get everything right that Saturday morning.

Where the Makers and the Gentry and all their other incarnations had basically been guitar-driven, leap-about, punky power-pop bands, this new version were based around a cheap synthesiser which Gary stood stock still behind and played with two fingers. They all did their best to look serious and posey with lots of fringes swaying. Movement was at a minimum, sangfroid was maintained, shapes were cast, stares were well practised.

Clearly Rusty's record selections at Billy's and the Blitz had been absorbed into Gary's songwriting, and the first track they played opened with a brittle but cinematic sequence of single synthesised notes, catchy and clever. When Tony opened his mouth and that big operatic voice came bellowing out, spouting Gary's splendidly pretentious lyrics about being beautiful and clean and so very, very young, the small audience, all of us, looked at each other in deep amazement: *Blimey, they're good.* And they just got better, including a brilliant instrumental version of the theme from *On Her Majesty's Secret Service* that was right on the money and even had us dancing. It was quite a relief: I had dreaded having to lie to Gary about it afterwards, as he was one of my best mates.

When we all gathered after the forty-five-minute performance in an old rundown Irish pub on the Holloway Road, we could all say with genuine honesty how impressed we were. Everything about them fitted the tone and tenor of the times; there was a certain detached coldness to the sound, a steely electronic sheen which came with the territory. This was supposed to be the antithesis of sweaty rock music, new and cool and arch, but there was also an almost classical lushness to some of it, especially Tony's voice, which made it feel romantic and epic. Plus, with that insistent beat from John's metronomic drums, you could do the Blitz jive to it. Gary dubbed it European dance music.

Even Steve Strange, who was desperate to be the first pop star to emerge from this scene (he hated Gary Numan for having beaten him to it with 'Are "Friends" Electric?' and banned him and his music from the club), admitted that they were great and asked them if they would become the first band to play at the Blitz at the Christmas party in just two weeks' time. Simultaneously, Chris Sullivan informed Dagger that we were planning the second Mayhem warehouse party for a week after that and asked whether they would play there too. They leapt at the chance. Steve's plan was underway. This band was about to be launched via its Blitz connections.

We asked what they were going to be called. Gary and Steve both saw the look on our faces when they said they were called the Gentry. I guess it was supposed to get across the idea that these kids, all from rough old Islington council estates, were somehow working-class aristocracy, dressed like lords and living the life of Riley. But no, surely not: *not good*. Chris Sullivan and I both shook our heads. We already had the answer tucked away from our trip to Berlin and I said 'You must call yourselves Spandau Ballet.' Gary and Steve thought about it for about thirty seconds and both nodded. They now had a new name and gigs planned at the two most fashionable venues in London. Somebody bought another round.

Since then, I have heard numerous elaborate theories on what the name means, but it genuinely did not mean anything. It just sounded good, arty, pretentious and posey, exactly like us. Most importantly, it did not sound like a rock band. The Spandau bit had that hard Mitteleuropa edge, a bit Berlin, a bit Bowie, while the ballet reference was sensual and feminine, sylph-like and glamorous. European dance music. And it was about to be launched at the most fashionable nightclub in the world, for that was, by now, definitely what the Blitz had become. And it was about to become my job to tell everybody.

9

THE
BALLET
BEGINS

After that Saturday morning on the Holloway Road, things changed. Up until then, the Blitz had been a weekly party and a lifestyle choice – it was always more than just a nightclub, and being part of this scene was full-on, a complete commitment – but nobody yet saw it as a future, a launch pad, a career path. We were having such a blast that nobody really gave a thought to what came next. Except for Steve Dagger.

The rest of us were still in the 'no future' nihilist, hedonist stage of our teenage years, but all of a sudden, because of the Spandau Ballet project, and because Dagger was determined to include as many people as possible from the scene, our futures started to emerge. Being part of this became something akin to a job, except nobody was paying us yet.

Steve, working from his mum and dad's fifth-floor council flat in Holborn, immediately involved everybody he could in the process of making this band big. Simon Withers, Melissa Caplan and Willie Brown were roped in to design clothes; Simon would also do the lighting; Steve Strange and Chris Sullivan would organise and promote shows; Ollie O'Donnell would do hair; Steve Marshall looked after the kit; Graham Smith would take care of photography and graphic design. I, meanwhile, was made minister for propaganda, which is literally how Steve Dagger put it.

That first Mayhem party had, in many ways, provided the blueprint for the early stages of Spandau's rise. The whole anti-rock'n'roll ethos of the time meant that they could not just go and play the 100 Club or the Marquee – that would put them in the morass with every other two-bit band in town. Instead, Steve had decided upon a ploy of only performing in front of invited audiences of the hippest crowd, at one-off events in unusual venues, and of making every gig unique, a happening. Was it elitist? Yes, but it was also very clever.

His strategy had the advantage of making each performance seem like an event, of creating a buzz around the band and making people desperate to get in to see them. But it also crucially meant Steve could control precisely who was present at the shows, including the press and the record companies, who were strictly not invited. The theory was that if the record companies couldn't get in, they would become desperate to do so once they heard the hype. And if the press couldn't get in, they couldn't give bad reviews, so you could create your own press, which was where I came in.

It was all about the buzz. In a pre-digital age, this was all done by word of mouth, getting the right people – which meant the Blitz people – raving about the band and harnessing the momentum of the movement. So they played the Blitz.

My recollections of that first Christmas party gig are hazy. I suspect alcohol had been taken. But I do recall that the place was rammed and the tiny dancefloor, which served as the stage, was way too small for five quite burly blokes. Because the stage wasn't raised enough, you had to go on tip-toes or stand on one of the stalls or chairs to see them, which meant that people were desperately peering over each other and craning their necks to do so, all of which just seemed to magnify the intensity of the event. The atmosphere was fervent.

Some of the people doing the craning were already established stars; Billy Idol, Midge Ure, Steve Severin and Marco Pirroni from the Ants were all present to check out the new kids in town. The band, who looked just right in their tartan sashes and constructivist strides, played the same short set they premiered at Halligan's and fitted perfectly into the ambience and aesthetic of the club. I do recall asking George and Philip Sallon what they thought, and both of them were excoriatingly dismissive, which I took as a very good sign. Everyone else seemed to love them, though, and they went down well among a very hard-to-please crowd.

Indeed, halfway through the set, so only four or five numbers into their first ever official gig, a conventionally well-dressed grown-up ambled up to Steve Dagger and asked him what the band were called. He replied, for the first time ever, 'They're called Spandau Ballet.' This man then offered to sign them to his record label on the spot. He was Chris Blackwell, owner of Island Records, who had come along by chance with his hairdresser, Keith from Smile. Dagger knew from that point on that his plan was working.

Smile, a stupendously trendy hairdressers in Knightsbridge owned by Keith Wainwright, plays a part in this story. It was where the likes of Bryan Ferry and Derek Jarman got their hair cut. It had pioneered the 'crazy colour' craze during the punk days and now it had become the epicentre of the tonsorial excesses of the Blitz crowd. As we know, Jimmy and Ollie O'Donnell both worked there – Jimmy for colour, Ollie for cuts – along with another ace face, Spike Denton. Almost all the Blitz crowd would go there at some point during the week to hang out and be seen as much as to have their 'do' done.

Smile was where Ollie razored off my asymmetric wedge and gave me a Buzz Aldrin flat top, and, later on, the General Custer curly long back and sides. It was where you went to find out what was happening and where the next party was. And it was where Steve Dagger went to put up posters and hand out invites to the next Spandau gig, just a few days before Christmas 1979.

The first Mayhem party had been a triumph, so we repeated the format. Again, Graham designed the invite, on my mum's kitchen table, as the three of us sat round thinking what to call it, finally settling on 'Mayhem 2 – A Crash Course For The Ravers'. It was a rave and this time we actually charged people entry, partly because of the added cost of putting on this new band everybody was already talking about. It was obviously a very attractive proposition, because tickets flew out and just about every member of every style tribe in London – the soul set and the rockers, the Blitz kids and the futurists – turned up and tried to get in, whether they had tickets or not. It was complete chaos as hundreds of people, all dressed to the nth degree, stormed the place, with only Chris Sullivan and Steve Marshall keeping them at bay at the top of those steep and wobbly stairs. The pass at Thermopylae came to mind.

Inside, with people literally hanging from the rickety rafters, it was even wilder. It all went psychedelic very quickly. The porn films projected onto the walls seemed to inflame a few couples, who started to get it on. A group of people had clambered up onto the stage we'd built and were showing off their slightly wonky Blitz jive. One person climbed up onto the roof, fell about twenty feet and just got up, dusted himself down and continued dancing. The whole place was jumping.

Inevitably, the police came again, stuck their helmeted heads inside, looked around with amazed stupefaction and left, defeated once more by the madness. It was loud, it was raucous, it was glorious. Amid all this, and already way past midnight, the band somehow had to get up there, get everybody's attention and play.

To try to get the room ready for a performance, I jumped up on stage, took the mic and said, in my best and loudest cockney aesthete's voice, something about how we must all concentrate, the Spandau Ballet being the dance of perfection. Somehow it worked and the place became still and hushed enough for the opening notes of 'To Cut a Long Story Short' to ring out. I felt quite proud of myself. We kept the porn films playing behind them while they were on, so that the more distracted members of the audience would keep looking at the stage. We needn't have, though: the band were fantastic and a perfect match for this crowd. They looked and sounded great, getting better by the week, although I'm not sure how many people were really in any condition to judge. None of that mattered; the whole shebang was so wonderfully riotous, so hip and so hot, and word spread so fast about the roaring night at Mayhem. The band's brilliance was magnified by being part of this event; success by association, just as Steve had planned.

I enjoyed my little slot up there on stage, showing off, and so I set about writing a piece of preposterous poetry to recite before the next gig. Dagger had resisted the temptation to get Spandau Ballet signed to Island Records, reckoning they could get a better deal if he got a bidding war going with a few more carefully chosen events and some press coverage.

The first task was to get the band photographed, so Graham Smith took them to Warren Street for their first ever photoshoot. He'd taken some snaps at their Halligan's debut, but this was their first shot at posing for a lens, which came fairly naturally to them, it turned out. He produced a series of stark black-and-white images of these five handsome youths looking stern and dramatic in their buttoned-up finery. They looked like time travellers from the 1930s, all high collars and floppy fringes, ballet slippers and jodhpurs – certainly not what post-punk rock bands looked like at the time.

There's (again) a touch of *Cabaret* and a bucketload of *Brideshead Revisited* about those shots, but you have to remind yourself that these are actually kids from the council estate being photographed in a condemned, derelict cold-water squat. It's the old mod saying 'clean living under difficult circumstances' made manifest. There's a certain trying-too-hard stiffness, but also a palpable hauteur about those pictures. It was the arrogance of ignorance; they didn't know what they were doing, so they posed and pouted for all their worth.

Graham tells of how, during the shoot, George O'Dowd came in and started barracking the band, showing off, playing up and telling them that he was a better singer than Tony Hadley and how he was going to be bigger than them. Later on, he admitted that it was all because he was jealous and that he really fancied Steve Norman. Later still, of course, he arguably did become bigger than Spandau, a huge global superstar, but he might not have done so if they hadn't shown the way. This was the first time he'd even mentioned singing; Spandau was creating a blueprint for Blitz kid success.

The next gig was back at the Blitz, the second of only two shows they played there and their third show in total. On that night, Rusty's mate Richard Burgess – who was often to be seen talking beats and beeps to Rusty at the DJ booth – was brought into the camp to act as producer. He was both a drummer and a synthesiser expert who'd actually taught Rusty to play drums and was a member of his own band called Landscape, who had a big international hit with 'Einstein a Go-Go'. Richard was also an inventor and innovator, specialising in electronica and computers, so he fitted the club's futuristic soundscape.

As one of the few adults in the room, Gary decided Burgess would be a good man to work on the band's studio sound, to capture both their essence and that of the Blitz. Richard went on to produce scores of hit records with dozens of bands and define the sound of the era, but he started with Spandau, as a result of having watched them live that night and seeing the potential.

By this stage, the press was starting to be interested in the scene and the band who now represented it. An *Evening Standard* journalist named David Johnson had tried and failed to get into the Blitz on a couple of occasions, but eventually Steve Strange relented and let him in and he wrote the first excitable piece about the club for what was then the leading London newspaper.

Despite being a relatively grown-up Fleet Street hack, David would become a proselytiser for the whole movement, falling in love with it in many ways, though along with everybody else he didn't know what to call it, so he just dubbed us 'Blitz kids'. A couple of fashion pieces appeared in *Tatler* and I was featured in a write-up in *Honey Magazine* with a picture in my PX top, the first time I ever appeared in the press. Interest was ratcheting up, but up until this point, the music papers had studiously ignored what was going down in Covent Garden.

It is hard to realise now just how important and influential the three weekly music papers – the *NME*, *Sounds* and *Melody Maker* – were back then. They each sold hundreds of thousands of copies a week and, throughout the 70s, could make or break bands almost at will. The *NME* was the trendiest and most arch of the three, with star writers like Tony Parsons and Julie Burchill, Danny Baker and Nick Kent, who were more famous than many of the bands they wrote about. But they were also mired in a crusty rock'n'roll mindset, which meant they dismissed the soul scene and disco, looked down on nightclubs and fashion, hated dance music, and would undoubtedly have despised and derided the Blitz if they'd heard of it.

But Steve Dagger knew that if he was to build the hype about his boys for the record companies, he would need to get them into the music papers as well as Fleet Street rags. He did the latter by walking up and down Fleet Street, where his dad worked, blagging his way in and using his considerable charm and chutzpah to convince people this young, unsigned band were the spearhead for a major new movement. This resulted in a piece in the *Sunday People* and a splashy two-page spread in the *Daily Mirror* on the wild happenings at the Blitz club, written by a reporter called Christena Appleyard.

Steve could, of course, have invited an *NME* or maybe a *Sounds* writer to their next gig, but he was far from sure what sort of review they would write. He was not the sort of man to leave things to chance, so instead told me that I would write a review for the *NME*, they would print it, I would become a music writer and Spandau would sign a major record deal. That was exactly how he put it and that was exactly how it happened.

By now, it was March 1980, and next up was the first of two gigs at the Scala Cinema, then situated in Fitzrovia and run by Steve's old schoolmate and occasional Blitz visitor Stephen Woolley. This was another example of Dagger calling in favours and keeping it in-house; we all pulled out all the stops to make it as achingly arty as possible.

Graham designed the invite in Russian constructivist style, Chris Sullivan oversaw the guest list; Simon Withers obtained a copy of Buñuel's classic surrealist film *Un Chien Andalou*, which would serve as the warm-up entertainment. He also designed 'expressionist' lighting, projecting shadows of the band onto the cinema screen while they played.

I was the pre-show DJ, choosing to play a set mixing classical music with intentionally unfashionable disco and funk tracks to highlight our soul-boy roots. It was decided (probably by me) that I would premiere my poetry, introducing the band on stage. I wrote it down on a scrap of notepaper, then committed it to memory. I stood at the microphone and read it in my most portentous voice to the slightly bemused audience as the band stood stock-still on stage, their silhouettes looming behind them:

> From half-spoken shadows emerges a canvas
> A kiss of light breaks to reveal a moment when all mirrors
>   are redundant
> Listen to the portrait of the dance of perfection
> The Spandau Ballet.

The show began. With the cream of the Blitz crowd present, dressed at their most ardently fabulous, transported to this back-street art-house cinema, it was as close as we ever came to an Andy Warhol-style happening. The atmosphere in that old picture house was crackling; you could feel the excitement. Again, there were crowds outside, including half the record company representatives in London. Steve refused to let any record company A&R men in, figuring that would just make them even more febrile; a couple tried to bunk in through the back door, but got caught.

The show was brilliant, probably their best so far. I think on that day Steve knew he had cracked it, as he had a massive Cheshire cat grin on his face. Those thwarted A&R men certainly heard the buzz about it afterwards because the phone in Dagger's dad's council flat did not stop ringing for days afterwards.

The next morning, I was back at uni. I was in my final year at the LSE and actually needed to do some studying for my degree, so despite the excitement of the gig the night before, I turned up for a class the next day. So did Dagger, although he had pretty much given up on his degree (managing this band was now his only aim). He came in specifically to badger me. 'Have you written a review of the Scala gig yet?' he asked. Of course, I hadn't. I didn't really think he meant it. But Steve is not an easy man to say no to. So he marched us both to his council flat and sat and watched as I wrote the review on a coffee table in his front room, trying to capture in a couple of hundred words both the essence of the band live and the scene they represented.

We then walked together, to save on the bus fare, from Holborn to Carnaby Street where the *NME* offices were, and Steve almost pushed me up the stairs to the reception on the first floor. Up until this point, I had been sceptical about this whole enterprise. I still held the *NME* in some esteem and assumed they would laugh at an odd-looking twenty-year-old with an exaggerated haircut and a review scrawled in biro, but to placate Steve I decided that I might as well give it a go. I asked the receptionist where the live editor was and he pointed at a scruffy-looking bloke on a desk at the far end of the room, which looked and smelled a bit like a sixth-form common room, with records, clothes and papers strewn everywhere.

When I got to the desk, this guy – who wasn't actually much older than myself – barely looked up at me, so for a second I stood there with my piece of paper in my hand not knowing what to do or say. Then I thought: Fuck it, I'm better dressed than him and I know about this stuff and he doesn't, and besides I quite fancy being a music writer, so I might as well go for it, give myself an edge.

My opening line was 'Your paper is shit,' which secured his attention. I then went into a breathless rant about this club called the Blitz, where the coolest, most modern people go and this new band called Spandau Ballet who have surpassed rock'n'roll and how the *NME* is so square and so behind the times that they know nothing about the new scene. Finally, with a flourish, I slammed my bit of tatty paper down on his desk. I then waited for him to throw me out. But give that man his due (if I knew who he was I would give him a credit) – he read the piece, said it was good and if we had any pictures, they would run it next week. In a state of shock, I said Graham Smith had pictures that I could get over to him that day.

When I went downstairs, Steve was waiting for me. I told him what had happened, expecting him to be as amazed as I was, but rather he just chuckled and said, 'I told you that would happen.'

That review I wrote for the *NME* was my first ever piece of journalism, the first ever mention of Spandau in print, and it came out on 29 March 1980. It began:

> Shadows dominate a white backdrop as five young figures
> dressed almost too well exude a soaring dance music that
> conjured up everything except rock'n'roll.

I then went on to regale the readers with tales of the elitism of the gig and the fabulousness of the audience, all intentionally provocative and deeply un-*NME* stuff, and finished up by stating that unless you are really in the know, you won't even be able to see this brilliant new band. The last sentence read: 'On the evidence of their latest performance, it really is your loss.'

Reading it now, I am simultaneously embarrassed and proud. It is arrogant beyond belief, but then so was I at that moment in time; we all were, it was our schtick. What I am not sure of is why the *NME* agreed to print it, because from that point onwards, they hated everything about Spandau and the Blitz. But print it they did, and the music-biz frenzy about Spandau escalated to new heights. They were now the hottest unsigned band in this or any town, and Steve upped the hysteria by refusing to let the record companies know when they were playing next or to let them hear any kind of demo tapes.

I got a cheque for £15 and, from that moment on, told people with some justification that I was a writer. Most importantly, I told myself I was a writer and then set out to prove it. Almost immediately, I was getting regular work as a commentator on contemporary youth culture, appearing on TV and radio and writing a column in *Girl About Town*, a freebie magazine that the Spandau boys handed out at Tube stations to earn a few bob. I became the nation's de facto hosiery and silly hair correspondent almost overnight. If Dagger had not been so insistent, none of that might have happened.

After the *NME* piece appeared, Steve was inundated with calls. One of them was from London Weekend Television asking him if they could make a documentary about both the band and the Blitz scene which had spawned them. It was for a show called *20th Century Box*, presented by Janet Street-Porter. They wanted us to recreate the Scala show for the cameras; they would shoot it in arty black and white, along with a documentary about the lives of these fashionable Blitz kids. And the kids they chose to concentrate on were yours truly and the lovely Jo Strettell.

Today, Jo is just about the most revered make-up artist in Hollywood, a proper star in her chosen field. Then, she was a penniless but fearless art student like half the Blitz crowd and the girlfriend of Simon Withers, who was deeply entrenched in the Spandau camp. They sent the two of us clothes shopping at Willie Brown's Modern Classics in then-deserted Shoreditch, filmed Ollie cutting my hair at Smile and the likes of Christos, Melissa and Chris Sullivan getting ready for the gig. They also filmed Spandau putting their gear together in a beaten-up old motor at drummer John Keeble's parents' council flat. We were supposed to look glamorous, but actually we came across as what we really were: a bunch of sassy working-class youngsters trying hard to find a way.

Me reciting my now-notorious poetry before the band came on was just one of the many extremely pretentious parts of the show as I did my best to seem both intellectual and fabulous, but came across as rather self-conscious and surprisingly camp. But I looked good in my buzz cut and a second-hand Italian-cut suit, exuding the confidence and chutzpah which comes from years of strutting about in ridiculous outfits.

The film is great. The shots of our mates Blitz-jiving in the aisles are priceless and the band comes across as very polished, but still with a punky energy and desire, the real deal by this stage. I recall watching the TV show with my mum, sitting together on her floral sofa, and she was completely matter of fact about her son being on the telly. 'You've always been a vain bugger,' she said with a proud smile. Within a few weeks, I would be doing this for a living and Spandau Ballet would be a household name. Within a short while, the Blitz would be the most talked-about, written-about and analysed nightclub in the world.

10

ASPIRATION, ASPIRATION, ASPIRATION

Margaret Thatcher arrived at 10 Downing Street just a few weeks after Steve Strange first presided over No. 4, Great Queen Street: these two grand dames with big hair, big shoulder pads and enormous egos both ruled their fiefdoms with a caustic tongue and a will of iron. Between them, they came to define the decade, reshaping Britain in their image, dismantling accepted mores, challenging long-held assumptions. They both encapsulated the libertarian, individualistic spirit of the times and propelled entrepreneurialism and consumerism to the fore. Alright, I'm going too far with this analogy, but we do have to address the question: were the Blitz kids just Thatcherites in fancy dress?

That suggestion has troubled me for many years. My dad, who died when I was but a boy, had been a life-long building-site socialist and militant trade unionist who would have hated Thatcher with every fibre of his body. I had taken on his bolshy views and considered myself a committed lefty as a student at the then-still-radical LSE – and I wasn't the only one. As we've heard, Dagger's dad was father of the chapel on a Fleet Street paper, while Melissa was and still is a genuine anarchist, Chris Sullivan a staunchly socialist valley boy from mining stock and Gary Kemp would become part of Red Wedge. Almost all the people at the Blitz who had any kind of political awareness would have deemed themselves to be on the left. But others saw it differently.

That we were somehow the nocturnal wing of the Conservative Party was certainly an accusation made at the time, especially from the left-leaning but largely middle-class music press, who were convinced that these dandyish New Romantics with their estuarine accents and libertine ways must be Tories in disguise. Why weren't we wearing Dr Martens, carrying SWP banners and going to Redskins gigs? It must be because we were posh fops, rabid right-wingers and allies of the milk snatcher. The accusation has continued to plague us to this day.

I chanced upon a reader's comment section in the *Guardian* online recently which accused Blitz girl Sade – a woman of colour from a single-parent family in Essex, who was a staunch supporter of the striking miners – of being some kind of yuppie Tory stooge. It also managed to call me every kind of loathsome right-wing shill, because I liked fancy clothes and wrote for *The Face*. We have been tarred by association, but it isn't just by people who never got it and never went near the Blitz.

Dylan Jones, a firm friend who became an editor at *i-D* magazine before going on to run *GQ* and the *Standard* and write scores of books, served his time in the club, usually down at the shallow end. He was very much part of the Tuesday-night chattering classes, positioned on the stools with myself and Perry Haines arguing the toss and debating the times, and as a prominent Blitz alumnus has bluntly stated, 'The whole Blitz scene was Thatcherite.' But was it, really? What was the relationship between the economic upheaval wrought by Thatcher and the cultural revolution forged in the Blitz? Which was the bigger bang?

To this day, I sometimes muse on whether I was an inadvertent Thatcherite without even realising it. My politics are still firmly on the red end of the spectrum, but I realise that I was an active part of the 1980s zeitgeist which undid so much of the post-war settlement and promoted an aspirational entrepreneurial spirit. By the end of that decade, this was a very different country from the one I had grown up in, and we undoubtedly played our part in the dramatic upheaval.

I was a child of the welfare state: delivered by a National Health midwife, I grew up in a council house and was educated by the state to the age of twenty-one, no fees and a full grant. I was fed by the state in the form of free school meals after my father died and funded by them when I became a play leader for the Inner London Education Authority, which Maggie attacked and later abolished for being reds under the desk. I voted against Thatcher, campaigned against Thatcher, marched against Thatcher. My story is similar to many others who gathered at the Blitz, so how come we've been branded Thatcherite?

Well, maybe it's because we rode the same tsunami.

It is hard for anyone to argue that George and Marilyn and all the out-and-proud gender-morphing gay guys were natural allies of that uptight upholder of traditional moral values, the prime minister who oversaw Clause 28. I'm not convinced that the Grantham grocer's daughter would have enjoyed spending time in the ladies' toilets downstairs at the Blitz, while two blokes were frotting next to a girl snorting speed and applying eyeliner to a soundtrack of Throbbing Gristle. The roaring trade in pharmaceuticals was not quite the kind of free market she espoused.

Thatcher was an economic libertarian, but as far from a libertine as you can get and would no doubt have been appalled at the sex, drugs and electro disco of it all. And what's more, the squat-dwelling, rave-holding, gender-bending piratical bohemians of the Blitz could not have been further away from her deeply conventional, philistine Little England taste, with its tweed and twin sets. Yet there is no doubt that we had some traits in common.

Aspiration was the by-word of the Thatcher years and it is indisputable that we aspired like crazy. Aspiration – the desire to move on up and make the most of yourself – had always been part of a particular kind of British working-class youth culture mindset. The mods of the early 60s were all about looking good, dressing up, feeling hip, becoming a face. It was an innately elitist and intrinsically aspirational culture which valued individualism and style: the sharpest suit, the coolest scooter, the thrill of being in with the in crowd.

The 70s soul scene was very similar, with its designer labels and import records, lurid-coloured cocktails in Rumours and saving up for a Ford Cortina and some Antony Price schmutter on South Molton Street. And, of course, many, if not most, of the Blitz crowd had come through the soul scene.

Punk meanwhile, for all its rebellious, anti-establishment trappings, was in many ways overtly entrepreneurial. Its abiding message of you can do it yourself, start your own, was the most liberating aspect of the whole ethos. It was a clarion call to the creative and the ambitious. Punk inspired a generation to get off their arses and do something. And, of course, many, if not most, of the Blitz crowd had come through the punk scene.

I have never been an adherent of the hippy-dippy John Lennon imagine-no-possessions definition of socialism. You have to have quite a lot to think that less is more. In our house, we only had to look around the living room to see very few possessions, some of which were on hire purchase. My dad and Steve Dagger's would both have wanted their trade union members to have as big a slice of the cake as possible. My idea of the promised land was cake all round, so in that respect I was definitely aspirational, a champagne-for-all socialist.

But there was precious little champagne to go round in that era: we could barely afford a can of Schlitz in the Blitz. We were skint,

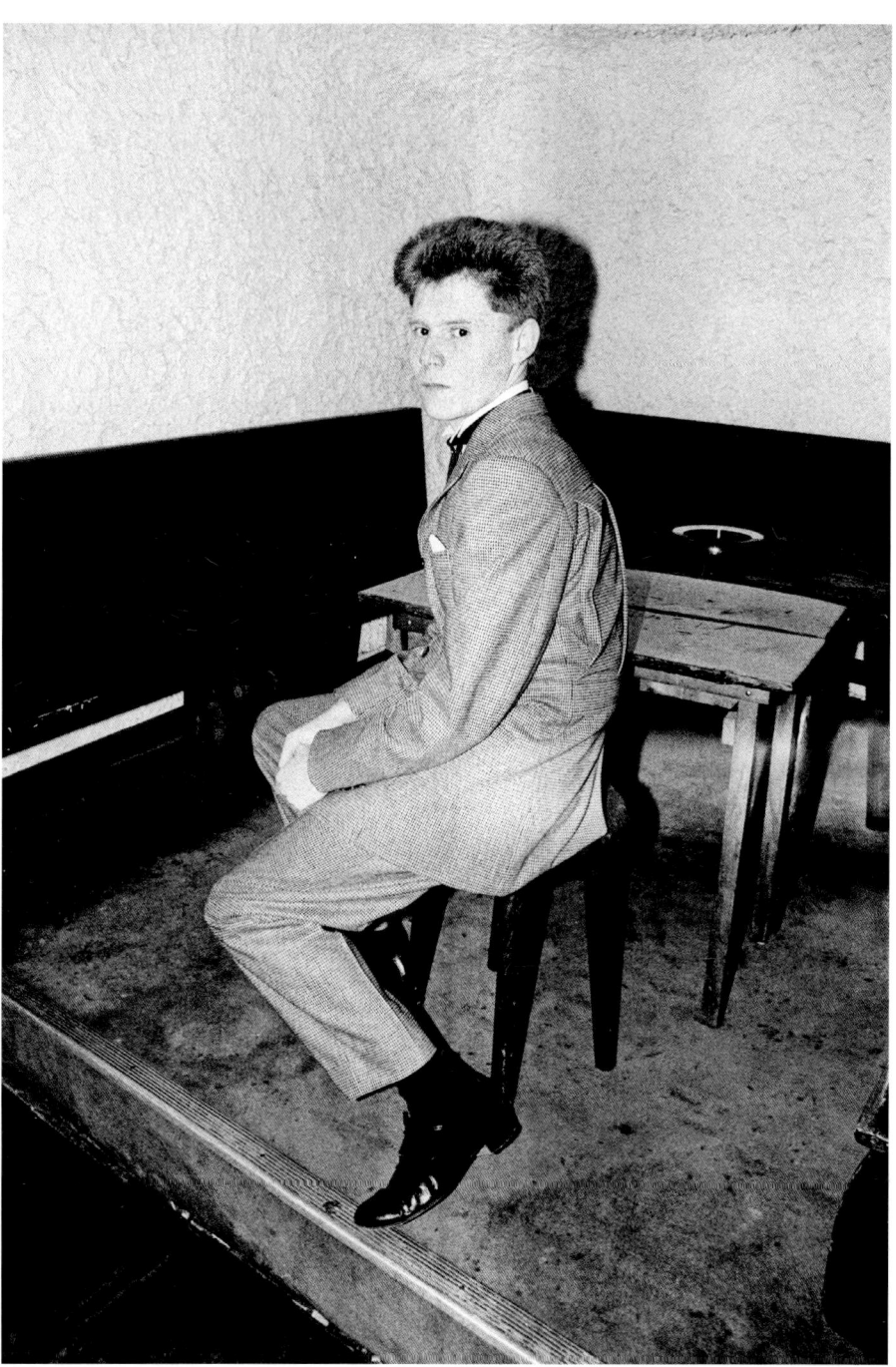

Me in the Max Baer-back suit at St Moritz.

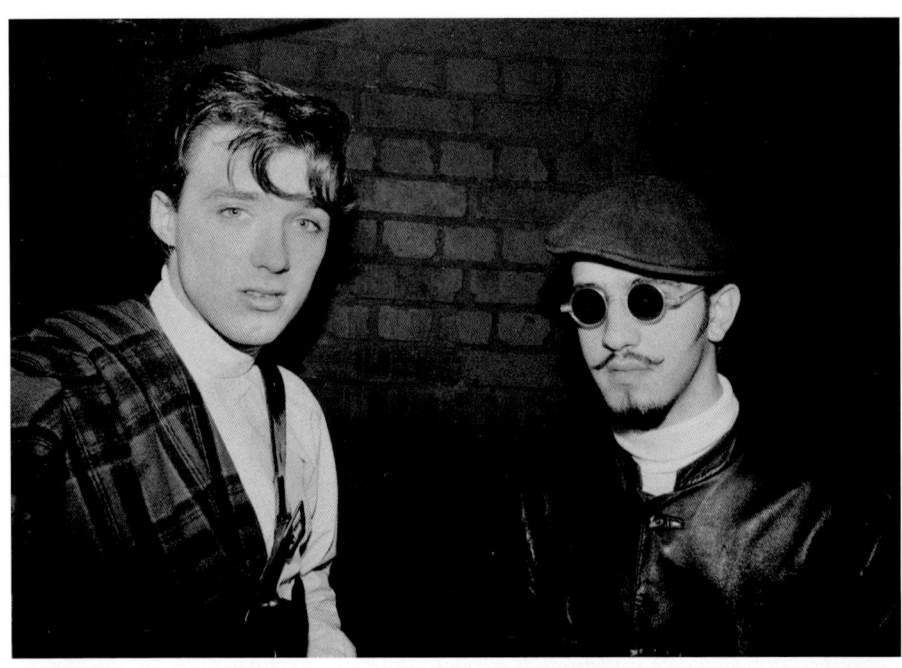

Martin Kemp and Christos Tolera.

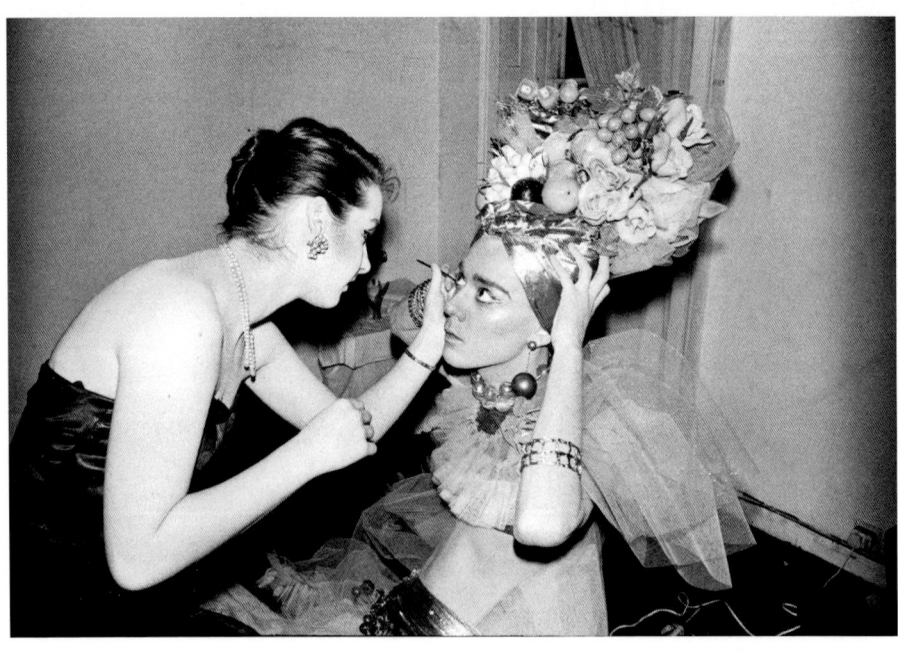

Kim Bowen applying Stephen Linard's make-up at Warren Street.

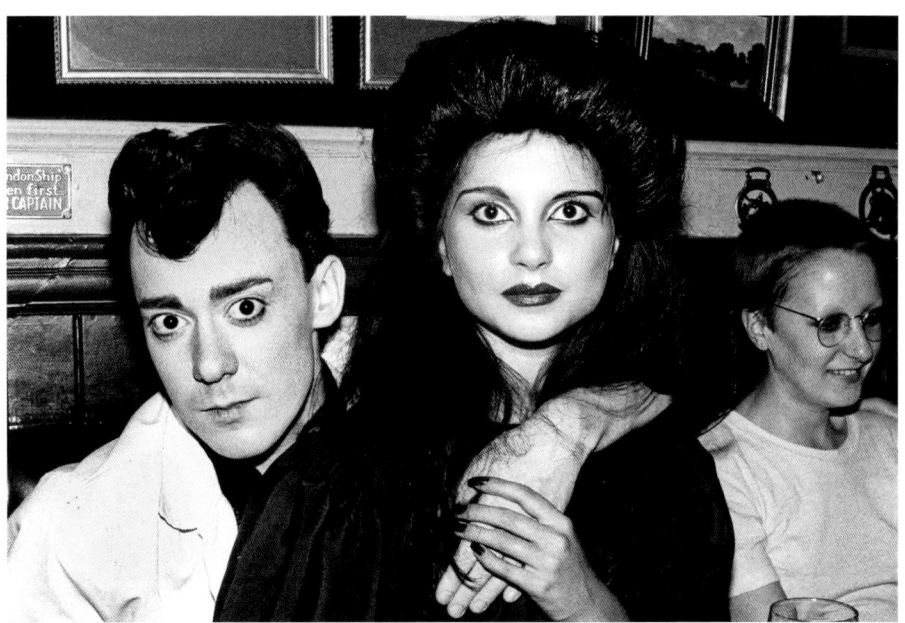

Stephen Linard and Princess Julia.

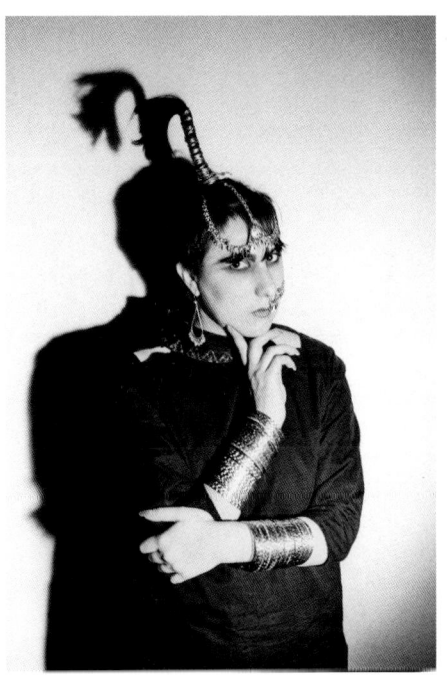

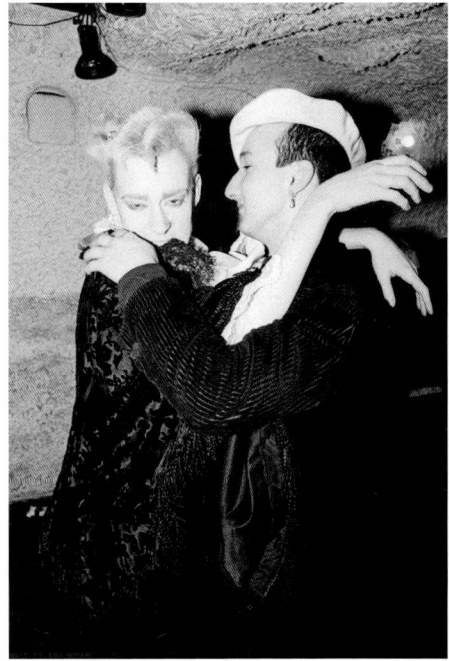

LEFT Melissa Caplan at Warren Street.
RIGHT Two Stephens, Linard and Jones, at St Moritz.

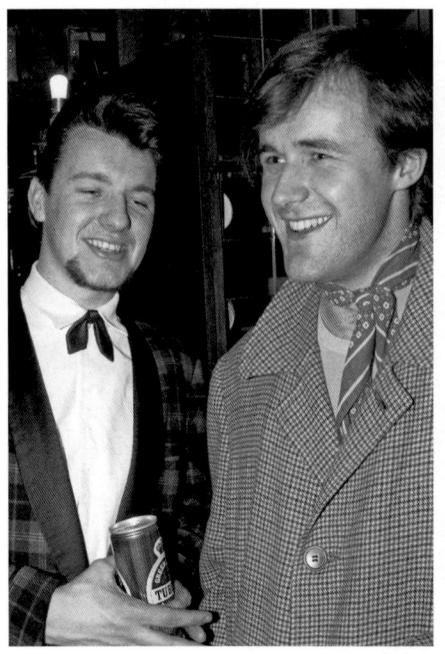 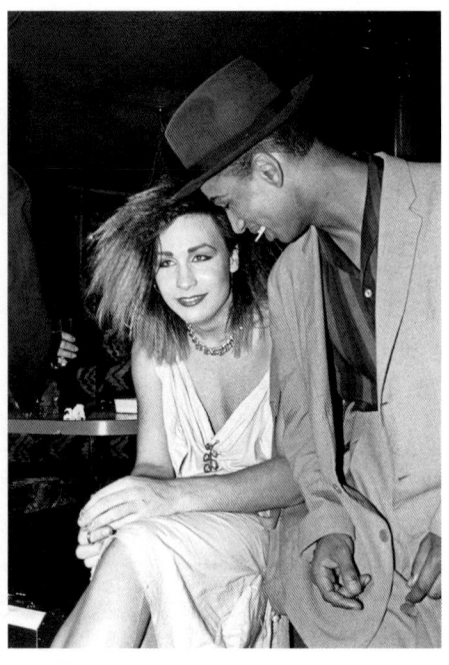

LEFT Chris Sullivan and Steve Dagger.   **RIGHT** Marilyn and Andy Polaris.

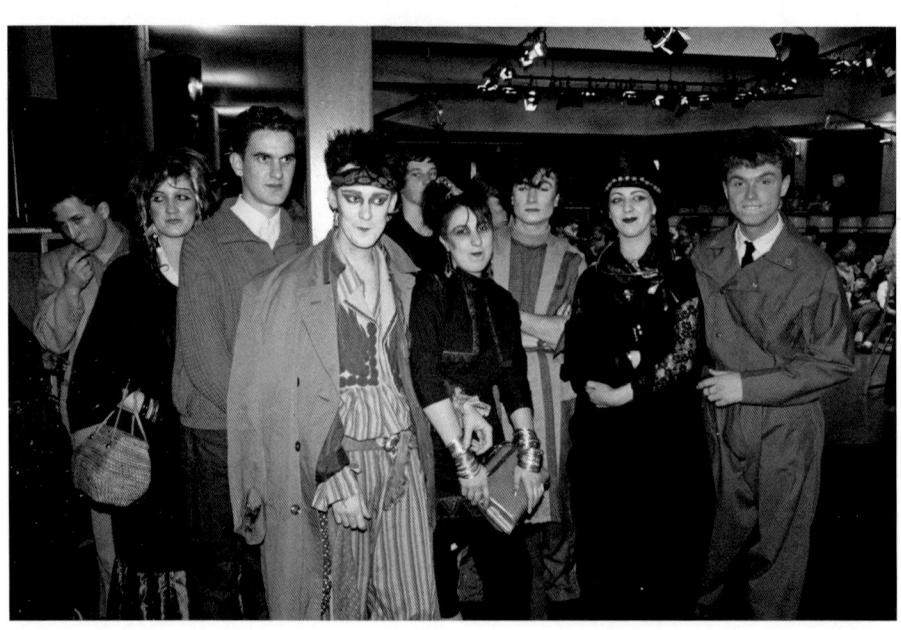

Perry Haines, Clare Thom, Simon Withers, Stephen Linard, Melissa Caplan,
Greg Davis, Michele Clapton and Gary Kemp at the Scala.

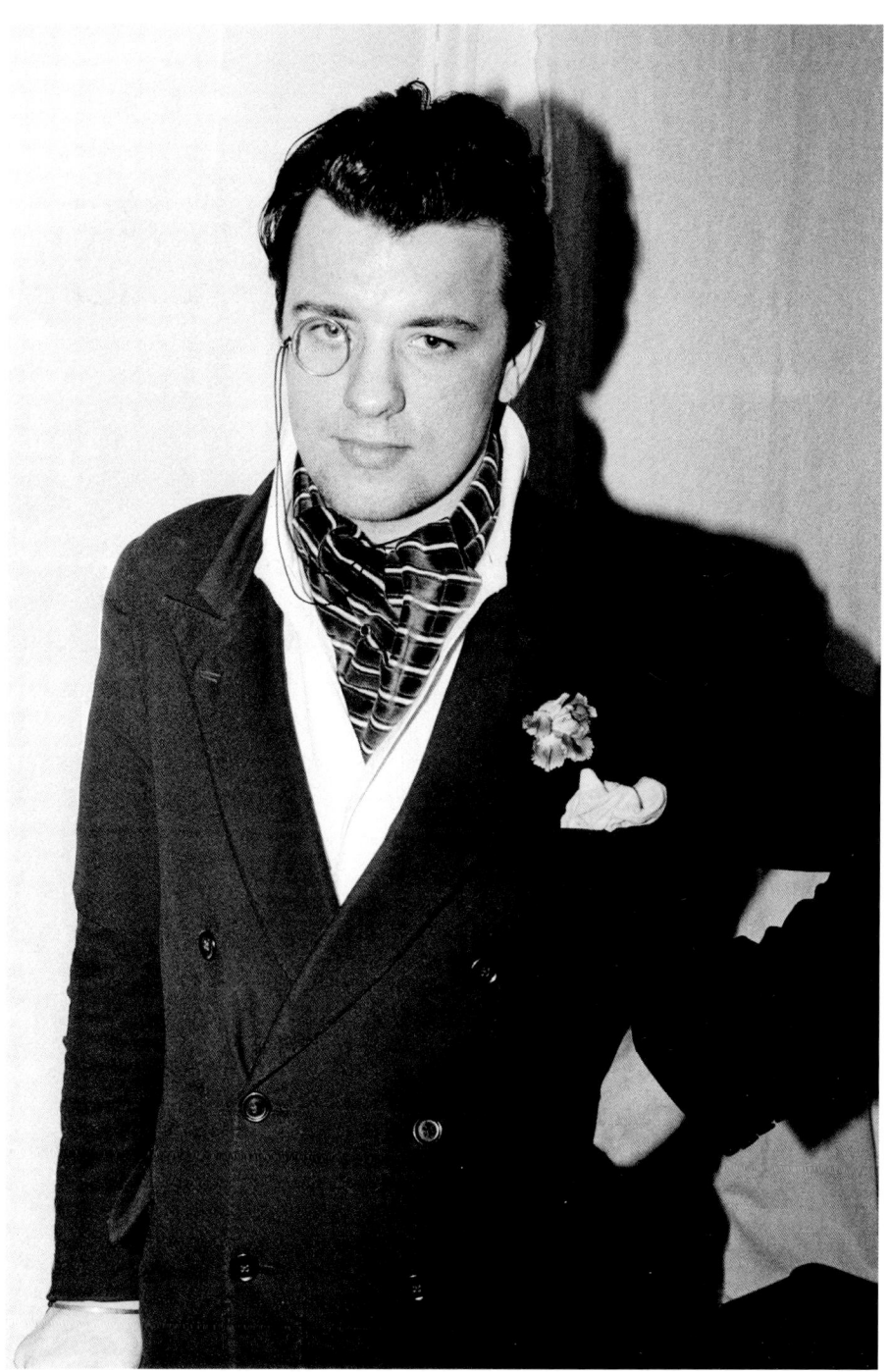

Chris Sullivan with monocle.

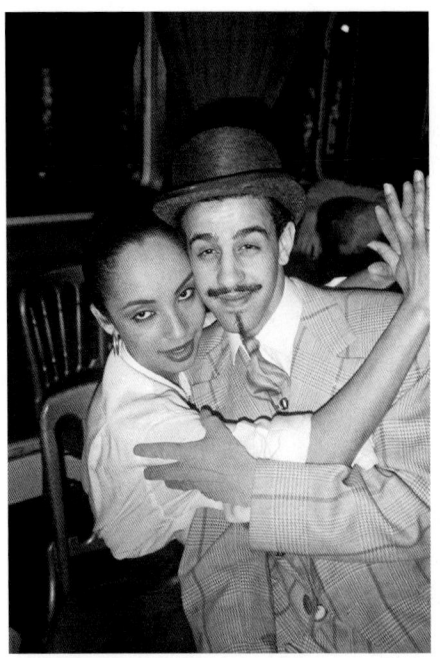 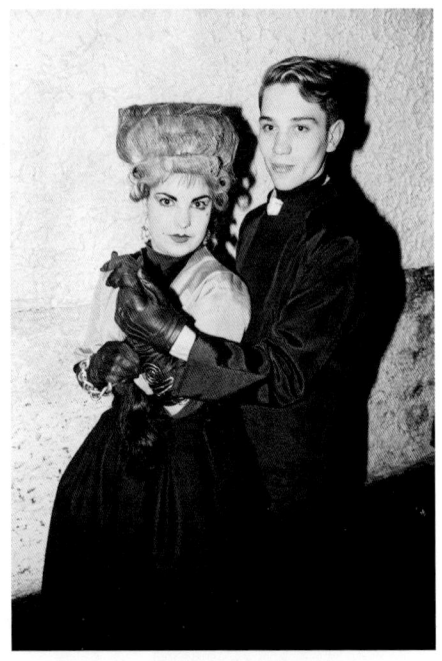

LEFT Sade Adu and Christos Tolera.   **RIGHT** Stevie Stewart and David Holah.

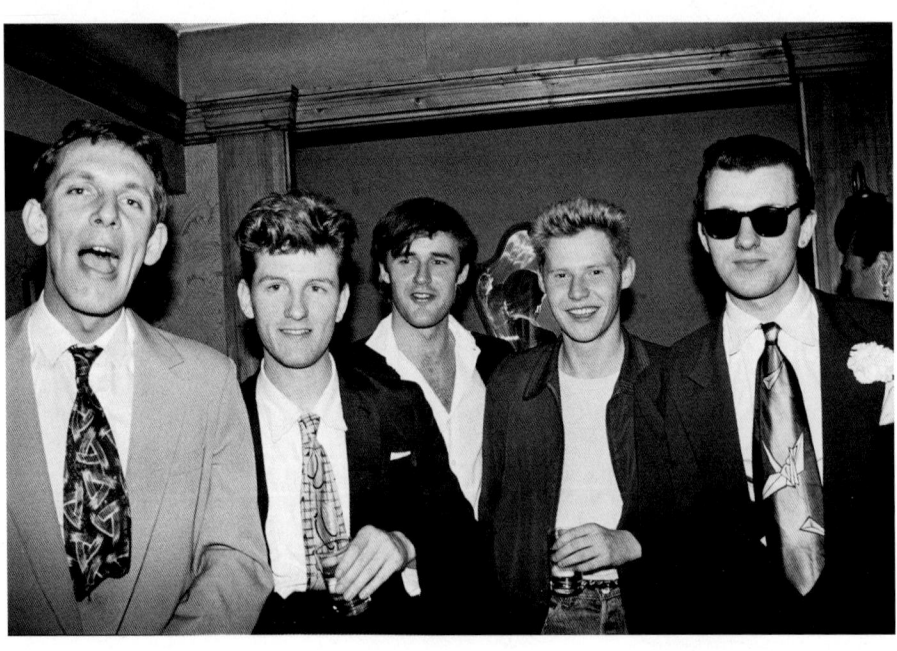

Graham Ball, Ollie O'Donnell, Steve Dagger, me and Chris Sullivan.

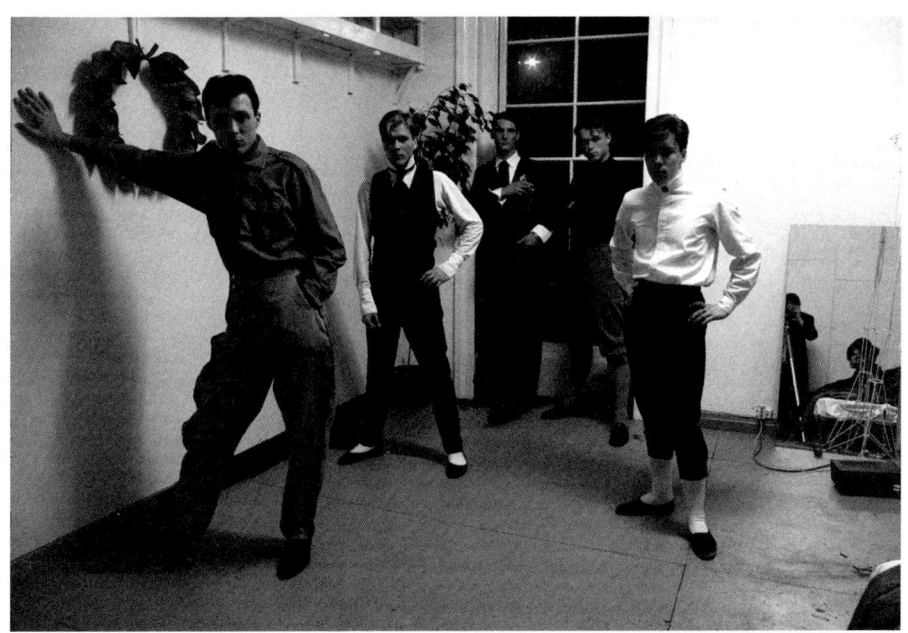

Spandau Ballet's first photoshoot at Warren Street.

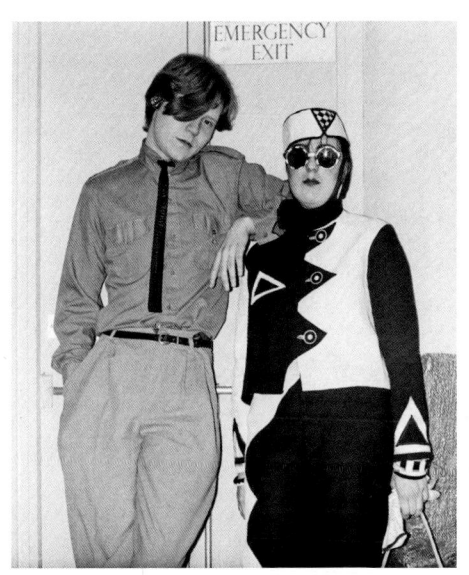

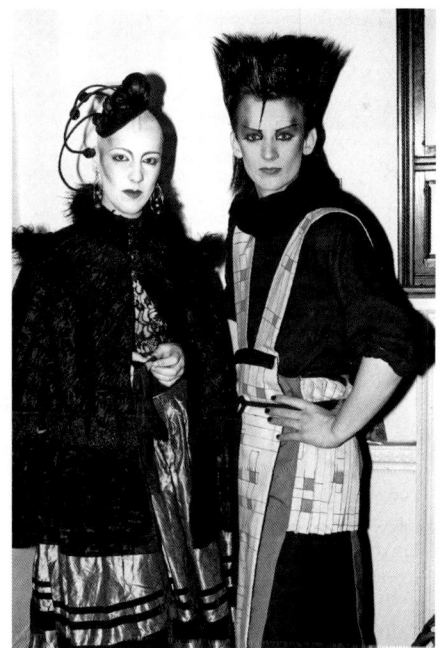

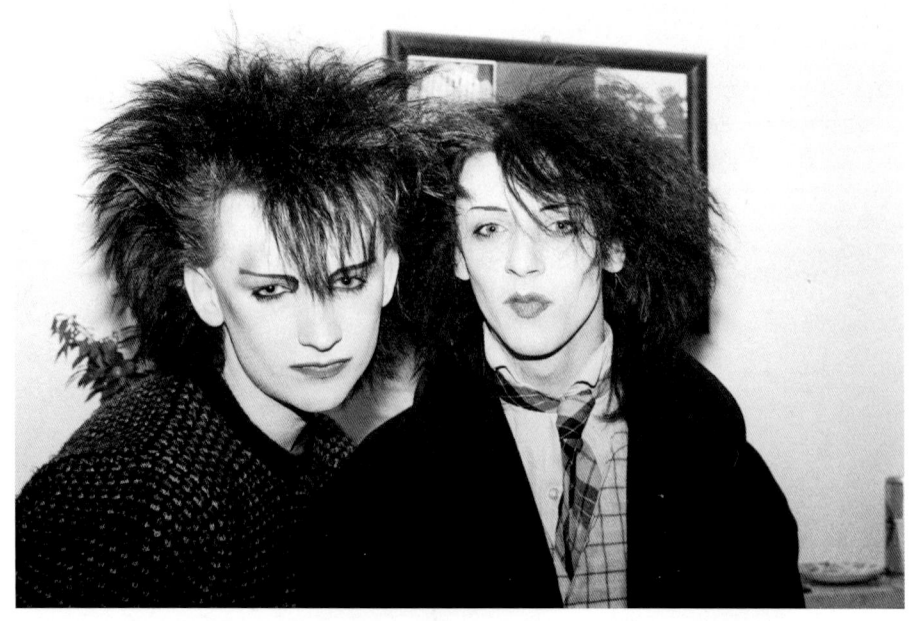

George O'Dowd and Jeremy Healy.

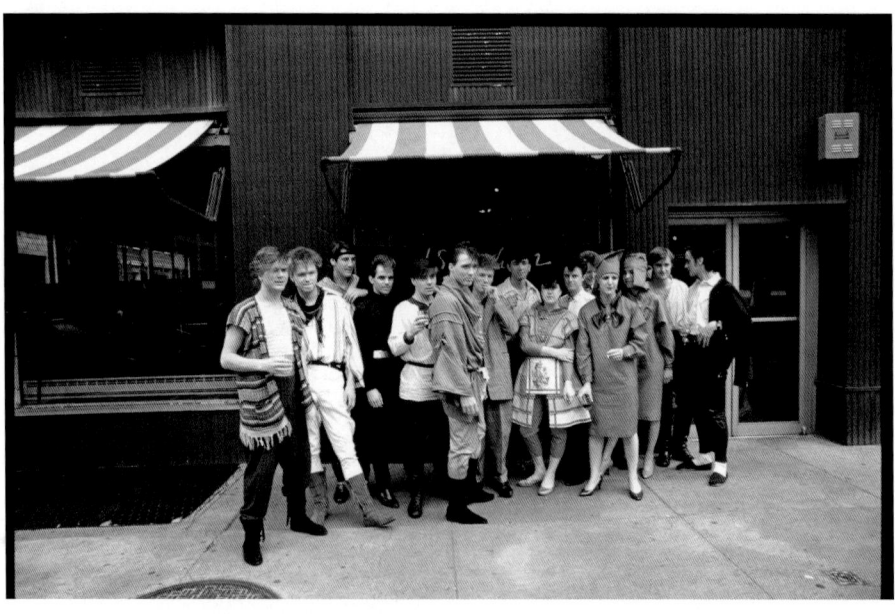

The gang in New York outside the Underground club:
Steve Norman, Gary Kemp, Tony Hadley, Richard Burgess, John Keeble,
Martin Kemp, Ollie O'Donnell, Jon Baker, Melissa Caplan, Graham Smith,
me, Sarah Lubel, Sade Adu, Steve Dagger and Simon Withers.

the country was skint, things were broken, nothing functioned and everybody was profoundly fed up with the way things were. In 1979, it was hard not to be. But rather than just moan about it, we decided to change it, and hopefully enjoy ourselves at the same time, to ensure we had a spectacularly well-misspent youth.

The statist, conformist, insular, early-closing, backward-looking, bleak Britain of the late 1970s, which at times felt like Soviet Bulgaria on a bad day, was rejected simultaneously by Thatcher and her neo-liberal ideologues and us, a bunch of rag-tag urchins who wanted to be fabulous. In that sense, we were certainly part of the same zeitgeist, a gust of positivity, energy and desire sweeping away the stale, the tired and the old. We were, whether we realised it or not, espousing some of the same tropes, encouraging the same changes as the neo-liberal individualist, risk-taking, money-making city boys in Porsches who became the face of Thatcher's Britain. We all wanted success. But there were big differences, too.

Thatcher saw the ruins of post-industrial Britain as a wasteland to be developed by and for hedge fund managers and property tycoons; we saw empty factories and warehouses as an opportunity to have a party. She opened up financial markets, we opened up nightclubs and clothes shops. She freed speculators in red braces to make loads of money, we freed young people in frilly shirts to wear make-up and make art, love whoever they wanted, become designers, play synthesisers, start magazines, shoot videos, make records. Her big bang made the City of London rich; ours made Soho swing.

They both still reverberate to this day, and I would argue that in hindsight, as a result of the winds of change blowing through the 1980s, our culture got richer and more open as our state grew poorer, more unequal; privatised wealth and public squalor. My lot were lucky to be nurtured by the welfare state and to grow up in that time of opportunity, a chance which has largely been denied to subsequent generations, enslaved by student debt, impoverished by greedy landlords, yet in thrall to bland, globalised culture and ensnared by the avarice of capitalists and the omnipotence of corporations.

Today we have a top-down culture, imposed by big business, big tech, big fashion houses, big global pop stars. The Blitz kids back then, with little more than the cobbled-together, homemade, slightly grubby clothes on their backs and the dreams in their heads, were working from the very bottom up, the epitome of the Wildean idea of being in the gutter but looking up at the stars. We were guttersnipes with grandeur.

In the early days of Billy's and the Blitz, nobody was doing it for the money because there wasn't any. We were undeniably ambitious, hungry for success and driven by desire, but not for money; it was the craic not the cash, the fame not the fortune, glory not greed. But, at some point, that started to change.

The first overtly entrepreneurial thing the Blitz crowd did was what they knew best: they opened other nightclubs – and this included myself and Chris Sullivan. The hegemony of Tuesday nights was about to be challenged. The St Moritz was an old swinging Soho institution fallen on hard times, a warren of tiny basement rooms beneath a Swiss fondue restaurant in Wardour Street, where the Kinks had played back in the day.

Chris had teamed up with another of the Taffy mafia called Stephen Mahoney* and they had a word with the management of

* Why is almost everybody in this story called Steve?

the St Moritz, persuading them to let us have Monday nights from January 1980 onwards.

Chris and Stephen would do promotion and the door, while myself and Graham Smith would select the records. We made a conscious decision to make the music as un-Blitz-like as possible. So where Rusty had gone for electro-futurism, we opted for romantic nostalgia. Turning our backs on synthesisers and drum machines in favour of pianos, string arrangements and brushes on skins, we literally went post-modern.

Playing up to the whole Weimar, Otto Dix and Max Ernst 'degenerate art' atmosphere of this place, which felt like a subterranean bierkeller, we spun Kurt Weill and Marlene Dietrich, Edith Piaf, Julie London and Billy Strayhorn, but also the Lounge Lizards and James White and the Blacks. I scoured the racks of the scores of local record shops for old film soundtracks and compilation records, for the kitsch and the cool. We featured jazz, lounge, chanson, tango, cabaret, crooners and New York no wave, all blasting from a single deck. Beautiful couples of every persuasion waltzed slowly cheek to cheek on the tiny dancefloor as if they were in a Brassaï photo, while people ate melted cheese above us.

St Moritz was wildly, self-consciously pretentious. We were full of ourselves and full of a jumble of stuff we'd absorbed at art school and university, that potent mix of St Martin's and the LSE. It was history, fashion, politics and cultural studies as lived experience; we were role-playing the stuff we were studying. We were also having a thrillingly decadent time, louche and sumptuous. St Moritz was very sexy, and many a union was forged on that dancefloor.

The whole Warren Street crowd adored it; tuxedoes and cocktail dresses came out, taffeta and silk, long gloves, high heels, veils, cigarette holders, gardenias in the hair and carnations in lapels. It was dressing-up heaven. The Derek Jarman and Toyah Willcox arthouse lot were deeply enamoured with the camp theatricality of it all. But not everybody got it. One week, a bunch from Birmingham came down to check it out, including the members of the band that would become Duran Duran, and went away amazed but baffled by how different it was to the Blitz. The paradigm had been broken.

St Moritz proved that Rusty's brilliant electro disco selection was only one possible soundtrack to a great night out; we weren't wedded to that sound. Unlike every other youth cult that had gone before us, we were not defined by one musical or sartorial style. That was what made this scene unique and its shapeshifting so difficult to pin down.

Once you'd begun to explore the options opened up by an open-minded, post-modern attitude and realised that there was almost a century's worth of recorded music to choose from, the records became like the clothes; you rummaged around in the big box of the past, picked the best of any style and put them together how you saw fit. Choosing the music for St Moritz was like selecting your outfit for the night. We knew no boundaries.

The eclectic taste of the time was later proven by the vast variety and wide range of musical styles associated with bands who emerged from this scene, from Bananarama to Boy George, Sade to Spandau Ballet, Blue Rondo to Visage, Ultravox to Wham!. There was no one style of music, but there was style in abundance. It was also a precursor of today's limitless digital library of sounds, where every song ever recorded is available at your behest. The second-hand record shops of Soho, bursting with cheap vinyl, were our Spotify.

The other thing which linked all those bands above is that they all wanted to be successful, to have hits, to be big. Pop, short for popular, was a dirty word in some quarters in 1979, but not for those who came out of this milieu. When you've come from a dodgy estate and lived in a crappy squat, when you hanker for good things that look good, you want to sell as many records as possible, make some money, enjoy success. The musicians, the club runners, the clothes designers, the would-be writers and photographers were all aiming high. Did that make us Thatcherites?

The success of Mondays at St Moritz provoked Steve Strange to also get involved in another nocturnal venture. Perhaps he felt his crown was slipping; his monopoly was certainly crumbling. The Blitz was still going strong. Indeed, now that we were firmly into the new decade, it was becoming famous. Where once we had been a secret sect on our Masonic street, we were increasingly in the public gaze and in the popular consciousness.

Frilly collared shirts, ruffles and big shoulder pads had started showing up in high-street stores as more and more pieces were appearing in the press about this fabulous new youth cult. TV crews were sniffing around, photographers standing outside. Most weeks, there was a piece in some magazine or other, and we became used to seeing ourselves in the press.

The club itself also started to change, with new faces appearing – older, already famous people, rich people, models and actors and artists. Even suave but dull Chelsea aristos, who would never have been at Billy's, were turning up and swanning around. Steve was cultivating a different crowd. As the Blitz got more famous, it became less familial, and some of the original scene-makers were getting a touch restless.

Steve decided to go back to his roots and hook up with Chris Sullivan, who through the success of the Mayhem parties and St Moritz was now his main competitor. Later on, at the Wag in Wardour Street, Chris would create the defining club of the second half of the 80s, a Soho institution and a brilliant launch pad for everybody from the Pogues to Neneh Cherry, Sade to George Michael. But when the two Welshmen, still just twenty years of age, got together in May 1980, they came up with a version of Hell on earth. Or maybe it was heaven in Hell.

★   ★   ★

If St Moritz on a Monday was strictly for the in-crowd, and the Blitz on a Tuesday was becoming famous, Hell on a Thursday was distinctly underground in every sense. A small, dark, subterranean, gothic gay drinking den with crimson walls and demonic murals, backing onto a graveyard in Henrietta Street in Covent Garden, Hell only lasted for a few months because it was so extreme; a brilliantly over-the-top imagining of Hieronymus Bosch-goes-nightclubbing. It was Dionysian, it was bacchanalian, it was hardcore.

This is where the full religious regalia look ruled supreme, all inverted crosses and nuns' habits, and hedonism was given full psychotropic rein in a sea of tinned lager and acid tabs, all played out to a background aroma of amyl nitrate and a soundtrack of early Elvis, prime Funkadelic, James Brown and Beethoven's Ninth. It was nuts.

Hell ended in a near riot, with policemen's helmets sent flying, fireworks exploding and windows being smashed in. But, before that, it was the most decadent, the most dramatic and the most outrageous fun. The tone was relentlessly hedonistic, but it was also fiercely popular. Bowie, who had only come to the Blitz once, turned up a few times and now felt like one of the gang; photographer Helmut Newton scouted for talent; Grace Jones descended into the underworld. Clubs run by Blitz alumni were now the talk of the town, and we were at the centre of a social whirlwind. Although we weren't necessarily aware of it, the whole Blitz scene was nearing a crescendo. But its influence was just beginning.

Partly, this was down to the fact that so many of the main movers and shakers were coming to the end of their college days. I was now approaching twenty-one – in my third and final year at uni along with Steve Dagger and Graham Ball – and so were most of the art and fashion students who had constituted the original in-crowd. That meant that as well as this plethora of new nightclubs, there were lots of final-year fashion shows to attend, lots of frantic late-night sewing and lots of people just starting to wonder what came next. The plotting and planning moved up a notch: the West End came alive.

Steve Strange celebrated his twenty-first birthday with an extraordinary event that reverberated round central London. The Pied Piper in pierrot costume gathered about twenty or so of the Blitz elite near his flat in Chelsea, all of them attired in their absolute dandy finery, and led them down into the underground. Only this time they weren't descending into the bowels of a nightclub but onto the Tube's Circle Line.

In those days, the Circle Line really was a circle, so you could just get on a train and keep going round and round to your heart's content. Back then, it was also legal to drink alcohol on the Tube, so they did – copious amounts – and when it ran out, they all rushed to the tiny bar at Sloane Square station for some more. Can you imagine the faces of the weary commuters going about their business, only to see this rowdy gang of magnificent macaronis partying for all they were worth? The photos made it into the papers next day. That was such a Steve Strange stunt to pull.

Another event on a very different scale, in which Steve and the Blitzerati were heavily involved, was the Alternative Miss World contest in October 1981. Andrew Logan had been celebrating this fabulous queer rival to the official Miss World contest since the early 70s. It was a festival of joyous freakery and transformation, a grandiose display of gay pride before Pride was such a big thing. And as the popularity of the original sexist and normative Miss World declined, so the high-camp alternative flourished, this time with support from Steve Strange and many of the Blitz fashionistas. It was truly massive.

They took over the vast expanse of Olympia, a hangar-like arena in west London, built a huge funfair in the centre and filled the room with every drag queen, surreal show-pony and extravagant exhibitionist in town. It was still very much the domain of Them, the older arty crowd, with Logan and Fenella Fielding presenting. But Steve Strange was one of the judges, and the likes of Michele Clapton, Judy Blame and Iain R. Webb, accompanied by their fabulous entourages, entered the competition. It was madly silly, funny and debauched, and marked the coming-of-age of the Blitz crowd in the eyes of the alternative establishment. It was also a big media event and, of course, provoked suitable degrees of coverage and outrage. The Blitz was becoming a very big story and Steve Strange was becoming a celebrity.

The stand-out star of the fashion design crowd was Stephen Linard, whose final show, 'Reluctant Émigrés', caused an absolute sensation, and who was already earmarked for major success and bound for an atelier in Japan, where he would boast he was paid more than Margaret Thatcher. Stephen forged a decent, life-long career in fashion, but never quite scaled the heights his talent should have commanded. This skinny, iconoclastic kid from Canvey Island was an absolute star, but he was also a rabble rouser and a hedonist who never took it all too seriously. He was a trailblazer and, without Stephen, there would have been no John Galliano and no Alexander McQueen. They were cut from the same cloth and had the careers Linard should really have had.

Melissa Caplan, with her medieval-meets-Mondrian style, was the designer who more than any other actually dressed the Blitz. She had Toyah Willcox, Steve Strange, Boy George and most of Spandau Ballet in her garb; her work was in every photoshoot and so was she. Melissa was one of the most prominent faces on the scene and one of the largest personalities. Later on, she would become an educator and an artist, and remain a truly staunch individualist, ever the rebel.

Stephen Jones, with Kim Bowen as his muse, rose to almost instant prominence. A softly spoken mad hatter, his exquisite high-art sculptural designs appealed to scores of high-society types, including Princess Diana, who became a regular client. He has been Britain's most illustrious milliner ever since, working with many internationally famous designers from Westwood to Gaultier, while his own shop on Great Queen Street, just yards from our old haunt, is where just about every pop star and film star has gone to get ahead in the fashion stakes.

Stevie Stewart and David Holah teamed up to form BodyMap, one of the most successful labels of the age, redefining the 80s idea of leisurewear with elaborate layering and geometry. They went from a stall in Camden Market to being the defining crossover brand from club culture to haute couture. Keeping it in the Blitz family, they worked closely with Michael Clark's ballet company, made videos with John Maybury, dressed Boy George and won almost every fashion accolade available. Both of them are still busy in creative spheres, and BodyMap clothes have been chosen to represent the 80s in numerous design exhibitions and events.

Michele Clapton was a dark horse of the Blitz. Always in black, Graham Smith's girlfriend – with her shaven head and Nosferatu-meets-Miss-Havisham image – was one of the most distinctive-looking characters in a scene full of arch individualists. But it was only much later on, after we had all gone our separate ways, that I realised just how phenomenally successful she had become. A multi-award-winning costume designer, her outfits for *Game of Thrones* at times resembled a normal Tuesday night in Covent Garden. She also dressed *The Crown* and numerous other hit shows.

Willie Brown went from Modern Classics to Old Town, a uniquely English celebration of quirky traditionalism still flourishing today. Fiona Dealey followed Michele Clapton into stage and screen design; fashion designer Judith Frankland worked in France and Germany; Darla Jane Gilroy is a prominent designer and teacher at Central St Martins; Kim Bowen became a fashion editor, then a Hollywood stylist; Jo Strettell, as already mentioned, is one of LA's leading make-up artists, while her one-time beau Simon Withers worked for Vivienne Westwood before moving into architecture and education. Dinny Hall is perhaps our most famous contemporary jewellery designer. They were a talented lot.

But as well as these Blitz luminaries, there were a couple of others yet to really make their mark on the scene, but who would become the most famous of the lot. Sade Adu, then studying fashion at St Martin's and living in the Wood Green short-life housing squats, was a half-Nigerian girl with a subtle, understated style, who was a stand-out beauty, standing quietly at the back. Then there was a skinny, nervous youngster in the year below called John Galliano, who first rose to prominence when he volunteered to make a shirt for Gary Kemp when he needed one for the next Spandau gig. Both Sade and John would go on to scale incredible heights.

The other name to throw into the ring is that of Jon Baker, now a major music-biz mogul and international hotelier with his base in Jamaica. Jon was studying at Chelsea School of Art and, like Dagger, he had a fascination with the whole 60s swinging London mythology. He had already displayed his entrepreneurial chops when he started his own business selling punky screen-print T-shirts from a shop in Kensington Market called Axiom. Kensington Market, which in the 60s had been the centre of the whole Afghan-coat-wearing hippy scene, was about to become the focus of a new alternative generation in the 80s.

Jon, known at the time as Mole, had this amazing force-of-nature positivity and gift-of-the-gab personality which was a galvanising force. He had the bottle to do large stuff and an ability to unite and organise the often disparate and wayward personalities in the Blitz. He was a catalyst and a provocateur.

He put on a provocative alternative Axiom fashion show at St Martin's featuring Melissa, Fiona, Simon, Willie Brown, Chris Sullivan and myself (as a rather inept model) and garnered loads of press. The son of a car salesman and a fashion designer, Jon was very definitely a 1980s entrepreneur who was bound for big things. And he was determined to take some of us with him.

Along with Steve Dagger, Jon Baker was one of the motorised personalities propelling this scene to international prominence. They had their eyes set on bigger prizes and would soon be dragging us all off to the Big Apple for an extraordinary extravaganza. But there was a far shorter journey across Carnaby Street which would be the making of me.

11

THE
FACE
OF
THE
DECADE

The one-room office of *The Face* magazine was on Carnaby Street, directly opposite the far grander suite of offices of the *NME*, which was quite handy because I got thrown out of one and landed at the other.

After the *NME* printed my review of Spandau, I hectored then editor Neil Spencer into letting me write a handful of live reviews, including those of Ella Fitzgerald at the Festival Hall, who I loved, and the goth darlings Bauhaus, who I panned. I took to hanging out at the office, making an opinionated nuisance of myself. The fact that it soon became apparent that I was trying to become a writer at the most famous rock paper in the land, but didn't much like rock music, was one obvious bone of contention.

But, more than that, it was soon clear that most of the other writers at the paper hated everything they thought I stood for and saw this new scene that I represented as the devil's (or Thatcher's) spawn. Neil told me this as he said that sadly I had no future at the *NME*, but he also told me that he thought I was a good writer and should go and have a word with Nick Logan over the road about his fledgling mag that might suit my tastes and passions better. So I did, walking from one office to the other. It was one of the most important journeys I ever made.

Nick Logan had been the editor of the *NME* before Neil Spencer, turning it around during punk, which it had also initially dismissed, by hiring Julie Burchill and Tony Parsons to chronicle the punk scene from within. But then he left to start *Smash Hits* for the publishing house EMAP, which under his guidance became a hugely successful photo-driven pop mag aimed at a teen audience – so he clearly didn't have any of the rock-snob superiority complex of so many of the *NME* mob.

As an old West Ham-supporting Essex mod, Nick really wanted to run a monthly magazine which combined great photography and writing, music with fashion and film, nightlife, design, style, art and attitude, glossy, hip, groovy – the antithesis of the militantly muso, irredeemably worthy black-and-white weeklies, a magazine unlike any other in the UK at the time. He put this idea to EMAP, who turned it down flat, so he mortgaged his house and started it himself, originally on his kitchen table, then in one small room at the *Smash Hits* offices.

The Face launched in May 1980, the name originating from the old mod vernacular for a cool dude, a face that stands out from the crowd. The first issue featured Jerry Dammers of the Specials on the front cover and sold respectably, but not spectacularly. There had been four or five issues in total when I walked the twenty yards across Carnaby Street and knocked on Nick's door. This time, I did the exact opposite of what I'd done at the *NME*; I told him I loved his magazine (though, truth be told, I hadn't read it), but that it needed to cover this amazing new scene which was based around the Blitz club and this still-unsigned band called Spandau Ballet, who were going to be enormous and would look great in his mag. I showed him some photos and said I was an established *NME* writer.

He looked me up and down, complimented me on my trousers and basically said welcome to the team, which at that point consisted of Nick, his lovely wife Julie, part-time designer Steve Bush and later charismatic ad man Rod Sopp. Nick has since gone on record as saying that my walking into his office that day was one of the most important moments in the story of *The Face*, not because I was a particularly great writer or anything of the sort, but because suddenly the magazine had a raison d'etre. Now it had a scene to chronicle, a scene in glorious technicolour – visual, exciting, provocative, new: everything *The Face* wanted to be. The defining journal of the 1980s was about to be defined by what was happening at the Blitz club.

My first feature was the Spandau story, the second was entitled 'The Cult With No Name', because at that stage we still didn't really have one (bar the generic Blitz kids) and the kind of people who went to the Blitz on a Tuesday night didn't want one – although lots of outsiders tried to make a moniker stick. The feature was a potted history of the scene from its origins in Bowie and Billy's, acknow-ledging that the rampant individualism and ever-changing look of the Blitz crowd made it impossible to categorise and therefore hard to pin down. The Blitz was a spaceship which could fly off in many directions, with numerous satellites and scores of little space cadets using it as a launch pad of their own.

Those articles launched me, Spandau Ballet and the whole gang into a torrent of attention. It also set *The Face* on a new course as the champion of the next big story. It wasn't the first time we'd appeared in print, but it was a big splash feature in a cool new magazine, with lots of great pictures and written passionately from the inside by someone who lived it. The effect was almost instantaneous, and I too started getting a torrent of calls at my mum's house asking me to write for or be interviewed by other papers and magazines, or TV and radio shows. We became a big story and I became a spokesman. I remember my mum putting on her poshest phone voice when we got a phone call from *National Geographic* magazine in the US and she had to call me downstairs to answer it.

Up until this point, the serious British press, the broadsheets and the BBC, had assiduously avoided covering much youth culture

– and certainly nightclubs, style and fashion, which were seen as entirely frivolous and peripheral. Serious newspapers were still foolscap, print was still black and white and came off on your hands, there were few photos, no glossy style supplements with the Sunday papers (style was something slightly dubious that the French did), or else it was all about the jet set in Annabel's ageing nightclub in Mayfair and Sloane Rangers in *Tatler*. But in the wake of *The Face* that was all about to change.

At almost exactly the same time that Nick Logan launched *The Face*, a magazine called *i-D* first appeared. Colourful and visual, but cheaply hand-folded and stapled, it was basically a street fashion fanzine, specialising in 'the straight up', head-to-toe portraits of young people on the streets of London – mainly the amazingly attired people who frequented the Blitz. The second issue of *i-D* is basically a Blitz alumni yearbook; they're all in there.

i-D was started by Terry Jones, an exile from stuffy British *Vogue*, and Perry Haines, one of the most charismatic and voluble of the Blitz crowd, a great raconteur and arguably the man who first coined the term New Romantics. He said we had romanticised our own lives, so used that moniker to describe the extraordinary creatures he lived among and who featured in his mag. Later on, Dylan Jones and Caryn Franklin, both Blitz alumni, would go on to edit *i-D* as it became an internationally influential fashion journal.

Perry, who has spent the second half of his life as an ornithologist and conservationist in the mountains of Andalucia, was a major player on the scene. Studying the fashion journalism course at St Martin's, he organised an alternative fashion show for the designers in his year, which caused a huge sensation, and he also put on the only catwalk show actually held at the Blitz. He co-founded *i-D*, then went on to open his own club night called, mysteriously, Dial 9 for Dolphins. He wrote, sang and released a minor club hit called 'Whats Funk', which was arguably the first UK rap record; managed a successful band called King, who did a collaboration with Dr Martens; discovered and managed Massive Attack; and styled videos, clothes and stage sets as an 'image consultant' for Duran Duran and many others. He was a very modern young man.

All of that he puts down to going to Great Queen Street every week and meeting the remarkable group of people who coalesced there. When asked in a BBC *Newsnight* documentary at the time if these New Romantics, as he called them, were just escaping reality, he said: 'It's not escapist. It's an alternative reality that we're creating.'

The Face, i-D and, to a lesser extent, a large-format, small-circulation, full-colour mag called *Blitz*, which Iain R. Webb worked for (and which seemed to have Steve Strange or Boy George on the cover most months), were revolutionising the look, feel and scope of British publishing, dragging it into the modern age. It was partly a technological leap. Just as the availability of cheap synthesisers had dramatically altered the sound of pop music, so inexpensive and easy colour printing was changing the look of the magazines that lined the newsagents' racks. Soon MTV and lavish pop videos would complete the transformation from monotone to multi-coloured popular culture.

Britain was changing from a primarily literary culture to a much more visually attuned one, where photography, imagery, graphics, style, design and the look would come to the fore. Nick Logan knew that the design of his mag was equally as important as the content, and once he linked up with the brilliant young graphic artist Neville Brody from the London College of Printing, the team was complete and it went from strength to strength. It would take our national newspapers much longer to catch up, and it would also mean the demise of the once all-powerful old school music papers.

The hullabaloo around the cult with numerous names – Blitz Kids, New Romantics, Futurists, Poseurs, Peacocks, New Dandies, the Style Tribe, Neo-Glam (every journalist came up with their own one) – was growing almost daily, but as yet, it still seemed to be very much a London thing. Indeed, it had begun to transform the fortunes of the near-moribund inner city.

There were now highly fashionable clubs to go to in Soho and Covent Garden almost every night of the week; add to that the Spandau shows, the fashion shows at the colleges, the arty warehouse parties at Mayhem and Butler's Wharf. On the retail front, Rusty Egan opened his own record shop in Chelsea, PX and Modern Classics were thriving, Swanky Modes up in Camden was uber-cool, Jon Baker's Axiom as well as Johnson and Johnson made Kensington Market a magnet, Ollie and Jimmy held court at Smile in Knightsbridge . . . The pendulum had started to swing again. But how would it go down outside the Big Smoke?

Those Bournemouth jaunts were perhaps an indication that this thing could travel, though they were largely down-from-London larks in an otherwise sedate old seaside town. Travelling out of town, especially in small groups, was not to be undertaken lightly, as the sight of Stephen Linard in a gold lamé Elvis suit or Melissa in her full Hindu goddess attire could still cause degrees of consternation and aggravation from Little England locals incensed by our sense of freedom. But we also saw that we could have the opposite effect, and that if we visited somewhere en masse, it might galvanise the local youth and a sympathetic club night may well open up for like-minded souls.

While Spandau was still in its incubation phase, the band made a pilgrimage to Cardiff for their first out-of-town gig at the behest of a group of mates of Steve Strange and Chris Sullivan, who both made the journey way out west – and suitably wild it was too. About half of the Blitz regulars decided to go by various means of transport, some hitching in all their glam finery, others taking the coach or the train. Inevitably, the band van, with Simon Withers driving, broke down en route, so they were late and a couple of stragglers never made it at all. But despite that, the Welsh capital was still invaded by hordes of slightly bewildered metropolitan macaronis in spectacular mufti.

The gig itself was in a rough old reggae club down by the docks, but despite Chris's pink zoot suit causing a degree of merriment among the more vocal locals, the place was packed with very sharply dressed Welsh folk, enthusiastically embracing the event in their Bowie- and Ferry-inspired outfits, with lots of skinny ties and quiffs on display. It was proof that we were not alone in our obsessions, and the band went down a sweaty treat. But it was after the show that it all went wonderfully wonky.

The promoter took this rag-tag band of forty or so Londoners to a lock-in at an all-night dockside pub frequented by the fishermen time forgot. This place was like some kind of Dickensian smugglers' den filled with grizzled geezers in sou'westers and stained waterproofs straight from the trawlers, supping pints of dark beer at 1 a.m. The look on their faces as we filed in . . . Steve Strange dressed as a spectacularly camp Will Scarlet in Lincoln green tights and pixie boots, Pinkie in her Little Bo Peep look, Christos in full

Second World War partisan mode. It was tartan, leather, bondage and lace as far as the eye could see.

For a moment or two the silence was foreboding and the atmosphere tense, until one of the fisherfolk proudly produced his catch and offered it round for our inspection. The sight of Steve Strange canoodling with a large cod is one that will stay with me for life. Pints of Guinness were ordered all round and sea shanties were sung. Looking back, that was probably my favourite night of this entire caper.

No fish were involved in our trip to a club in Rayleigh in Essex, though there were crocodiles. This little jaunt was instigated by Rusty, who had become mates with an eighteen-year-old kid called Stevo (another one) Pierce, who was a maverick DJ, record producer and manager of electronic musicians. He was involved with a band called Soft Cell, who were allied to their own 'futurist' hangout in Leeds called The Warehouse. Somehow, we all got roped into going to see this Soft Cell lot play at another 'Blitz-style' club called Crocs, which had opened up out in the far east. All these clubs scattered across the country were a sign that the scene was really gaining momentum.

There was obviously some kind of three-line whip in operation that night as many of the proper in-crowd headed for Essex. It was as if we were missionaries going to visit the natives and lend spiritual support to the congregation. And that supercilious attitude was only heightened when we pulled up at a dreary suburban parade way out in the Essex Badlands to be told that this was the local outpost of all things New Romantic. It didn't look particularly romantic.

We knew this place was called Crocs, but nobody had explained that its name came about because you were met with live crocodiles in a cage as you walked into the club. We were used to some pretty surreal experiences, but a coachload of London's startled finest staring at a pair of scaly reptiles in a typically over-the-top Essex nightclub took some beating. What kind of place *was* this?

In fact, it was an absolutely thriving local hub, full of enthusiastic kids in frilly tops and exuberant eyeliner who treated us as visiting dignitaries – Stevo rather embarrassingly bowed down before Steve Dagger as he entered. It's a shame we were so stupidly superior about the whole evening, because not only were Soft Cell very good, but this Crocs place had a house band who opened the show and who we rather ignored, assuming they'd be rubbish. They were called Depeche Mode and I don't remember a note they played.

Somebody who did recall the place fondly, though, was Boy George, because a year or so later, when he had got his own band together, one of the first gigs that Culture Club played was out in Rayleigh – only by then the crocodiles had gone and the place had been renamed the Pink Toothbrush. Only in Essex.

The most exotic trip we took at this point was a direct result of the *20th Century Box* television show. As well as all the desperate record company A&R men, Steve Dagger got a call from a club promoter in France who had seen the TV show, and consequently asked if Spandau would play a two-week residency at his illustrious nightclub, the Papagayo in Saint-Tropez, and could they bring some of those famous New Romantics with them. Now at this stage, Saint-Tropez – spiritual home of Brigitte Bardot, Alain Delon and all that – was about as alien to us as Mars. Was it even a real place? We were all kids from council estates in London for whom the Riviera was Southend-on-Sea. Steve said yes, but assumed it was a wind-up. It wasn't.

The Papagayo had been *the* Côte d'Azur club du jour back in the 60s, and Steve regaled us all with tales of the beautiful demi-monde. We had no idea what to expect; I remember Gary Kemp and I discussing whether or not we should wear ankle bracelets on the beach to display a touch of dandyism while sunbathing. That was about as sophisticated as we got.

A few weeks later, we found ourselves crammed into an old, beaten-up hired minibus with all the band's kit stuffed inside and our clobber strapped to the roof. The bus was so crowded we could only get in and out via the windows. We were driving further south than most of us had ever been in our lives: Simon Withers, Graham Smith and I had accepted the offer of a free jolly in the sun and unwittingly very nearly signed our death warrants in the process.

Spandau's dreadful luck with vehicles continued as Tony Hadley drove as fast as this overloaded jalopy would go down an autoroute somewhere in Provence. Suddenly the tyre burst and we veered across three lanes of traffic, narrowly avoiding a terrible collision which could have wiped out a large chunk of London's nocturnal glitterati. Thankfully we survived and even managed to change a tyre so we could finally get to the fabled Côte d'Azur.

The Papagayo was in the centre of Saint-Tropez, down by the docks. We looked spectacularly out of place in our PX and Modern Classics gear among all the Gallic sybarites wandering the chic streets and cobbled alleyways of the Old Town – although I have to say, Martin Kemp looked very dashing in a pair of speedos with an almost instant Mediterranean tan, whereas I managed to take all the skin off my forehead by trying to bleach my hair with lemon juice.

The real revelation was watching the band play live every night. Given that they had only ever done a handful of gigs, the improvement from performing regularly was remarkable, and so was the crowd's reaction. Before Saint-Tropez, Steve had made sure they had only ever performed in front of carefully selected audiences of their own kind – it was a keystone of his masterplan – but here were a jaded jet-set crowd watching an unsigned band, and they were blown away. They were a little confused by my poetic intro and shocked by boys jiving hand in hand (so much for French liberté and egalité), but the songs went down a storm. Steve's grin grew steadily wider.

Later in the trip, as the band's reputation was spreading locally, a bunch of the guys from the local Gitane community let it be known that they found our appearance a trifle unsettling, and also implied that somehow we might be inflaming the passions of their female folk and they were going to run us out of town. At one point, myself and Gary, in all our gear, were chased through those cobbled alleys by a gang of enraged vigilantes. Thankfully we were quite good at running away after years of practice, and also perhaps secretly relieved that we still had the ability to wind people up with the way we looked.

Back in Britain, tanned and toned from our exertions in the South of France, and with the band's live performances considerably sharpened by playing every night, Spandau had one last gig to play before signing a record deal, as dictated by Steve's masterplan. Luckily, they had better luck with boats than they did with vans, because the culmination of the 'get Spandau Ballet signed' project took place on board a warship moored on the Thames. Steve was trying to find a suitably memorable venue for the big finale gig which would finally seal the deal, when his dad, who had served in the navy, suggested HMS *Belfast*, a Second World War light cruiser permanently parked up by Tower Bridge.

Steve discovered that you could hire the ship for parties and told the old salts who ran it that this was a graduation event for students with a quintet playing. This was technically true, as 26 July 1980 was just about the time many of us were finishing college and there were indeed five members of the band. What followed was one of the legendary larks and one of the most memorable nights.

Yet again, Graham designed the invite and Chris assisted with the guest list, which consisted of every single hipster in town and became the most scorching ticket I've ever known. Such was the clamour to get on board that some of the west London style warriors from Dave Mahoney's band of buccaneers 'borrowed' a rowing boat and attempted to scale the ship from the river. Someone walked across the gangplank festooned in fairy lights and, once on board, found a socket to plug himself into. People came as admirals and pirates and Jolly Jack Tars; bell bottoms and matelot tops were de-rigueur.

The interior of an old warship is rather like the set of *Eraserhead*, all metal pipes and tubes, valves, gauges and tight stairwells; more safety hazards than you can shake a swagger stick at. It was made even more precarious by the fact that the licence of the ship was such that food had to be served, so a buffet of various cheeses and cold meats was laid out in the officers' mess, where the band were set to perform. New Romantics don't often eat, so inevitably a food fight started and mess was indeed the operative word as almost immediately the floor was slippery with dairy products and Spam.

The crew who manned the ship, mainly old sailors, were in a state of complete shock at the debauchery all around them, but there were already far too many people on board to call the thing off. At one point, one of them complained to Steve Dagger that he'd just seen two blokes rogering each other in the toilets, and I remember thinking it can't have been the first time.

It was the last time I ever performed my poetic intro and the last time Spandau Ballet would play as an unsigned band. They were immaculate, the night was a roaring success and Steve could pick from every major record company in London, eventually signing a record-breaking agreement with Chrysalis Records for what was then the largest advance ever given to a new band.

Part of the deal was that the band would be given control of their own label as part of the Chrysalis group; their debut LP *Journeys to Glory* came out a few months later on the Reformation imprint. That name, with its grandiose historical associations, was suggested by Simon Withers. The album was produced by Blitz regular Richard Burgess, while the embossed neo-classical LP sleeve, designed by Graham, featured another piece of my preposterous poetry, for which I still don't think I've been paid:

> Picture angular glimpses of sharp youth
> Cutting strident shapes through the curling grey of 3am
> Hear the soaring joy of immaculate rhythms
> The sublime glow of music for heroes
> Driving straight to the heart of the dance
> Follow the stirring vision and the rousing sound
> On the path towards journeys to glory.

★   ★   ★

There was also a journey to Birmingham.

When Steve Dagger badgered me into writing that first piece for the *NME*, he had said something along the lines of 'Write a review and within six months we'll end up on *Top of the Pops* and you'll be a famous writer.' It was actually seven months before 'To Cut a Long Story Short' was released and became an instant hit, but indeed there they were on Thursday evening in their sporrans and their spats, looking very, very young and rather self-conscious, but absolutely spot on, on the nation's TVs.

The whole thing was about to explode. Britain's youth embraced this whole New Romantic thing with amazing alacrity. Spandau made it to number five in the charts and tartan sales went through the roof; there were high collars and ruffles in Top Shop within a week and New Romantic haircuts on offer at your local salon. I wouldn't say I was exactly famous, but by that stage I was the most prominent writer on the most glamorous magazine in the land and about to land a TV gig myself. Steve had been right.

He'd also been proven correct in his tactic of including as many of the Blitz crowd as he could in the process. He was effectively selling a whole scene, which was so much more potent than just another band. The video for 'To Cut a Long Story Short' was shot on one freezing night in the London Dungeons and featured a surfeit of candles and a pair of binoculars, but also Chris Sullivan and Christos looking conspiratorial, Chris's girlfriend Holly with a cigarette holder and a couple of the finest female dancers doing the robotic/erotic Blitz jive. It was a masterclass in self-mythologising in three minutes.

As 1980s pop videos go, it was pretty basic, but it set the tone and made the point that we were entering a more visually striking age, that guitar bands in blue jeans with long, lank hair were a thing of the past. The band also embraced the dancefloor as the group insisted the single was released in an extended 12-inch dance version, which was truly radical. This was the EDM of its age. This was the future.

The night after their *TOTP* appearance, Spandau were booked to play only their second gig outside London, at the Botanical Gardens in Birmingham, a fabulously flouncy venue amid the hothouses and palm trees. Yet again, London's most flamboyant fruits clambered on board a coach in Covent Garden, this time headed for the Midlands to see what the second city had to offer. We knew there was a club called the Rum Runner which had a similar vibe; Valentine and Eddie from the Bournemouth beanos had told us all about it while George had actually lived in Brum for a bit and his dramatic mate Martin Degville was a main player in the scene up there.

When the coach-load of fans made it to the Botanical Gardens, there was a minor kerfuffle going on as the Spandau band bus had yet again come a cropper. This time it was driven by Dagger's chum, photographer Neil Matthews, who had managed to wedge it beneath the low-lying roof of the venue and could not get it out. As we filed off the coach in all our fancy slap and tackle, we were instantly press-ganged into pushing the van free of the trap it was caught in. Eventually we released the vehicle to a loud cheer and filed into the gig.

Again, the details of the show have faded, but the after-party at the Rum Runner remains vivid. There was a tangible tension between the two camps, the lairy Londoners up from the Blitz, buoyed by Spandau's *TOTP* appearance, and the Brummies who were already rightly proud of their own scene and also had a band of their own, who had been at the gig to check out the opposition. Indeed, Steve had spurned the offer of having them as a support act, saying no one could share the stage with his band. They were, of course, Duran Duran. Nick Rhodes said that they had massive smiles on their faces during the concert because they could see their own route to future success mapped out by Spandau. Afterwards, it was more snarls and sneers than smiles.

The Londoners, myself doubtless included, were somewhat sniffy about the Birmingham scene, which was more goth/futurist, all high, bright hair and big frilly collars of the kind we'd abandoned months before. Our undeniable hauteur riled the locals and there was not a lot of mixing between the two camps. What none of us realised at the time was that, in that club on that night, a large section of the future of the British pop scene had gathered. There was Spandau Ballet and Duran Duran, Boy George, Visage, Ultravox, Blue Rondo à la Turk, Animal Nightlife and even Sigue Sigue Sputnik.

12

YOUR
FIFTEEN
MINUTES
START
NOW

The 2i's coffee bar at 59 Old Compton Street back in the late 50s was the closest historical precedent for the Blitz. Steve Dagger was always berating us with tales of that one tiny Soho basement room with an espresso machine, a minuscule stage and no drinks licence, where almost the entire first generation of British rock'n'roll and pop emerged. From 1956 onwards, a series of teenagers –Tommy Steele, Cliff Richard, Hank Marvin, Johnny Kidd, Joe Brown, Adam Faith and a host of others – went from kids sipping coffee to stars almost overnight, while Terence Stamp, Michael Caine and Francis Bacon were watching in the crowd, Lionel Bart and Mickie Most were waiters and the bouncer was Peter Grant, who went on to become the notorious manager of Led Zeppelin.

Like the Blitz, the 2i's was home to a varied assemblage of as-yet-unformed youth culture tribes: skifflers, beatniks, rockers, folkies and, of course, would-be Elvises aplenty. There was no single 2i's look or sound; it was a sounding board for a whole new generation, an incubator where the future was given breath.

And pretty soon, just as with the Blitz, there was a host of similar Soho joints to cater for this burgeoning burst of youthful musical and stylistic creativity: coffee bars, nightclubs, record shops, tailors and boutiques appearing to provide for their every need. Teenagers were practically invented down there in the subterranean fug of a throbbing W1 basement. The transformation from ration books and dreary post-war austerity to cool, swinging London, from the 50s to the 60s, effectively started with a swig of frothy coffee on Old Compton Street.

Something similar happened in Liverpool at the Cavern a few years later when the whole Merseybeat sound emerged fully formed from that one room, and when Manchester went Mad at the Haçienda towards the end of the 1980s. Every now and then, a nightclub and its young denizens don the vestments of their new creed, learn the songbook and become the focus for the spirit of the age, a conduit for the zeitgeist. It is especially true when one era is transmogrifying into another, when there is a changing of the guard. And as the 80s really started to kick in and make its presence felt, rendering the 70s stodgy and monotone by comparison, so the Blitz became the undeniable nocturnal totem for the times. But with things being so transient, by that point it was already on the way out.

The Blitz club, with Steve on the door and Rusty on the decks, officially ran one night a week from 6 February 1979 to 14 October 1980, nineteen months of Tuesdays, plus that one Christmas Wednesday, seventy-seven fabulous nights in all. But it didn't really. By the time Spandau Ballet had signed what was then the most lucrative record deal in British history and the New Romantics were on everybody's lips, the Blitz was on the slide. So much so that when I spoke to people for this book who had been absolute Tuesday night die-hards, most of them thought it had ended by the summer of 1980. I don't think we stopped going; it was more that there were so many other things going on that it stopped being the centre of our world. The energy moved elsewhere, but the spirit sustained and flourished.

The last few months of the Blitz have faded from memory, largely because its job had been done. For Rusty and Steve, it was now a side hustle as they put their considerable efforts and energy into furthering their own careers. Rusty always wanted to be a success-ful musician, Steve always wanted to be famous. All of us by now wanted to be something or somebody and were ready to branch out into adventures of our own.

The Blitz had dramatically altered the landscape. For eager, aspirational young things looking for an exciting time, London was already a very different city. After the bleak prospect of the winter of discontent, things were now buzzing, and an extraordinary percentage of those Blitz kids were pushing the buzzer. So much of what happened afterwards, so much of what went on to define the 80s in terms of music, fashion, nightlife, publishing and art, happened not at the Blitz, but *because of* the Blitz. Its aftershocks were the real story.

Some of the success stories were almost instant. Spandau were quickly followed into the charts by Visage, when Rusty and Steve finally got their act together, joined by such established musical luminaries as Billy Currie and John McGeoch, and had a huge international hit with 'Fade to Grey'. Rusty had been trying to distil the music he loved into a complete package of his own creation from Billy's onwards – recording demos, trying different permutations – but inevitably it always involved his mate on the door as frontman.

It was Spandau's emergence which ultimately gave them the drive and the opportunity to get their own project sorted, as the major labels were now hungry for more of that Blitz magic and Visage were snapped up by Polydor, who financed their foray into the charts, paying for recording and, most importantly, a video.

Steve Strange, unlike, say, Tony Hadley or Boy George, was not a natural vocalist – his voice was thin and limited – and nor was he a great live performer. Steve's undeniable charisma worked best up close and in person. Visage was very much a studio project, and Steve's contribution was limited by Rusty and the musicians in the band, making the most of his breathy, monotone delivery. His visual presence, however, was paramount and priceless. I remember at the time thinking that Steve didn't have what it took to become a true pop star, but he was always an icon.

They weren't called Visage for nothing. Steve's face, artfully caked in make-up, was everywhere, and his demeanour – haughty, ethereal, camp – became the mask that was adopted by so many acolytes and admirers. It became the visage of the age. And 'Fade to Grey' in particular still holds a potent place in the memories of many people who saw them on *Top of the Pops* and rushed out to buy a piece of this extraordinary new scene – or maybe rushed to the bathroom to secretly apply some slap.

Midge Ure (now OBE, then of Visage) – a Blitz fixture down at the shallow end with Steve and the musos, or conspiring with Rusty and his records – had been one of the few relative adults in the room, already well into his twenties when most of us were still teenagers, and a veteran of the music scene from his first band Slik onwards. He was a canny, charming character, his soft Scottish burr full of sage advice to us youngsters with our flights of preposterous fancy, ready to bring us down to earth, yet never to squash our ambitions. He was good company at the bar.

Having been through punk and power pop, and being adept at adapting to changing tastes, he soaked up the vibe of the place and honed it into a commercial package with Visage. But his vision truly came to fruition with Ultravox and 'Vienna', a moody, *Third Man*-inspired, synth-driven masterpiece which fitted seamlessly into the Teutonic soundscape of the Blitz. Its video, suitably operatic and romantic, a preposterous piece of baroque-and-roll stuff and nonsense, full of extras from the scene, didn't mean very much to anybody, but it was perfectly pitched for the overblown imagery of the time. And the song remains a classic.

Even Spandau's producer Richard Burgess and his band Landscape – who, truth be told, were old studio boffins who'd been around for yonks – pulled on leather trousers, shoulder pads and fedoras and scored a hit with 'Einstein a Go-Go', a gnawingly catchy piece of danceable synth pop. Suddenly, the airwaves sounded like Rusty's playlist. Suddenly, Blitz alumni were having hits and making money, and that is exactly what they wanted.

Selling records wasn't selling out. Steve Dagger always modelled himself on the larger-than-life managers of the 60s who piloted their bands to enormous fame and wealth. Unashamedly ambitious, signed to major labels, intent on adulation and world domination, these artists craved number ones and fancy limos.

That first wave of Blitz bands who garnered instant success were very much in that pulsing four on the floor synth-pop mould, which is all down to Rusty Egan's tutelage on the decks. Also, established acts like Japan, Orchestral Manoeuvres in the Dark, Adam and the Ants and Human League, who weren't from the Blitz, began to move their sound and style more in the direction of the nightclub, the dancefloor and the charts. Meanwhile, the likes of Duran Duran in Birmingham, Dead or Alive in Liverpool, Soft Cell in Leeds and Depeche Mode in Essex were waiting in the provincial wings, each of them allied to a Blitz-style club. There was a discernible shift in the emphasis of British music back towards pop songs and visually striking performers.

There was also a second wave of Blitz musical graduates waiting to be unleashed. The variety of acts who finally emerged from that one space underlines the truth that the Blitz was never primarily about electro music, any more than it was just big hair and frilly shirts. Like the 2i's, it was a place to be inspired, to experiment, to invent yourself and find your metier.

George and Marilyn, the terrible twins from the cloakroom, both emerged a year or so later to massive sales, public gasps and international notoriety, though one of their careers lasted a lot longer than the other. Siobhan Fahey roped in a couple of her mates and named their ebulliently coiffured trio Bananarama, after the Roxy Music tune 'Pyjamarama'. Chris Sullivan and Christos started Blue Rondo à la Turk; Andy Polaris fronted Animal Nightlife; Jeremy Healy and Kate Garner, with their dreadlocks swinging, formed Haysi Fantayzee; Corinne Drewery, studying fashion at St Martin's, was the lead singer of Swing Out Sister. Matt Bianco, Sigue Sigue Sputnik, the Patsy Kensit-fronted Eighth Wonder . . . All had Blitz heritage and degrees of success in the early to mid-80s.

★   ★   ★

Within a few months of my first walking into Nick Logan's office at *The Face*, his mag was being called the bible of street style and the world's best-dressed magazine, catapulted to international renown and influence on the back of the whole fashion-obsessed, New Romantic, nightclub hullabaloo. The success was all down to Nick's inspiring editorship, his hands-on hard work and his ability to let the talent run. He decided to go all in with the New Romantic scene and got the best people to do it, especially Neville Brody with his brilliant constructivist-inspired design. Nick even came to the Blitz a couple of times in his sharp mod suits.

By then, he was editor of the hottest title in town. For artists and bands, blagging a full-colour cover shot on *The Face* had superseded anything the weekly inkies could offer in terms of promotion. Even a mention in the mag put you on the cultural map. Its seal of approval was like a royal charter and that would play a part in the next generation of bands to be unleashed.

As well as writing for *The Face*, I was also freelancing for just about every major newspaper and magazine in Britain, who now had an insatiable hunger for the kind of youth culture and style stories they had so assiduously ignored for so long. Suddenly everybody wanted a slice. Simultaneously, I was being written about by them on a regular basis, sometimes even favourably. I was featured on the front cover of the *Observer Magazine* as 'The face behind *The Face*' and in numerous papers as the mouthpiece for a generation, though the *NME* still saw me as the enemy and was incredibly sniffy about me, Spandau and the whole scene.

By January 1981, still aged just twenty-one, I was presenting (not very well) a live weekly youth culture and music TV programme for BBC2 called *The Oxford Road Show*, had my weekly column in *Girl About Town* and was a regular commentator on LBC. Within a matter of years, and still in my mid-twenties, I would become a published Penguin novelist. All down to Steve Dagger and the Blitz.

It was like the famous Andy Warhol adage about fame: every fifteen minutes, one of our gang was becoming famous, and sometimes it lasted a lot longer than a quarter of an hour. A photoshoot was organised by David Johnson at the suitably lush Waldorf Hotel entitled '21 at 21', which featured twenty-one of the prime movers and shakers with an average age of just twenty-one.

In retrospect, what was so remarkable is that this did not seem at all remarkable at the time; we just took it for granted, feeling somehow that this was our due. It's amazing how quickly you get used to things. It's not surprising how big-headed we got.

The other would-be media types were also doing well. *i-D* magazine went from strength to strength with Perry Haines and Dylan Jones both becoming leading figures. Caryn Franklin found her niche as a writer, presenter, campaigner and broadcaster on *The Clothes Show*. Iain R. Webb was writing for *Vogue* and editing *Blitz*. We went from talking to each other at two o'clock in the morning in the Blitz echo chamber to being called the voices of youth.

Other writers took longer to emerge from the melee. John 'J. J.' Connolly in particular, a member of Ollie O'Donnell's rollicking north London posse, was working fixing track for London Transport at the time. But, years later, his sensational debut novel *Layer Cake* was released and followed up by an even more successful film script. Similarly, Liz Fremantle, another Blitz stalwart, found her voice as a bestselling author of historical fiction for both novels and movies in the 2000s. The ripples of the Blitz's impact went well into the future.

Michael Clark CBE became easily the most exalted contemporary British dancer and choreographer of his generation, with his own internationally renowned company. A couple of years younger than us, he was truly an enfant terrible, who would use shock, awe and technical brilliance to propel the conservative world of ballet into the twenty-first century. I went to see one of his extraordinary shows in the 1990s and it was like being transported back to the Blitz in all its joyous excess and untamed creativity. Whenever I see him out now, we both smile. Perhaps oddest of all, David Claridge, who'd been with us from Billy's onwards, became the saviour of TV-am when he invented Roland Rat, at the time the most famous rodent in the land. Oh, how we laughed.

The fashion crew – Steve Linard, Stephen Jones, Stevie Stewart and David Holah, John Galliano, Pam Hogg, Simon Withers, Melissa Caplan et al. – were renowned and fêted almost as soon as they left college and started to radically alter the perception of British style. By the end of 1980, British mainstream fashion was awash with rip-off New Romantic gear. You could not move for taffeta and tartan, britches, shoulder pads and high collars on the high street and every frothy teen magazine published articles on how to get the New Romantic look. Jean Paul Gaultier started turning up in the clubs in London looking for inspiration.

The most famous teenager in Britain, Diana Spencer, went almost overnight from Sloaney nursery assistant to ruff-collared, big-shouldered, high-haired romantic princess, recruiting Stephen Jones for hats and Sam McKnight – himself a die-hard Soho nightclubber – to restyle her barnet. Her iconic pearl silk wedding dress was later described by its co-designer Elizabeth Emanuel as being 'typical of early 1980s style: overblown, romantic, flouncy'. That sounds a lot like the Blitz to me.

Up at the other end of the schmutter spectrum, Vivienne Westwood, who was the progenitor of so much of this haute-rebel style, an inspirational figure to all, followed suit with her now-famous Pirate collection, with Bow Wow Wow and Adam Ant wearing her designs. The tables had turned. That look, with its romantic re-imagining of history, owed a direct debt to the likes of Steve Strange and Stephen Linard and all the Blitz pioneers, who had been pillaging the past so remorselessly. When Vivienne and Malcolm opened a new shop called Nostalgia of Mud, Philip Sallon and George O'Dowd were the shop assistants. As a result, of course, the true innovators simply moved on to other looks.

Artists took a little longer to come to the fore, but soon Grayson Perry, always a genial madcap character, would become one of the best-known and most recognisable visual creators in the land, a loveable cross-dressing potter. John Maybury went off into film and video directing, including the legendary 'Nothing Compares 2 U' video for Sinead O'Connor. Cerith Wyn Evans is now a hugely respected sculptor, represented in major public galleries worldwide. Peter Doig, who barely registered as a quiet one of the St Martin's crew at the back of the club, would emerge years later to become the highest-priced living artist in the world and credit the Blitz as being a vital part of his education. These were all Young British Artists before anybody had coined the term.

In terms of nightlife, Chris Sullivan, after his Blue Rondo adventure with Christos, went on to run the Wag Club with Ollie O'Donnell, who also ran Le Beat Route. Philip Sallon ran the Mud Club, Phil Dirtbox ran the Dirtbox and Dave Mahoney virtually invented the illegal rave scene with his wild outdoor parties. Princess Julia, Fat Tony and Jeremy Healy became and remain superstar DJs. London's nightlife scene, with its EDM, its house music and its mega clubs and raves, would not exist without those Blitz-trained pioneers.

Steve Dagger quickly established himself as one of the most respected music biz figures in the land, as did Jon Baker, who later moved to New York where he set up Gee Street Records and managed PM Dawn, becoming among the most influential movers and shakers in the world of hip hop. Graham Ball managed Blue Rondo and Sigue Sigue Sputnik before starting the whole Westworld/Wetworld club extravaganza. Lee Barrett guided Sade to global success. The list goes on and on, and so did the beat.

Morrissey sang 'We hate it when our friends become successful,' and Boy George claimed to dislike Spandau Ballet, but he was undoubtedly spurred on by their success. Without Spandau, there would be no Visage, no Culture Club, no Sade. Each one followed the other. Watching people around you suddenly become famous is a pretty big kick up the butt to get on with it.

A blend of envy to wind you up, but also admiration and inspiration to drive you on, is a potent combination. As soon as one or two people from within the group started to achieve some kind of prominence, the possibilities opened up for all of us. If he or she can do that, so can I. If they can do it, so can we. We didn't really hate it when our friends became successful because it meant we might well be successful too. Success felt contagious.

Spurred on and wound up by our mates doing well, we all started to work out how we could emulate them, what potential we could call upon. There undoubtedly was talent in that room on a Tuesday night: all those art and fashion students had already displayed a degree of aptitude to get into St Martin's or Central, and there were some very bright minds as well as a handful of decent musicians. But more important than skill or nous or talent was belief, the infectious collective belief that we could do whatever we wanted, a positivity born of punk and intensified by the weekly process of crossing the threshold into the most exacting, exciting and ultimately uplifting environment I have ever entered. If you could make it there, you really could make it anywhere. Going to the Blitz was the greatest education of them all.

Our next move would dramatically broaden our horizons, open our eyes and further our education, as well as spread the word about this scene which was causing such a scene. New York was next.

13
WE'LL TAKE MANHATTAN

We had already been bitten by the bug in the Big Apple. Myself, Chris Sullivan, Ollie O'Donnell and a handful of others had headed to New York for a couple of weeks in the summer of 1980, staying next door to the Hell's Angels clubhouse on 11th and 1st, which despite being in a dodgy neighbourhood, turned out to be the safest address in town for a bunch of wildly attired young Londoners in search of the craic. Our hairy biker neighbours took to us immediately and we were safe in their patronage.

Manhattan back then was a very different city. London has changed dramatically since the early 80s, but New York's premier borough has been gentrified beyond any recognition, away from the dilapidated, dangerous, thrilling and incredibly inspiring metropolis we first encountered. This was before Rudy Giuliani robbed it of all its glorious edge and energy and the developers excluded all but the exclusive and the expensive.

It was rundown, drugged-up and avowedly tough, yet open and welcoming. We quickly made contact with like-minded souls like August Darnell and James White, John Lurie and Jean-Michel Basquiat, and Jim Fouratt and Rudolf Piper, who ran the newly opened Danceteria, which was the closest club New York had to the Blitz – kindred spirits all. We basically befriended a whole host of our nocturnal New York equivalents, who adopted us and took us under their wings. It was apparent that there were parallel worlds in our two towns.

It is no coincidence that both New York and London were at their most vibrant and fecund as they were falling down. Punk had emerged from the rubble of these broken behemoths in the 70s because people were angry, but also because they were free; free from high rents, free from the need to get a job, free to take over abandoned spaces, free to party and play, and boy did they party. By 1980, punk had been and gone in both cities and even disco, once the joyously deviant NYC soundtrack, was flagging. But a new, fashionable, danceable, arty party scene was emerging downtown – in the summer of 1980, we were thrown in at the deep end.

Somehow Chris had a ready-built network of contacts of friends of friends who welcomed us into their world. He would stand in a zoot suit at a public phone box on teeming 14th Street armed with piles of dimes, organising our social life for that night. I told everybody who would listen, and plenty who didn't want to, that I was a writer for *The Face*, which had already developed an exalted reputation over there, and doors opened. Everybody wanted to know about the scene they had heard about in London.

We went out every night, all night, and deep into every day, at places like the Mudd Club, the Peppermint Lounge and the wonderfully named after-hours joint Save the Robots. We were on every guest list and in every fashionable bolt hole from seedy S&M clubs in the Meatpacking District and arty jazz lofts in SoHo to swanky uptown soirées in parkside mansions. I was even invited to DJ at Danceteria (I told them I was rubbish, but they thought it was just exaggerated English modesty) and stood in the booth next to Mark Kamins, Madonna's then beau.

★ ★ ★

After that first trip in 1980, we came back down to earth with a bump in London. Chris and I were still living with my mum at this stage and didn't have two pennies to rub together, but in New York we were somehow twenty-year-old royalty, fêted and invited. When we got back to Blighty and the Blitz on that first Tuesday night, we would not stop talking about how brilliant the city was. Steve Dagger was one of the people doing the listening.

As soon as Spandau Ballet was established in their hometown, Steve wasted no time in planning the next phase of his global domination: it centred on Bournemouth. On New Year's Eve 1980, Spandau had appeared at Richard Branson's vast venue Heaven, the biggest club in London, which many of us had known as the Global Village back in the mid-70s soul era. It was easily the largest venue they had played so far, but it still wasn't large enough as the queues outside were enormous and hundreds were locked out. It was effectively to be their last London gig as standard-bearers of the trendy club world. But there was still the seaside to come.

By 1981, the tradition of heading down to Dorset for the Easter bank holiday had become absolutely enshrined in club lore, a major pop culture conclave. The Bournemouth Beano was how new trends, sounds and styles got circulated. Thousands from all the various tribes converged on this otherwise staid seaside town, mainly from London but increasingly from all over – Cardiff, Birmingham, Bristol – for non-stop hedonism; dancing, drinking, drugging and, if you could still manage it, fucking. We were on it from the moment the Buccaneer, the Fox and the Palace Vaults opened at 11 a.m., stopping only for some tucker in the Double O Egg then on to the nightspots, the Village Bowl or the 81 Club, and finally all back to whatever hotel bar you could cram into and whatever bed you could blag your way into.

Behaviour was disgraceful, liberties were taken, drinks stolen, runners done, fun was had. It was both a recreation of the old mod tradition of seaside bank-holiday excursions and also a foretaste of the whole Ibiza club culture extravaganza, a few hedonistic days with hopefully some sunshine, sex and a great soundtrack. Except we were snoozing in deckchairs by the English Channel rather than chilling on sunbeds by the Med. In 1981, Spandau, who had been there in previous years as punters, were set to play at the largest venue in town, the Exeter Bowl, a kind of jolly for all of us who had been part of the journey thus far.

Being soaked in beer and deprived of sleep, I remember very little of the weekend, except that Steve Dagger, who by now had his own office on Carnaby Street, actually booked and paid for a room in the poshest hotel in town, the Merville. He got repaid for his flashness by getting invaded by about thirty of us at four in the morning, demanding to sleep on his floor, including Chris Sullivan, who collapsed on his bed and proceeded to snore loudly in Welsh.

But I do remember that Gary introduced a striking new song during the set, which he dedicated to me, called 'Chant No. 1', a major musical departure away from electro and into brittle, blue-eyed funk, heralding one of the major changes by then underway. It even included a Soho 'rap' at the end, a direct if slightly gauche nod to the big new thing emerging from New York. In London too, in the post-Blitz landscape, a whole new sound and style was coming to the fore. We were about to bring the two filial cities together: we were all bound for Gotham.

★   ★   ★

Twenty-one young nightclubbers flew from London to New York, our suitcases full of schmutter and heads full of tales of New York nightlife. We had no idea where we were going to stay, or how it was going to work. But, by that stage, we were so full of ourselves that we just assumed it would be a roaring success – after all, we'd done it in Birmingham and Bournemouth – so we just got smashed on the flight out to JFK and hoped for the best.

The trip was organised, sort of, by Steve Dagger – who was paying all the air fares from Spandau's advance, but didn't stretch to accommodation costs for anybody but the band in their swish hotel – and Jon Baker, under whose Axiom banner a fashion show would take place. Between them they had assembled the cast list. The Spandau contingent consisted of Dagger, Gary, Martin, Tony, Steve and drummer John Keeble, their producer Richard Burgess to oversee the live sound, and their roadie Steve Marshall, my old punky mate from the Watling Estate. Ollie O'Donnell was there to do the hair for both the band and the fashion show, Simon Withers was taking care of staging and lighting, and Graham Smith was the official photographer, along with Neil Matthews, who doubled as security dressed as a Basque freedom fighter. I was there as an embedded journalist reporting for *The Face*. Little did I know I would also have to walk the catwalk.

Jon Baker had cobbled together the fashion show side of things, including his own take on swashbuckling corsairs' clobber, Simon Withers' strap-heavy Reformation collection and Robin Archer's teasing fetish wear. The star turn was provided by Melissa Caplan, whose neo-medievalist robes were Spandau's predominant look at that moment in time, with Martin looking particularly striking as a hooded warrior monk.

Chris Sullivan, who doubled as social secretary for the trip, had designed a wardrobe of modified 40s-inspired zoot suits, spearpoint collar shirts and kipper ties, and, at the last minute, a couple of girls no one really knew were added to the line-up. They were Sarah Lubel and Sade Adu, both from the St Martin's fashion course, who had teamed up to produce an unusually subtle set of silk dresses and headgear.

The trip did not get off to an auspicious start when we were, perhaps understandably, given a torrid time by the grimly officious officials at immigration. They were decidedly troubled by our attire and by the fact that most of us had East German stamps in our passports from that Berlin trip. They took a particular dislike to Chris, holding him in a cell for three hours of intense interrogation. But eventually we all got in, piled our suitcases into Checker cabs and set about finding somewhere to stay. Chris was straight on the phone to the contacts we had made the previous summer, and somehow we all got assigned a bed or a sofa in somebody's apartment. I stayed in Gramercy Park in the spare room of a woman called Rhonda Paster, whom I'd met when she was waitressing at Danceteria. She became the absolute star of the trip.

Jon Baker had come out to New York on a scouting trip a few weeks earlier, hooking up with a girl we all knew as Little Debi, who worked the door at Danceteria. She later became famous as the actress Debi Mazar, appearing in *Goodfellas*, and it might even have been because of us. Jon and Debi's job was to recce all the potential venues, of which there were plenty in the city at that time. Dagger's theory was that there was a huge nocturnal void in Manhattan at that precise moment, caused by the demise of disco. Studio 54 had just closed and its owners were in jail, and discos generally were struggling to fill their vast dancefloors. This meant not only loads of eerily empty spaces all around Manhattan, but also that they were eager for a new sound and style to take over and fill their clubs and their coffers. Jon and Debi settled on somewhere called The Underground, a cavernous, under-used discotheque with an industrial feel and an amazing sound system, situated directly beneath the offices of Andy Warhol's magazine *Interview* on Broadway.

Jim Fouratt, the gay activist co-founder of Danceteria, who Chris and I had befriended the previous summer, was the promoter for the event. He'd flown over to London to see the scene first-hand and to persuade Dagger he was the right man for the task of launching Spandau and the whole Blitz crowd in the US. Jim ended up coming with us to Bournemouth to see Spandau play, and, despite having been an integral part of the decadent New York club scene throughout the 70s, was wide-eyed, shocked and amazed by both the debauchery and the creativity of a bunch of louche Londoners by the seaside. He ended up in a lock-in in a damp B&B at 4 a.m. with a load of rockabillies in eyeliner and loved every minute of it. He went all out to make sure he got the gig.

The guest list for that night was an absolute Who's Who of New York's finest and fruitiest. De Niro and Scorsese walked in together and met both Little Debi and her mate Madonna, who was then a dancer at Danceteria with not-so-secret ambitions to conquer the world. Basquiat and Keith Haring, the two stars of the street art scene, were there with an entourage of downtown B-boys in baseball caps, while Warhol himself sat stony-faced throughout, staring blankly at the scene. Kid Creole, John Lurie and Billy Idol, a former Billy's boy who had relocated to New York, all came, as did Paula Yates, who happened to be in town. Diana Vreeland, the grand dame and doyenne of New York fashion writers, sat sternly in the front row with a phalanx of reporters from just about every major paper and journal in the land and a few, including David Johnson, who had come over from London. And we had to try to entertain and impress them.

The run-up to the show was splendidly chaotic. Spandau spent most of their time doing interviews and photoshoots, while we slept away the day and prowled by night. We did not have enough models for the fashion show, so we were all sent out to clubs to recruit pretty or interesting people to wear the clothes and walk the catwalk, with the proviso they would not be paid, as we had no budget.

So our nocturnal jaunts became even more intense as we tried to select and cajole the beautiful people of Manhattan into modelling with our supposed English charm. The accent certainly helped, as did the fact that MDMA was the new, still legal, drug of choice among New York's night people and so everybody was feeling proper loved-up. That might also account for the fact that, when we had an official photo call for the publicity shot for the show, outside the venue, only fifteen of the twenty-one participants turned up. The others were too wasted.

Rhonda's apartment, known colloquially as 'The British Embassy', served as our HQ and it was frantic, with rails of clothing being wheeled along 21st Street and into her lift at midnight and half-naked people trying on bizarre garb in her hallway. There was a perpetual stream of press-ganged party people and a few proper models who would arrive for fittings under the eagle-eyed scrutiny of Melissa, who was choreographing the whole thing, and the slightly more laidback gaze of Jon Baker, who played Mr Cool.

There were bikers from New Jersey modelling Chris's suits; his mate Lisa Rosen, a top Milan catwalk model, adding a much-needed air of professionalism; Perri Lister, Billy Idol's then girlfriend; a suave Venezuelan bloke with a superb moustache; a gorgeous but dead-eyed Russian sex worker from Coney Island; and seemingly half the staff of Danceteria, who Rhonda had recruited.

Amid this mayhem, the two new girls on Jon Baker's Axiom squad arrived at Rhonda's straight off the plane from the UK. I stupidly mistook one of them, the almond-eyed beauty with the corn rows in her hair, for one of our model recruits until she told me in no uncertain terms that she was not a bloody model, she was one of the designers and her name was Sade. I should have known, as she was part of the St Martin's crew and had been to the Blitz a few times with her squatmate Greg Davis, a lovely, flamboyantly queer designer who was a real regular. She was obviously strikingly beautiful, but more than that, she had an instant stature, a solidity and a down-to-earth charm with an easy smile, which certainly charmed me.

We were still in need of models, so we did eventually persuade Sade to wear her own gear on the runway, knowing she would look great. Even I, not the most obvious contender for male model, was fitted with an outfit and told to walk the plank. That was how we met.

Eventually, the night of the show came amid a veritable pyrotechnic display of flashbulbs and film crews, TV reporters delivering live pieces to camera, red carpets and limos lined up outside as we caused a huge hullabaloo on Broadway, with the queue stretching round the block. It was potty; we were the hottest ticket in town, yet we remained cool. None of us had slept for days, and we were under-rehearsed and under enormous pressure, but nobody panicked, except perhaps Jim Fouratt, who had gone out on a limb with this one and had his reputation riding on it.

Jon Baker and Steve Dagger strolled around with big smiles on their faces, Chris Sullivan greeted everybody arriving personally and seemed to know them all, while Ollie O'Donnell worked absolute miracles backstage with an endless supply of hairspray and pins. Rhonda, meanwhile, seemed to be everywhere and doing everything. She was a model, a maître d' and a tough taskmaster, keeping this very unsteady craft afloat.

The place was absolutely heaving and amazingly full of New Yorkers trying desperately to look like colourful New Romantics, when just a couple of months before they had all been in all black. We certainly changed the colour palette. The fashion show was first up and Jim Fouratt made the on-stage announcement, saying, 'I offer you not just music and fashion. I offer you London.' No pressure there then. I waited backstage, feeling incredibly nervous.

Trying to walk with some kind of insouciance and style on a thin, rickety platform, in time to music, between rows of eyes staring intensely at you, while you wear a weird outfit, might just be the most difficult thing I've ever done. And I'm pretty sure I did not do it very well. Caked in make-up and trussed up in clothes pinned to fit, my stint flashed by in the blink of an eye, probably because I rushed through, desperate to get to the end, almost hitting the model in front and toppling over. After that, I had nothing but respect for the people who do catwalk modelling for a living.

Everybody else did just fine and, by the time it came to Melissa's finale, with the sound of Burundi drums echoing round the room and more than a few whoops and hollers from the crowd, we had definitely won them over. By this stage, the atmosphere was febrile. Backstage, there was a mixture of joyous relief from the fashionistas, many of them slumped against walls or lying on the floor, but nerves from the band, who now had a lot to live up to.

I recall Dagger giving the boys a managerial pep talk along the lines of 'Give 'em hell' and walking them in single file up to the stage: Steve in front like a wise corner-man, Martin shrouded in a hood with his hands on Steve's shoulders like a prize fighter about to step into the ring for his big shot, all of them hyped and ready to rumble.

Later on, Spandau Ballet became a slick, showbiz affair in their swanky outfits and extravagant hair, playing giant stadiums with a super-smooth show, all swooning saxophone solos and choreographed moves. But not that night. This was still a bunch of punky Angel boys from the council estates of Islington, rough not just round the edges but to the core of their souls, and desperate to prove their mettle. Sweaty, impassioned, raw, they knocked the crowd off balance with their energy and attack, Tony's booming barrow-boy voice cutting through and those pounding disco rhythms getting the crowd onto their feet. They went about as wild as New York crowds can get. We had a major success on our hands.

In retrospect, Spandau Ballet's debut performance in New York, that May in 1981, supported by a fashion show promoting some of the best of young London design talent to have emerged from the club scene, was the apogee of the whole Blitz caper – a band with barely a dozen songs and a bunch of penniless fashion students who had made a handful of frocks taking on the toughest and coolest city on earth. It was an audacious exercise in self-promotion and brazen front from a bunch of wayward kids, and despite being underfunded and overhyped, alcoholic, shambolic and shamelessly hubristic, somehow, by the seat of our fancy pants, we pulled it off.

The reviews were phenomenal; 'Show-Blitzness has launched its American invasion' one paper said. 'A conquest. Not since the heady days of Studio 54 has a Manhattan club crackled with such intensity,' said another. The super-hip *SoHo News* even proclaimed: 'We are jealous, London has done it again.'

My emotions were mixed. I was thrilled certainly, knackered definitely, but it was all tinged with just a hint of melancholy. I think I knew even then that this was the end of something, that this amazing event was the finale of at least the first part of an incredible adventure, which had begun when I first walked into Billy's almost two years before. The Blitz had been and gone, and our job was done with Spandau. They were going to sail off into mainstream success and I was about to reach the ripe old age of twenty-two. I was also falling in something like love.

The date of that memorable extravaganza in Manhattan was 4 May 1981. I know that because the next night, the 5th, has gone down in history as the night Bobby Sands, IRA volunteer, H-Block prisoner and hunger striker, died. That tragic event played a part in this story. Flushed with the success of the night before, a whole load of us blagged our way into a gig uptown with an amazing line-up of New York's finest. James White and the Blacks, Richard Hell, the mighty Defunkt and Blondie, fronted by the wondrous Debbie Harry – the perfect combination for our punk/funk musical tastes at the time.

At that gig, I found myself dancing with that beautiful designer from Essex via Ibadan and having a great night in her company. It was late when we emerged onto the streets and it so happened we were right by Hell's Kitchen, the old Irish quarter of Manhattan. I suggested we go for a nightcap in a bar, trying to extend my time in Sade's presence, not knowing that news had just reached the city that Bobby Sands, by then an elected MP, had died after sixty-six days of starvation in the notorious H-Blocks of Long

Kesh, Margaret Thatcher having refused to grant him political prisoner status.

Suddenly we found ourselves amid a riot, windows being smashed, angry people roaming the streets protesting. This was the one time and place in New York when it was definitely not an advantage to have an English accent, and a drink in one of those famed Irish bars was out of the question. We had intended to go our separate ways back to our digs, but we were genuinely scared and, in an act of self-preservation, we jumped in front of a Checker cab and persuaded him to take us both down to my apartment.

★   ★   ★

One other thing happened in New York on that trip which is worth mentioning. Myself, Chris, Ollie and Jon Baker went out one night to yet another downtown club, but rather than the usual mix of no wave art house funk and punk, and the usual crowd of wasted-looking Lower East Side trendies, this place was full of Black and Hispanic kids in baseball caps back to front, spinning on their heads, while DJs were spinning and scratching cut up funk tracks and talking over the top. We'd all heard of hip hop but had never really seen it in action, and it certainly stopped us in our tracks. I remember thinking it was great fun and all that, but rather gimmicky and it would never catch on, which is perhaps a sign that you should never trust my judgement. Jon Baker did not agree: I think he saw his future right there.

Jon introduced us that night to a friend of his called Ruza Blue, or Cool Lady Blue, as she was known to these spinning kids down from the Bronx. She regaled us with exciting plans to start her own club called the Roxy where she would showcase this incredible scene. And, of course, she did just that, becoming one of the biggest players in the early days of hip hop in New York, managing Grandmaster Flash and Afrika Bambaataa. She said all this in a broad English accent, because she was a Londoner. It turned out she was a veteran of both Billy's and the early days of the Blitz. It seems we were everywhere.

14

THE BLITZ IS DEAD, LONG LIVE THE BLITZ

By the time we'd taken on New York, the Blitz was no more. After a year and half of almost unchallenged nocturnal supremacy the most influential, the most consequential club of the age just fizzled out: no last hurrah, no grand finale, no one remembers a final farewell, probably because we were too busy going out, because there was so much going on. By day, Britain was mired in misery and conflict, but the night is a different country. There was a goldrush going on out there in the dark.

The last night of Steve Strange and Rusty Egan's masterpiece was on 14 October 1980. I didn't even go. By then, the Blitz had run its course, done its job. Given that the essence of this scene was perpetual change, it is remarkable that it lasted so long, testament to how brilliant it was. Everything that came afterwards was in its wake, was because of the Blitz. The prospects for those of a nocturnal bent were far different by then; London was rocking.

Chris and I had discovered Le Kilt as we scoured Soho, looking for a suitable venue for our next adventure, a follow-up to our kitsch *Cabaret* extravaganza at St Moritz. Up some stairs from a simple doorway with a brass nameplate, behind a scarlet awning, this venerable old discotheque was up on the quieter Soho Square end of Greek Street, opposite the ancient Gay Hussar restaurant and a non-stop strip club, and next to a Dickensian doss house for female sex workers.

Run by a charming if dodgy French chancer called Jean Pierre, the kind who proliferated in the warren of W1 back then, Le Kilt was strictly old Soho, post-war, pre-gentrification, past its best. There had been a raft of these supposedly sophisticated whisky discos for men in Jags and girls in mini-skirts and Le Kilt was the last one left. Swinging London in a hunting lodge.

Decked out in a grand Scottish baronial style, with dark wood panelling, tatty tartan carpets and wall hangings, and moth-eaten stags' heads staring at you on the stairways, it had changed not one iota from its groovy 60s heyday. The DJ booth was an old ornate eighteenth-century sedan chair, the sound system was a single deck like your mum and dad's hi-fi and the place stank of single malt, cigars and desiccated antlers. It was perfect. We opened our one-night-a-week special at Le Kilt on the first Tuesday of November 1980. The Tuesday bit was significant: we were directly picking up the baton from the Blitz, which had closed just a couple of weeks before.

Chris and Graham Ball would take care of the door, and myself and Graham Smith would select the music. Chris and I had made a decision that we would be going back to our collective soul-boy roots and playing strictly funky tunes; no electro, no cabaret, instead a mix of old Crackers classics (what later became known as rare groove), the new no wave and hip hop stuff coming out of New York, angular punk funk from the likes of A Certain Ratio and The Pop Group in the UK, and a bit of jazz, a touch of Latin. So you'd hear Gil Scott-Heron and Was (Not Was), James Brown and James White in the mix.

There was a brilliant record shop round the corner in Dean Street called Groove Records, run by a rotund elderly Greek lady named Jean (the groovy granny) who would sit knitting while recommending the latest 12-inch import single on ZE Records. I would be in there every weekend getting the new sounds for our session at Le Kilt. This place was for dancing and the more intricate, exhibitionist soul moves from some of Chris's old reprobate mates replaced the Blitz jive as the dance de nuit.

It was an instant success, despite the fact that the sound system broke down for nearly an hour on the first night, but then many of the punters were so high they didn't even notice and just kept bopping. The look was very retro: 40s and 50s, lots of matinée idol suits and ties for the guys and Hollywood glamour for the dolls, a little less make-up and gender-bending fancy dress. In hindsight, a fault line was appearing in the scene.

We all appeared in a BBC *Newsnight* special on the New Romantics, filmed at Le Kilt, introduced by a baffled-looking Peter Snow in a dreadful beige acrylic 70s-style suit, contrasting with Chris in a resplendent plaid zoot, myself channelling the Rat Pack, Christos as a moustachioed Low Rider and Graham Ball as Tom Mix. Steve Strange was now our guest for the night and looked slightly worse for wear as a kind of glam Wurzel Gummidge, but he still made lots of sense as he spoke about the positivity of these particular dandified youth of today.

Le Kilt was youthful, exuberant and more open than the Blitz, as we welcomed newcomers. A skinny south London teenager on the scene made his debut appearance at Le Kilt. He said he wanted to be an actor; he was called Tim Roth. Another one spotted dancing with his mate was known as Yog, though his real name was Georgios. His friend was called Andrew. Wham! were about to be born, another classic gay-and-straight double act, though of course George's sexuality was not known at this time, possibly even to himself.

There had always been two camps in the Blitz: the usually queer fashion student crowd and the more or less heterosexual old soul boy/punk contingent, personified by the pairing of Steve Strange and Rusty Egan, and held together by the fact that we all looked like weirdo deviants to straight-goers. We all got on just fine and benefitted enormously from the cross-pollination, but after Covent Garden closed and a raft of new clubs opened in its wake, so the factions drifted apart a little, starting their own evenings in their own venues with their own distinct styles.

There was never any segregation; we'd all go to all the clubs, you'd still see George and Marilyn at Le Kilt, and you could still fancy whoever you wanted wherever you were. But Le Kilt and, a little later, Le Beat Route, and certainly the Dirt Box, were more muscular, hedonistic and hetero, while Philip Sallon's Mud Club and later Taboo were aimed at the flamboyantly camp camp, pushing the avant-garde boundaries as far as Leigh Bowery and his outrageous performance art. On one side, Mark Powell suits from his new shop in Archer Street and Demob jeans from Brewer Street; on the other, BodyMap, Pam Hogg and Rachel Auburn outfits from Kensington Market.

By the time we had arrived at 1981, there were so many clubs opening, most of them the work of Blitz alumni, that it is almost impossible to create a timeline. Perry Haines had that place of his own in Marble Arch called Dial 9 for Dolphins where knee-high Dr Martens were de rigueur. Philip Sallon started a one-nighter called Planets in Piccadilly where Vivienne Westwood was the default designer and pirates and highwaymen abounded. George O'Dowd, still yet to find his métier, was the DJ, and his assistant was a chubby, feral sixteen-year-old street kid dubbed Fat Tony. Philip made the most spectacularly catty front-of-house of all time.

After a few months concentrating on being pop stars in Visage and planning their next nocturnal move, Steve and Rusty finally opened Club for Heroes, another Bowie night by any other name.

They switched to Thursdays, always a more traditional night out for a more traditional West End crowd in the swanky environs of the Barracuda Club. This was an upmarket jet-trash disco on Baker Street, all mirrored walls, marble and cocktails. And that was very much the vibe Steve Strange was aiming for now.

Kim Bowen, looking incredibly glamorous as a greeter on the door, was a link back to the Blitz, but this place had none of the transgressive yet inclusive camaraderie of the old club. Steve, always a shapeshifter, had now shed his avant-garde skin and reimagined himself as a suave Antony Price-suited entrepreneur and international celebrity as he shmoozed the beautiful people: the models and actors, the cosmopolitan A-listers, as nobody called them then, the famous-for-being-famous figures who would never have got past the door of the Blitz but who were fêted at his shiny new night. Steve was now a famous name himself and loving it.

The music Rusty played was indicative of the way his original electro soundtrack was beginning to dominate the charts: Heaven 17, the Human League, Orchestral Manoeuvres, Depeche Mode, Spandau Ballet, Duran Duran, ABC, Haircut 100 . . . Many of them were there in person to listen to their own tracks and bask in their new-found stardom – commercial, successful, contemporary shiny pop, which just about summed up Club for Heroes. Michael Jackson turned up one night with a massive minder and Steve paraded him around the club like a little lost boy.

We all still went to Club for Heroes and got in free because of our status as original Blitz kids, and it was a good glam night out, but seeing Jimmy O'Donnell and Phil Dirtbox in ripped-up denim and biker boots saunter past the likes of Bryan Ferry and Jerry Hall, Karl Lagerfeld and Francesca Thyssen, with their drivers waiting outside and their wealth on display, was a sign of another fault line opening up. Le Beat Route and the Dirtbox were calling.

My favourite year of this era is probably 1981; it was certainly the most hectic. Sade and I had moved in together when we got back from New York, originally into her short-life, semi-legal house-share up in Wood Green, but then into our very own squat in a disused fire station in Tottenham. Her brother Banji had scrambled across the roof of this imposing but decaying red-brick Victorian building in a sleepy Haringey backstreet and discovered that, although it had been long abandoned, the large rooms where the firemen used to sleep were all in good shape, even if the bath was in the kitchen and the toilet was out on the balcony. We got in, connected the electricity, sanded the floors, paid the rates and informed the council that we were now living there. That was how it worked then.

Chris Sullivan had rented a flat above a kebab shop in Kentish Town which became our de facto social centre as he spent hours on the payphone on the wall organising the night and the rest of the time deciding what to wear. Running a club like Le Kilt, just one night a week with the proceeds split between four of us, didn't bring in a fortune, but we were alright. Money was never really our motivation: we kept prices as low as possible and were still doing it for the craic and the kudos.

And after half a dozen months of great fun on Greek Street, we decided to move on again. The place was as popular as ever, but we had this idea that you had to keep doing new things, keep it fresh, which was so much part of the Blitz ethos. Le Kilt, however, had a major lasting effect, in that it re-established funk and soul as the primary sound and rhythm which would drive London's nightlife throughout the 80s right up until the hegemony of house music in the 90s.

The whole concept of club culture – of London as a thriving, groovy twenty-four-hour city – came from this period: Le Kilt, Le Beat Route, the Dirtbox and the Wag, right through to the Boilerhouse, Blackmarket, Special Branch, Talking Loud, Soul to Soul and Shake and Fingerpop . . . The musical formula and the dressed-up but down-and-dirty ethos pioneered at Le Kilt kept this city dancing for a decade.

Sade was trying to make a living in the fashion game, but it was tough and she augmented that with a spot of modelling, which she hated. I was earning enough from my writing and presenting to go out most nights of the week, but it was still hand to mouth, and it was very handy that we had a rent-free flat to live in. For other people, it was becoming tougher still.

Out there in the big, bad real world, times were getting harder and harder; unemployment had doubled in the first two years of Thatcher's regime and the streets were seething. The Brixton rising took place in April and there were IRA bombs almost every week. National Front attacks and countless strikes and protest marches were part of our every day, and there was a palpable edge in the air wherever you went. So we went dancing. While all this was kicking off, we were dressing up and going out for all we were worth.

There was undoubtedly an element of escapism: why wouldn't you want to escape some of that stuff, and enjoy your youth while you could? But also, rightly or wrongly, we still saw ourselves as part of the resistance, an outsider counter-cultural movement, albeit one which responded to Thatcherism by refusing to be kow-towed, by having fun in the face of oppression, rather like the alternative rave scene of the 1990s which picked up the mantle of partying as protest. I'm not sure that was how we were universally viewed, however.

The music press continued sniping away at us, resulting in a brief punch-up at Steve Strange's new club, the Camden Palace, between myself and an *NME* writer; we were parodied in the press and on TV, memorably by *Not the Nine O'Clock News*. We definitely divided opinion. At the other end of the spectrum, the whole New Romantic shebang was increasingly being commercialised and commodified. People wanted to latch on to this new trend, as they saw it, flogging whatever they could, which only served to speed up the process of change. By the time any style had hit the high street, it was already discarded by the people who had pioneered it. And I was partly to blame.

A new magazine called *New Sounds New Styles* opened and offered me a salary to be features editor. It came from the EMAP/*Smash Hits* stable of mainstream pop magazines and concentrated exclusively on the shiny new acts in the now-ubiquitous New Romantic style. Lots of colour photos of Steve Strange and Martin Kemp and articles on eyeliner and hairspray. I really should have said thanks but no thanks.

I was never sold on the format, and I was loath to leave *The Face*, but Nick Logan never offered me a proper job, or any kind of regular wage, and was still effectively running the show from one room. By now *The Face* was incredibly influential, but still only just scraping by financially, with Nick still doing almost everything himself. Selling sufficient advertising space was the toughest part as big brands with big budgets hadn't yet cottoned on to the commercial potential of this latest youthquake. That was certainly about to change. Within a year or so, Levi ads would be featuring *Face* covers, Buffalo boys and Russian constructivist graphics.

Nick never seemed to mind me writing for a competitor. I'm sure he realised that *New Sounds New Styles* would not last the course and, a year later, he was proved correct. But for twelve months at least, I had some money to spend and an official job title to my name. I also got to appreciate what a great magazine *The Face* was and why Nick Logan was the best editor I would ever work for.

The live Friday night BBC2 TV programme I presented, *The Oxford Road Show*, was filmed in Oxford Road in Manchester and tried rather clumsily to blend youth culture, music, fashion and politics, but ended up in a complete mess, not helped by the fact that I had no idea what I was doing, and nor it seemed did anybody else. Trying hard to be cutting edge and 'dangerous', it was chaotic and amateurish, and the only real danger was to our career prospects. When I put this to the producer, he actually said to me, 'I'm not trying to make good TV. I'm trying to start a revolution.' But at least I managed to get Blue Rondo and Sade on there. I left after one series.

The energy and effortlessness of youth was such that I could go out – and I really do mean out, often leaving the flat just before midnight to go to various clubs and events – get up in the morning, dust myself down, wake myself up and do some writing about where I'd been and who I'd seen the night before. It didn't really feel like work at all: we were working hard hardly working.

My job was chronicling what my mates and I were doing, a kind of gonzo journalism, although I had never heard of the phrase. It wasn't just me: many, if not most, of the original Blitz kids had by now found ways to make a living out of their lifestyle and life of style. We were all putting together what would now be called port-folio careers; a bit of this and that, a pay cheque here, some cash from there. Zero hours but maximum effort.

You could also argue that, essentially, we were influencers way before anybody had ever coined that term. People wanted to know what we were wearing, where we were dancing, what we were listen-ing to. How we lived became news. Even supposedly serious papers like *The Times* and the *Observer* sent reporters to our squat to inter-view me for features – and this was before Sade became famous. Then it really went berserk. The newspapers were cottoning on to the fact that we were witnessing a sea-change. The *Sunday Times*, for example, was about to launch its own *Style* section, the first of its kind and an acknowledgement that we were now in an age when style mattered.

We were fêted and defamed in equal measure, but what people thought of us was water off a duck's back; we had thick skins and big egos. What really mattered to us, above all else, was having fun. And believe me, Le Beat Route was fun.

If the Blitz was the most important club of its era (and it was), then Le Beat Route in Greek Street – a large, tacky subterranean disco, done up in a quasi-Hawaiian style – was the most enjoyable. Started by a couple of Blitz faces – yet another Welshman (and yet another Steve) Stephen Mahoney and Ollie O'Donnell, the arch hairdresser from Smile – Le Beat Route broke the midweek mould by going for the Friday slot, always the busiest of the week and a sign that our lot were now in charge of the night. Prior to that, we had still shied away from weekends for fear of the beer monsters on the prowl, but also club owners were still confident they could fill their premium nights themselves. By mid-1981, we were pretty much the only show in town.

Stephen and Ollie recruited Steve Lewis, one of the wild west London lot, as DJ, even though he'd never done it before. It was a masterstroke. A veteran of both the soul and punk scenes, he had immaculate taste in the harder, sharper end of dance music, a hunger to seek out new stuff and a genuine political belief – he DJ'd in front of a picture of Lenin and played 'The Red Flag' as the last tune of the night, which was perfect for such riven times. Was it gesture politics? Of course, but then we were good at gestures. Steve was also brilliant at selecting, the best I ever heard; he could have become the first of the new wave of superstar DJs, but refused to play the game, his low-key personality and his staunch politics preventing him from cashing in.

Le Beat Route, which immediately had chaotic queues back into Old Compton Street, lines forming way before it even opened, was a very different proposition to the arty posing and posturing of the Blitz. It was rougher and tougher, less refined, more visceral, yet the vast majority of original Blitz kids were there: Andy Polaris still a star dancer, Stephen Linard trying to look butch, Marilyn looking fabulous, Fiona Dealey helping Ollie take the money on the door. The soul of the Blitz had moved on and morphed into something much bigger.

The new club attracted a completely mixed crowd in every sense: sexually, racially, musically, stylistically, but still thoroughly trendy, with Ollie positively puritanical on the door. People came from all over, getting coaches and trains down to town in the hope of getting in. Others tried week after week until Mr O'Donnell finally relented and let them into the wicked wonderland. Friday nights on Greek Street took the scene way beyond its Blitz/art-school roots. It was a sign that what had been a handful of hipsters in a wine bar had now grown to a much wider constituency of switched-on, dressed-up youth. Everybody wanted to be part of the gang.

Le Beat Route – dark, subterranean, sweaty, sexy – somehow suited the tougher tenor of the times. Riotously hedonistic, it was a warren of little booths and niches where people could get up to every kind of mischief, and they certainly did. It was soaked in alcohol and wired with cocaine – chaotic, glorious, down to earth and up to no good. It was a celebration of excess: more was definitely more.

It was also the most uninhibited dancefloor I've ever witnessed: Fatback, P-funk and Brit-funk, cutting-edge New York disco and Steve Lewis's carefully curated political tunes coming from Reagan's trickle-down America; 'How We Gonna Make the Black Nation Rise?' and 'Money's Too Tight (To Mention)'. Soon some old-time rebel rockabilly was being mixed in with the beats to create a furious soundtrack made for abandon. The sweat ran down the walls and people slid down them, wasted, prone bodies sticking to the carpet as they collapsed.

If any celebrities turned up and got past Ollie, they were treated exactly the same as everybody else. They joined in the mayhem or left. There was no VIP area, no private tables, no quarter given, so you might see Grace Jones and Jean Paul Gaultier dancing with or snogging a rockabilly from Ealing and a rubber-clad fetish freak called Ron. Le Beat Route was so cool it was positively scorching.

There's a sense of that blistering intensity in the video Spandau Ballet made there for 'Chant No. 1 (I Don't Need This Pressure On)'. It's a sub-Scorsese mean streets of Soho short, in which a perspiring Tony Hadley definitely doesn't need that pressure on as he makes his way to the club on a colour-saturated Friday night. Shot through with punchy congas, blaring horns and street paranoia, it features both Ollie's quiff and Steve Lewis's Lenin. It was the last time Spandau would really be associated with the club scene and, by being at Le Beat Route, they got it spot-on for their farewell.

Whatever you wore on a Friday night was likely to be trashed by the end of it, which was one of the reasons for the most dramatic sartorial volte face of this whole story. Le Kilt, just a couple of months before, had been zoot suits and cocktail gowns, itself a change from the am-dram, anything-goes stylistic shock value of the Blitz. But by the time Le Beat Route became, as Gary Kemp would rap at the end of 'Chant No. 1', 'the place to shoot', a startling new look had emerged. There were still plenty of 50s Brando touches, but if you wore a suit, you had to accept it would be in the dry cleaners or the trash can by Monday morning, so a startling new look emerged. I called it Hard Times.

That was the title of a piece I wrote for *The Face* chronicling this dramatic change in the scene and equating it with the hardening of attitudes in Margaret Thatcher's increasingly torrid and turbulent Britain. It was a cover story featuring the shapely bottom of Lee Barrett, soon to be Sade's manager, wearing a plain white T, a pair of my old ripped and torn Levi 501s, a studded belt, a patterned hanky in his back pocket in classic gay village style and a fag in his hand.

For a magazine previously associated with glamour, it was both shocking and radical, the first time *The Face* had ever put anything but a pop star's face on the cover, and it was an anonymous arse. My prose was a hectoring, self-mythologising piece of over-the-top pop sociology linking fashion, music and politics, but it really struck a chord and became the most noted and notorious piece I ever wrote.

227

It also kicked off a craze for ripped jeans which has persisted to this day. After that *Face* cover came out, you could almost hear the nation's youth taking razorblades to their denims.

The first person I saw wearing a tatty old pair of ripped and torn Levis was Ollie's rocking brother, Jimmy, always a punk at heart, and he wore his most decaying pair over other slightly less worn ones – double denim indeed. Throw in a ruined biker's jacket, a pair of biker boots or tattered espadrilles, a cap-sleeved T or an old Vivienne Westwood 'Cowboy' top for credibility and a flat-top rockabilly crew cut and you have the essence of the Hard Times style.

It was as much a rejection of the slick glamour of Club for Heroes as any real political comment, but there's no doubt that it was getting serious out there: our response was always to counter depression with passion, hard times with good times. This stripped-back, dance-til-you-drop, take-no-prisoners approach to nightlife reached its zenith a while later at a peripatetic club called the Dirtbox, which was Le Beat Route on steroids, or rather on snake-bite and smack. They specialised in finding the grungiest, dirtiest venues for the most wild and wanton parties of all. Times were hard and so was keeping up with it all.

The best illustration of how quickly and dramatically styles changed was when Granada TV bussed a coachload of Le Beat Route's finest up to Manchester for a live special they were filming with August Darnell in his guise as Kid Creole and the Coconuts. The producers wanted loads of Cab Calloway lookalikes to wear the biggest, brightest zoot suits and kipperest ties in the crowd, and paid fifty or so of the Friday-night regulars to travel north. They had not bothered to come to London to check out the latest trend, however.

Tony Wilson, who was presenting the show, was dismayed when their expensive coachload of specially bussed-in London scene-makers all traipsed into the studio looking like dishevelled extras from *The Wild Ones* rather than glamorous members of the Cotton Club. Zoots were out, boots were in. Things move on.

Back at Le Beat Route, which lasted for three long, hard years, there were a couple of events worth noting. One was when those young Bushey boys first seen dancing at Le Kilt brought in a test pressing of their first-ever record. George Michael and Andrew Ridgeley could always be seen among the first in the queue on a Friday night in their leather jackets and frayed jeans, desperate to get past Ollie's fierce gaze.

They loved the club, leaping about enthusiastically to Steve Lewis's selections and incorporating his taste into their early tunes as they tried to harden up their suburban soul-boy sound. When they weren't formation dancing, they were always trying to get tips from the music-biz types like Steve Dagger and Jon Baker, and seeking Simon Withers' professional advice on styling their band.

One Friday in 1982, George and Andrew came into the club proudly clutching a white-label 12-inch single of their own. They were anxious to know how their debut disc would go down with the denizens of Soho's hippest redoubt. Steve Lewis agreed to play their tune and we all watched as they did an especially enthusiastic formation dance to 'Wham Rap'.

The lyrics of that song were almost a manifesto for the age, all soul on the dole, positivity in spite of hard times, a very English rap about having fun and not having a job. They even feature a copy of *The Face* in the video, and clearly it struck a chord with the nation's youth as it reached number eight in the charts. But it never got played in Le Beat Route again. Nobody there that night would have predicted that the pair would become the next massive pop sensation – and one of those gauche lads would go on to be among the most important performers of his age. Oh, and that their backing singer and dancer Shirley would become Martin Kemp's wife.

The woman who would become the highest-selling British female artist of her age also performed for the crowd at Le Beat Route on a Friday night. Sade was now one of a trio of singers in a sprawling north London soul and funk band known as Pride. Their manager, Lee Barrett, he of the 'Hard Times' bum and Blitz credentials, had an idea that they should play on a flat-bed truck outside the club at 3 a.m. to gain the attention of the in-crowd as they filed out.

They practised on the truck with a generator, parked up in the quieter streets north of Oxford Street, then drove into Soho and managed somehow to get a parking space right outside Le Beat Route. As the clock struck three, they began their set and, indeed, a stream of punters filed out of the club to be confronted with a nine-piece band playing songs that included 'Smooth Operator'. The only problem was that anybody coming out of Le Beat Route at the end of a long Friday night was likely to be so wasted that they could barely see or stand, let alone remember what they had witnessed. Sade hated that night performing in the street, but she needn't have worried. Pretty soon she was going to be performing at Live Aid and making a very good living indeed.

15

MAD
ABOUT
THE
BOY

There were those acts and artists who emerged directly from the Blitz while it was still going and who used the club as a springboard to success, but there were many more who bided their time before taking their chance, most prominent among them the person who has perhaps come to best symbolise the club and the age.

From the moment I first saw him on the arm of Philip Sallon walking down the stairs into Billy's on that inaugural night nearly half a century ago, I knew George O'Dowd was a remarkable man. I thought he was a star and so did he. He was barely seventeen, but already an imposing figure. He was big, bold and, in a way, beautiful, giving off an incredible aura of look-at-me arrogance, backed up with an almost tangible toughness, a don't-mess-with-me stare that could cut you across a crowded room, but also perhaps a certain wounded vulnerability. Of all the amazing characters who made it into that tiny basement, he was the one who stood out most, the boy most likely to.

As we all got to know each other at the Blitz, and in and out of Warren Street, so George became one of the dominant personalities among the group. Razor-sharp, argumentative, funny, bitchy, clever, brave, brazen and volatile. He was a proper street urchin, charming and challenging in equal parts, an absolute linchpin of the scene.

With Philip Sallon, his older mentor who had been a fixture on the queer scene since the Dark Ages, and his teen partner in catty repartee Peter Robinson, who soon morphed into Marilyn, he formed part of a triumvirate of performative vitriol, usually positioned by the cloakroom at the back. Marilyn was the pantomime villain, theatrically rude to just about everybody, unfiltered, often seemingly unhinged, but funny and very much a template for the current vogue for entertainingly sharp-tongued drag queens. That was their shtick.

George was always a complex character, capable of falling out with everybody, especially Steve Strange. The two of them fought like cats and dogs, often in full earshot of the whole club. But he was thoroughly charismatic; you always knew when George was in the room. He had a very strident voice and wasn't scared to use it. But he also had a soft side, a vulnerability which could make people fall in love with him, and an intellect which was bound to impress. He was quietly capable of genuine kindness as well as flamboyant nastiness. For some of the Blitz crowd, despite regularly feeling the full force of his tongue, George could do no wrong. He was our totem.

George and I never got close. Truth be told, I was both a bit in awe of him and a little wary of him – not physically, although it was obvious he could hold his own. A working-class south London Irish lad who looked and dressed like that had to be twice as tough as all hell, and he was. It was more the force of his vast, volcanic personality. I'm not at all sure George was very impressed by me, a cocksure little cockney know-it-all. I was not his cup of tea, and we all know George likes a nice cup of tea. We were never friends, though never enemies. Larger than life and twice as loud, the only mystery about George O'Dowd is why it took him so long to become a star.

Apart from the occasional thirty-second snippet as he wandered round Warren Street hunting for hairspray, I never really heard George sing until I saw him on *Top of the Pops* doing 'Do You Really Want to Hurt Me?'. I had no idea he had those pipes. But apparently those who were closer to him always knew he had a beautiful, soft and lilting voice, practised at singing the sentimental and stirring Irish rebel songs he'd grown up hearing at home. This makes it even more surprising that it was a full two years after Spandau Ballet and Visage made it into the charts, when every record company in the land was looking for the next New Romantic thing, that he finally cracked it with Culture Club.

After the Blitz closed, George went quiet for a while, working in various shops around Carnaby Street, doing a spot of DJing for Philip Sallon, getting closer to Malcolm McLaren, seemingly searching for an angle. I would see him out and about and would wonder when he was going to make his move.

He'd already acquired the whole red-gold-and-green, locks-and-smocks look designed by Sue Clowes that he would parade for the first time on *Top of the Pops*, but hadn't yet adopted the moniker Boy George, which no one who knew him ever called him. We were perfectly aware of his gender, not exactly shocked or confused by a man in make-up. He was just George.

He hooked up with Bow Wow Wow, fleetingly calling himself Lieutenant Lush, but they had a falling out before their collaboration had even begun. Then I remember hearing that he had formed a band called Sex Gang Children, which reeked of McLaren's influence, as Malcolm was obsessed at that point with the shock value of underage sex.

Then it was the much more middle-of-the-road Culture Club and Boy George, a family-friendly move towards the mainstream. But their first couple of singles passed me, and just about everybody else, by. In this pre-digital age, you couldn't just listen to things at the click of a button, so I still hadn't heard them when I sat down with Sade on a Thursday evening in our squat and watched him on the telly. I was just about as amazed as the rest of the nation, though for different reasons.

Spandau had caused a big fuss when 'To Cut a Long Story Short' was unleashed. 'Fade to Grey' is still vividly remembered by people who first saw Steve Strange on a Thursday evening. Ultravox with 'Vienna' and its video was a major hit. But Culture Club and their pretty/handsome, big, tough, effeminate lead singer – with ribbons in his hair, rouge on his cheeks, scarlet on his lips and honey in his voice – made arguably the biggest impression in a single performance since the Star Man with his arms round Mick Ronson back in 1972. You could almost hear the neighbours shouting at the television.

The furore surrounding George and his mellifluously gentle performance of a terrific, lilting cod-reggae love song was extraordinary. People were shocked because that sort of androgyny was still considered shocking. I was shocked because I had no idea he could sound so lovely and appear so sweet. I'd always assumed that George O'Dowd, one of the most confrontational men I'd ever met, would go full-on, in-your-face, tough-nut gender-bender glam, but instead he skipped about whimsically in front of his straight-looking band and crooned lightly in an impeccably rich and smooth tenor, thereby causing the entire country to talk about him next day. It was a masterstroke.

The whole 'is it a boy or is it a girl?' debate raged in the media while the single flew to number one here and number two in the US charts. That fantastic voice aside, I could not understand what the fuss was all about, which just proved that those of us who had been schooled at the Blitz lived in a very different world to most everybody else – and how far the masses still had to travel. The media were suitably outraged by his make-up and his manner, but most people decided they adored this apparently gentle soul who your grandma liked too.

The hullabaloo did George no harm whatsoever and, in retrospect, was an important staging post on the journey to acceptance for gender diversity. It was precisely George's contradictions – his down-to-earth south London ordinariness mixed with his flamboyance – which threw people and made them question their preconceptions.

The whole New Romantic phenomenon, with George eventually at the forefront, was a massive nudge in the direction of equality. Elton John, for example, was still a decade away from publicly coming out. But then, when George was asked about his sex life by chat-show host Russell Harty, he came out with the now-infamous line about preferring a nice cup of tea. Yet again, full of contradictions, but also perhaps feeling understandably defensive in the face of such prurient prying on national TV.

I never really saw George much after he was catapulted to fame, as he leapt immediately into a different sphere. But a few years later, we met again one day on Clapham Common when he was due to appear at a massive Artists Against Apartheid event; Sade and Gary Kemp were also on the bill. We were all backstage when we saw this stick-thin, haggard-looking soul with what appeared to be flour plastered all over his face, behaving completely irrationally as he was about to stumble on stage. So the rumours about his heroin habit were true.

I felt really sad for George that day and genuinely feared for his life; a very big man had fallen. Once again, he became both the centre of the nation's debate and the front page of every paper, hounded and derided when he needed help. Heroin, which had flooded into the UK from Iran and Afghanistan in the early 80s, became an epidemic as the decade wore on and that insidious drug inveigled its way into so many veins.

Smack, as it was popularly called, had first made its presence felt in our world at Le Beat Route, when some of those people sliding down the walls were not just drinking snakebite. I saw good friends, vivacious, outgoing souls, tumbling down that rabbit hole, nodding off, throwing up and dropping out; brilliant lives closing down as they sought the succour of oblivion.

In retrospect, the fact that George, Steve Strange and Marilyn all succumbed to heroin addiction perhaps indicates just how hard it was to be them back then, to live those lives in the full public gaze. They achieved great fame, but at a great cost, and George certainly sailed about as close to the wind as you can get without being blown away. But he survived and since then, of course, all the many sides of his character have emerged – the good and the bad – but he has made it through. We still collide occasionally at some event or other, and I still think often of that fabulous creature I met all those years ago.

I also muse upon the fact that George has somehow become the face of the Blitz, and, in many respects, the face of the 1980s. Whenever New Romantics and the Blitz are remembered or portrayed now, the overriding image presented is usually of a club full of identikit Boy George and Marilyn wannabes, or cartoon glam-goth Tik and Tok lookalikes. The Blitz is shown as a place chock-full of extravagantly OTT gender-bending caricatures in theatrical slap, though it was never predominantly like that.

A few years later, Leigh Bowery's club, Taboo, which inspired the stage musical very loosely based around George's life, was much more genuinely in that vein. The Leicester Square club took one extreme strand of Blitz style and magnified it. Bowery was a big figure in every sense, a larger-than-life personality who was totally inspired by the Blitz, and his dramatic take on self-expression was unique. Taboo was extraordinary, but very different to the Blitz, where the main strength was its stylistic diversity.

Marilyn, of course, had his own fifteen minutes in the limelight, his striking looks and his androgyny enough to secure a record contract. Just being Marilyn was the real selling point at the time. He had one big hit and a series of little mishaps before his own steep decline into addiction. Where George had the undeniable talent to go with his persona, Marilyn was proof positive that looks and opportunity alone can take you only so far.

Bananarama, meanwhile, were going all the way. It is important to note that two of the most commercially successful acts to have emerged from the Blitz and its offshoots were female-fronted. Too often the women have been excluded or marginalised in the story of the Blitz, but the powerful female energy of the place was phenomenal and, despite the sexism of the time, many of the women went on to have great success in their chosen fields – none more so than spiky-haired Siobhan Fahey and her partners in pop, with a world-record number of chart entries by an all-female group.

Siobhan was a proper pre-Blitz, Billy's original: a big-barneted, gothic-inclined ex-punk who studied fashion and lived in a squat in Denmark Street above the Sex Pistols' rehearsal rooms. She was a creature of the Soho night, always out and about, a prominent face who took the three-chord punk message of 'you can do it' and married it with the go-ahead, go-for-it pop positivity engendered at the Blitz to create an unashamedly commercial combination of sight and sound: ra-ra skirts and catchy tunes.

With Sara Dallin and Keren Woodward, the other members of the trio, she produced a seemingly endless string of terrific pop singles and a unique style, which was every bit as emblematic of the 80s as Spandau or Culture Club. Bananarama effortlessly straddled the arty and the mainstream, maintaining their position as a hip, alternative act while selling bucketloads of records. And when she decided to leave the band a few years later, Siobhan was replaced by Jacquie O'Sullivan, herself a Blitz alumna who had grown up a few streets away from me on the Watling Estate.

Mark Moore is a talented DJ and producer who got his big break from Philip Sallon at the Mud Club, but started his nocturnal career as a punter at Great Queen Street. He was part of the younger second wave of Blitz kids who came in on our coat-tails, along with John Galliano and Peter Doig, so I never really knew them, but he had a massive number one hit with his band S'Express, which marked the start of the UK house scene, and he remains an important figure in UK music.

Ian Shaw, perhaps our finest living, gigging jazz singer and pianist, is another of the second-generation urchins, puffing up his chest and his hair, who sneaked in, soaked it up and then went on to become a full-time performer. He was yet another Welsh teenager, a gay exile in the Big Smoke, who got his first taste of London nightlife and lowlife at the Blitz, going with his friend Scarlett Cannon when still far too young, before transferring his allegiance soon after to Ronnie Scott's. He's been a Soho institution ever since.

Haysi Fantayzee were a one- or two-hit wonder who emerged fully formed from the Blitz stable, hit the charts running and claimed their allotted slice of fame when it was being dished out to almost anybody who had ever waltzed through the doors of No. 4, Great Queen Street before heading off in different creative directions. Jeremy Healy was an old – or, rather, incredibly young – school friend of George O'Dowd, a kid who was there that first night of Billy's and there for just about every event in this book. Jeremy was a Warren Street veteran and the lover of Kim Bowen, and he is now an internationally famous DJ and musical director for huge fashion houses.

For a couple of years, though, Jeremy was part of this madcap pop-art combo with photographer Kate Garner. They wore dreadlocks and tribal robes before George did and danced in a quirky fashion to a song called 'John Wayne Is Big Leggy'. It was completely preposterous, tongue firmly in cheek, cheque quickly in bank. Haysi Fantayzee were great fun, silly fashionable fluff, all executed with a massive grin, destined to be short-lived but proof positive that this pop lark is not all that difficult, at least in the short run.

With video becoming an increasingly important medium, looking good was half the battle, and all the pop stars – no matter how fleeting – who emerged from the Blitz had mastered the look a long time before they ever sang a song. MTV had launched in 1981, totally shifting the dynamic towards the visual, and Blitz kids could definitely do visual.

Two other groups who emerged directly from the Blitz took the look and the music in a very different direction. Blue Rondo à la Turk and Animal Nightlife were both deeply embedded in nightclub culture and chock-full of Blitz kids. They were perhaps the acts most genuinely representative of the club's denizens, and they were both great live bands who never really managed to trouble the charts.

As mentioned, Blue Rondo were originally put together by Chris Sullivan, who recruited Christos Tolera and the O'Donnell brothers with the vague idea of starting a band which mixed Latin, jazz, soul and funk, but with a rough punky edge; kind of Kid Creole on a council estate. Mark Reilly and Moses Mount Bassie, a pair of brilliant dancers from the northern soul scene, joined in on guitar and sax, Graham Ball, working with Steve Dagger, was recruited as manager and Graham Smith took some photos before a single note was played. They looked fantastic – southside LA in 1955 meets gritty north London – and, at my behest, *The Face* printed the pictures and a piece about the cool new kids on the block waiting to take the world by storm. Half the job done.

But it soon became clear that some proper musicians were needed, so Jimmy and Ollie moved on and a handful of competent and suitably hedonistic South American and African players joined, giving the band a solid basis on which to build a set. Chris, always a polymath, wrote songs, took lead vocals, danced, designed the visuals, painted the artwork and set the sartorial tone. Christos did almost nothing whatsoever, but looked absolutely mesmerising and captured the anarchic, DIY spirit of the band perfectly. The others created a driving, percussive sound, heavy on cowbells and congas with choppy, propulsive polyrhythms over which there was lots of chanting while the trio of dancers flew in all directions and Christos twirled his moustache.

I can honestly say that Blue Rondo à la Turk live were among the most exciting and explosive bands I have witnessed in half a century of going to gigs. Ramshackle, raw but contagiously funky, with a shamelessly showbiz bent, they were the polar opposite of the whole posey, self-serious electro sound: uninhibited and rumbustious, sweaty and joyous. They were gargantuan fun.

They perfectly captured the cinematically hedonistic side of the Blitz crowd, all those down-and-dirty wild boys and girls in great vintage gear. Chris's band was the embodiment of those hardened veterans of the soul and punk scenes, who graduated from Crackers and the Roxy, went to the Blitz but also to Bournemouth every year for wild nights of dressing up, dancing and debauchery.

And, indeed, it was down in Dorset where they convinced Richard Branson to give them a large sum of money to sign to his record label. The band played under aliases in a couple of very low-key local shows in pubs and community centres in and around London to get their chops worked out, before an official unveiling in our favourite seaside watering spot on the May bank holiday in 1981.

Partly down to me championing them in *The Face*, the buzz about the band, who almost nobody had seen or heard, was already intense, to such a degree that the Virgin main man himself trekked down to Bournemouth to check them out. It was one of the most stupendously rollicking nights of this entire tale, a complete sell-out with crowds storming the venue and an atmosphere so charged it could have fed the National Grid.

Chris, with all his connections and his clubs, had already built a solid fanbase based on rumour alone. The Soho crowd turned out en masse and it must have looked like Blue Rondo were the hottest new band in the world with a fanatical following decked out in all the gear. Zoot suits a go-go. Truth be told, just about everybody who had ever heard of them or was likely to buy their records was down there in Bournemouth.

Of course, they were late on stage and the atmosphere became tense, but when they finally strolled on looking immaculate and unleashed a barrage of whirling dervish kinetic energy, fuelled by huge reserves of premium-grade chutzpah, the place went bonkers. Branson saw this and immediately brought out his cheque book. As someone said at the time, 'You could see his jacket growing longer as the night wore on.' Blue Rondo à la Turk, just a handful of shows in, were now the major new signing on Virgin Records and supposedly the next band to dominate the charts.

They did have a massive hit in Brazil with 'Me and Mr Sanchez', which was number one for three months and was the theme tune for the 1982 World Cup, but truth be told they never really managed to translate their live brilliance onto record. Their appeal was simultaneously visceral – you had to be there – and oddly intellectual. They were essentially a concept band formed from Chris's trained art-school eye and encyclopaedic knowledge of pop culture; films, music and fashion. Today, they might qualify for the Turner Prize, but people out buying pop records don't always buy into clever concepts linking be-bop and B-movies, low riders and high steppers. They want a tune.

Ultimately, Blue Rondo were a Blitz band too far – all the hype and none of the hits. But their legacy was substantial. Anyone who was present for their performance on the eve of Charles and Diana's wedding, just round the corner from St Paul's Cathedral in a disused print warehouse in the rundown backstreets of Clerkenwell, will surely recall it still.

Every renegade anti-royalist and overdressed anarchist was there, determined to party while others fawned and genuflected. The place was heaving. Blue Rondo were on fine form and the room, up in the eaves of this old industrial building, was rocking to a salsa beat, when something happened out there in the steaming crowd which provoked the biggest mass punch-up I have ever witnessed. To this day, I have no idea who or what started it, but suddenly two large groups, one from west London, the other from the east, were at it like something from a cheap western movie, bottles smashing, chairs flying through the air. Besuited bodies launched in all directions while, up on stage, the band played 'Klactoveesedstein', providing the perfect soundtrack for this epic brawl.

The fight spilled out onto the wrought-iron stairwells and then onto the rooftops of Clerkenwell, while down below vast crowds were gathering with their Union Jacks to wave for the nuptials taking place in just a few hours' time. Some of the mob from the East End who were part of that massive bar-room brawl were a band of left-wing herberts, originally known as the Mile End Philharmonic, who later became Animal Nightlife.

We'll come on to Andy Polaris and his band in a bit, but before we do, I mentioned that Blue Rondo had an important legacy beyond some great gigs and a couple of albums. Mark Reilly, who was the guitarist and dancer in the band, left the madness of Blue Rondo to form his own slightly less frenetic group called Matt Bianco, who had a string of international hits and still play live now; a properly successful band to this day.

When Blue Rondo eventually split, Chris Sullivan took all the ideas and energy he had bundled into the group and turned them into the defining nightclub of the second half of the 1980s, along with his partner in crime, Ollie O'Donnell. The Wag Club in

Wardour Street, Soho, in the shell of the old Whisky A' Go Go, was Sullivan's hip manifesto made manifest. It was cool yet wild, nicely sleazy but hugely popular, hard to get into and harder still to leave, retro yet so achingly now as to predict the future. It was a great club, which we'll hear more about later.

From the first US hip hop acts in London to Shane McGowan and the Pogues, Gil Scott-Heron to Sade, the Wag Club championed the best live music of every kind, but it also became the home of rap, rare groove, acid jazz and acid house – just about every nocturnal trend from 1984 onwards started under Chris's tutelage. And, speaking of Sade, it was directly because of Blue Rondo à la Turk that Sade became a singer, but we'll come to that story in a bit. First up, Animal Nightlife.

If I did a list of the most quintessential Blitz kids of them all, Andy Polaris would be right up there. Stephen Linard, Melissa Caplan, George O'Dowd, Kim Bowen, Princess Julia, Chris Sullivan . . . None of them were more at home in the Blitz than this gentle, beautiful, mixed-race waif from a children's home who wafted into the place and onto the dancefloor every Tuesday night. Gay, feline and feminine, but with that innate steeliness which comes from growing up in truly tough conditions, he was a squatter because he had no home to go to, yet he always presented himself with maximum panache.

So when that bunch of lefty, second-generation Irish soul-boy roustabouts from Hackney and Islington – Michael McDermott, Billy Chapman, Steve Brown, Declan Barclay and Steve Shanley, all of them former Blitz regulars – started putting a band together, they picked Andy Polaris as their frontman. Animal Nightlife, as they became, were an unlikely combination of staunchly socialist views and slick soul moves, Dr Buzzard's Original Savannah Band meets *Doctor Zhivago*, and they chose Steve Lewis, the Lenin-loving DJ from Le Beat Route, as their manager.

Supporting Blue Rondo at gigs, they developed a smoother sound, with Andy's softly swaying vocals as the focus, later augmented by two female singers, Leah Seresin and Chrysta Jones. They were a kind of jazz/soul big band. They had a few hits, developed a big gay following both here and in Europe, and in many ways pre-dated the whole acid jazz style of Jamiroquai, Loose Ends et al. Animal Nightlife, now largely overlooked, were in many ways the most quintessentially Blitz band of them all.

★　★　★

There is one final musical artist who emerged from the Blitz world, who we need to look at in more detail because she was arguably the most successful of the lot. She has sold more than 75 million records worldwide and was, until very recently, the biggest-selling UK female artist of all time. Sade was effectively the last of the line and the top of the tree.

Sade is both the name of that girl I first got to know in New York on the night of the Spandau Ballet gig and Axiom fashion show in 1981, and the name of the band that have been with her for more than forty years. Born in Ibadan in Nigeria to a local academic and an English nurse, Helen Folasade Adu is her passport name, but her Yoruba family were never going to call her Helen and so she became Sade, which stuck when she moved to Clacton as a kid with her mum, when her parents split up.

She excelled at art, loved soul music and clothes, and, at eighteen, became a fashion student at St Martin's, in the same year as Sullivan, Linard and the rest. But she was one of the quiet ones.

Truth be told, prior to the New York trip she was far from a Blitz devotee, although she had been a few times with her college mates, especially the lovely Greg Davis. In many ways, she was not a Blitz type, in that she hated showing off, wasn't a natural party person, didn't much like electro music and didn't really see herself as part of a gang. But when Jon Baker dragged her into the fray by including her and her design partner Sarah Lubel in the New York extravaganza, she was pulled into this vortex and began to make her mates and make her mark.

On that New York sojourn, Sade and I became a couple, while Sade and Melissa Caplan and Rhonda Paster became firm friends, three incredibly strong-willed women who are still best buddies to this day. Sade keeps her friends close. She also kept her options open. Sade is good at pretty much most things: her fashion designs were accomplished, she was an excellent photographer, she could paint, she could model, she could write, but she couldn't quite make up her mind where to focus her talent. I think she knew somehow, from that night in New York onwards, that by becoming part of this scene, she would find her way, and so she did.

Amid all the craziness and the partying, the Le Beat Route nights and Dirtbox days, she knew this madcap collection of friends that she had fallen in with – Christos, Ollie, Sullivan, Graham Smith; designers and musicians, photographers, writers and chancers – might just proffer a way forward, might just be her future.

We were ensconced in our squat in the fire station which she made effortlessly chic with a collection of skip finds and charity shop discoveries. I was building something that looked almost like a career as a writer and presenter, and she was casting around, trying to pick her path, earning a little money as a mannequin for rag-trade brands, until one day when we were en route to see Blue Rondo à la Turk play in Barry Island. That's when it began.

Lee Barrett, the bottom in the jeans on the Hard Times cover, the north London mate of Ollie O'Donnell's who had been part of the Blitz crowd from the very beginning, was driving a transit van full of Blue Rondo fans west and insisted that Sade and I sit up front with him. He was plotting something. Now, by this stage, Lee had seen Steve Dagger and Graham Ball and Perry Haines become successful managers and thought he would have a go. So he put together a band of aspiring young musicians from his manor called Arriva. They were based around the songwriting talents of his mate Ray St John and played a kind of Latinate funk sound, a bit like a poppier Blue Rondo, and they were still very much in the early rehearsal stage.

On that journey to Wales, we got about as far west as Reading when Lee turned to Sade and asked, 'Can you sing?' Without missing a beat, she said yes. Lee asked if she wanted to join his band as a backing singer and, again, she answered in the affirmative. I just sat there thinking, 'What do you mean you can sing?' There had been no prior evidence of this. When we stopped at a service station, I asked Sade why she'd said yes. She more or less responded, 'Well, it can't be hard, can it?'

The assumption that she could just get up on stage and sing, that 'it can't be hard, can it?', was born directly of the Blitz spirit she had bought into. We had seen so many people around us go for it and make it, learning on the job, that we were all imbued with a rampant positivity which told us everything was possible. I'm sure that whether or not Sade could really sing was not Lee's biggest criterion – he obviously wanted this very beautiful girl to look good up on stage, and also wanted to give his band a direct link to the in-crowd, assuming perhaps that it would be a short cut to success, with me already having a name and access to the media, to have my girlfriend on board.

But it didn't happen that way. The band, who morphed from Arriva into Pride, never made it, despite a couple of years of trying. Musicians came and went. When Lee recruited Stuart Matthewman and Paul Denman from Hull, the sound switched to a more soulful, jazzy style – precisely the music that the Essex soul girl Sade had grown up listening to – and, almost imperceptibly, the emphasis switched to the beauty with the cherry-red lips, the high pony-tail and the hoop earrings, a look that was in place right from the start.

The band had one song called 'Smooth Operator', which Sade would step forward to sing solo, and it was obvious to anybody with ears that here was the star. She had worked incredibly hard at finding her voice: a subtly sensual contralto with an understated delivery, stripped of all vibrato or vocal gymnastics yet full of direct emotion and empathy, just like her.

And as time went on, so Pride became Sade, still very much a band, but slimmed down and with the focus now very much on her. They needed some new songs, so she wrote them – it can't be that hard, can it? It turned out that not only could she sing in a truly distinctive style, but also write fine songs to suit her voice.

Despite having had no musical training and not being able to play any instruments, she could sit in our kitchen, with the bath in the corner, and come up with the lyrics and melodies of songs like 'Your Love Is King', 'Hang on to Your Love' and 'When Am I Going to Make a Living'. And yet still she didn't – make a living that is. Despite regularly playing live at the Wag and Ronnie

Scott's, there were no takers from the record companies, who were still looking for yesterday's thing, all New Romantic synthesisers and big beats. Sade doesn't do big.

It so happened that I was in the office of *The Face*, showing some photos of Sade to Nick Logan. There was one black-and-white shot by Graham Smith, of her in a backless black dress designed by Fiona Dealey, that he loved. An advert which was supposed to go on the back page of the next issue had just fallen through and so Nick decided there and then to put Sade on the back cover. Suddenly, the cloth-eared record companies were very interested indeed.

Sade, the band, eventually signed to CBS, and the resulting album, *Diamond Life*, went on to become the biggest-selling debut album ever by a UK female artist, going top five on both sides of the Atlantic and winning the Brit award for best album of the year, handed out by Pete Townshend to this smiling but still effortlessly cool young woman. That was quite a night.

My favourite story of that period came on the day Sade first appeared on *Top of the Pops* singing 'Your Love Is King'. The record company had sent a long black limousine to pick her up from our squat in Tottenham and it waited outside while she got ready. It was winter and the toilet out on the balcony had frozen over again, so Sade had to pee in a bucket before getting in the limo. We literally did not have a pot to piss in. It was a perfect Blitz spirit moment.

By the time she came home that night, she was very wealthy and our lives were about to change dramatically. But Sade never really changed. She is still kind and warm and private, still the essence of understated style and grace. Perhaps the most galling thing about being by her side then was the ridiculous accusation from some of the British press, a slur which still persists, that Sade was some sort of arch Yuppie, a card-carrying, coffee-table Thatcherite, because she possessed a natural sophistication and poise and because she did not shout about her politics. Listen to the lyrics to learn about her life and views.

Diamond Life did become the smooth soundtrack for the mid-80s because it was ubiquitous. It did play in just about every wine bar in the world, but it also played in just about every African American home and still does. Every record she has released has been huge in the US, where she is lionised. She touched people, especially people of colour like her. Yet, to white middle-class music critics in the UK, she was somehow to blame for the bland excesses of the age.

Here was a strong, fiercely independent, mixed-race, working-class Essex girl, the daughter of a single-parent NHS nurse, who, from the first royalty cheque she received, gave a hefty contribution to the striking miners. In a hugely successful international career lasting forty years, Sade has never once betrayed her principles or forgotten her roots or her friends. She is loyal, generous and fun.

And without those friends from the Blitz and the extraordinary movement and momentum of the time, it might never have happened. Sade would have been a success whatever she did, but if she had not got on the flight to New York with all the Blitz kids, or if we had not got in the front of the van on the way to a Blue Rondo gig, and if she had not thought 'It can't be that hard to sing,' who knows?

The onset of her huge success did also mean the end of something. As soon as the cheques started arriving, we left the squat behind us, as she bought a beautiful apartment with smoked-glass windows and an indoor toilet. I was twenty-five now, successful in my own right, surrounded by my famous mates all reaching new heights. Leaving the fire station felt like the end of an era, an era which had started on a Tuesday night in 1978.

16
THE
ROARING
80S

illy's, Blitz, Hell, St Moritz, Le Kilt, Club for Heroes, Le Beat Route, the Mud Club, the Dirtbox, Camden Palace, the Wag.

Spandau Ballet, Ultravox, Visage, Bananarama, Blue Rondo, Haysi Fantayzee, Culture Club, Marilyn, Animal Nightlife, Jo Boxers, Swing Out Sister, Sigue Sigue Sputnik, Wham!, Sade.

Those two parallel lists tell the story of the clubs started by Blitz alumni and the music acts which emerged from them, a distinct and interconnected lineage in London in the early 1980s, all of which leads back to Strange and Egan. There was a hard core of clubbers, the extraordinary characters who have peopled this book, who went all the way with that journey, and a generation of musicians who fed off the communal creativity. They were a gang of garrulous and ambitious nocturnalites who carried the spirit of the Blitz with them. Long after the club closed, I was still a Blitz kid. Perhaps, forty-five years later, I still am one.

But as the scene spread, there was also a broadening of the gene pool, a widening-out of both the sounds and the styles; bigger venues, larger crowds, not so much club culture edging towards the mainstream as the mainstream adopting club culture en masse. Everywhere you looked there was street fashion and vibrant new pop music emerging. It was on the radio and TV, in magazines and newspapers. Duran Duran from Brum, ABC from Sheffield, Frankie Goes To Hollywood from Liverpool . . . Hot Gossip dancing on TV looked like a tableau from the Warren Street squat; shoulder pads and high hair had gone from PX in Covent Garden to Joan Collins in Hollywood; Katharine Hamnett and John Galliano had gone from art school to international stardom.

England was swinging again like the proverbial pendulum, and foreign film crews were crawling all over us to get the story. Tourists from Paris, Milan and Barcelona were heading to London, going to the clubs to see and be 'scene'. In the 70s, we'd been defined as 'the sick man of Europe', but now, once again, London was the epicentre of cool.

More and more people were becoming more like us Blitz kids, but we were changing too, buying into the consumerism, enjoying the success, spending the money. And there was indeed money being made. Steve and Rusty took their earnings and their profile to another level by taking over a big old former Edwardian music hall by Mornington Crescent which had been the scruffy Music Machine in the punk days, where we'd all seen the Clash and the Banshees.

They now had investors who spent plenty of money on the place and called it the Camden Palace. They installed a sprung dancefloor, a massive sound system and banks of giant video screens where thousands of people could watch themselves dancing to Rusty's music. And they certainly did, every night of the week. Long queues of kids from all over the country tried very hard to get in in their recently acquired New Romantic gear, desperate to parade among the pop stars and famous faces who would be ushered in the side door and up to the VIP room at the top.

Madonna made her UK live debut there, Grace Jones played, Kylie Minogue later became a regular. It was the closest we ever came to a Studio 54-style venue: champagne corks popping, pop stars misbehaving, film crews and photographers everywhere, people posing for paparazzi on the balustrades and balconies. It was glitzy and glam – and all a very long way from a Second World War-themed wine bar.

In many ways, there are two very different 1980s. The early part of the 80s was still essentially a hangover from the 70s – dark, DIY, punky, anarchic, wild – whereas by the middle of the decade, after five years of Thatcher, it starts to get a lot sharper, brighter and slicker; more sophisticated, less confrontational, more commercial, designer duds and super-clubs. We were all growing up and so was this shiny new England. But we were losing things too: social housing was being sold off; squats were disappearing as property was now so much more valuable; free college education would soon be gone; and the whole post-war consensus, which created the conditions in which the Blitz kids could prosper, vanished as the market prevailed.

Yuppies and gentrification were two of the themes of the age, with young urban professionals moving into hitherto rundown parts of town and turning them round by doing up dilapidated properties and opening up delicatessens. 'Pioneers' they called these brave city types for daring to live in Fulham rather than Chelsea, for braving an elegant Georgian square in Islington which, a few years before, had housed working-class families like the Kemps. We, too, were young and decidedly urban, though never professional in the sense of having a job. Our profession was being us.

Residential gentrification was already a well-known phenomenon in London by the 70s and 80s. My own family was originally from Notting Hill, which witnessed jet-powered gentrification as people like us were forced out of our supposed slums to be replaced by nice middle-class families with floppy-haired children. My aunt was told her house was unfit for human habitation and moved out; it is now worth many millions of pounds. But a different process was occurring in other areas of town, and I think of it as trendification.

Soho in the 70s had been a grubby little enclave of seedy sex shops and dodgy dives. Covent Garden was a ghost town with tumbleweed blowing where the market had once been. Clerkenwell was completely forgotten, its once-thriving Italian community scattered and its cobbled streets bereft. Hoxton and Shoreditch were unknown, off the map – there be dragons in the far east. But all of those areas were already in the process of being trendified by the Blitz kids and their allies, partying by night or opening businesses by day.

The Face moved its offices to then-deserted Exmouth Market in Clerkenwell, beginning the revival of the area. Warehouse parties and clubs were now a regular occurrence in Shoreditch, utilising its tumbledown old factories. Hip clothes shops like Flip, which fed the craze for vintage gear, joined Willie Brown in those neglected backstreets. The same applied to Butler's Wharf and the whole riverside stretch where mighty Tate Modern now stands, a forgotten part of town with an abandoned power station, which was dead by day, but at night was now home to numerous raves. Many an evening was spent wandering its eerily silent riverside streets looking and listening for the big bash de nuit. Pretty party people appearing where once they would never have gone does a lot to shift the perception of an area.

Kensington, which had been a bland land of posh old women and bored Middle Eastern potentates, suddenly became a place of pilgrimage for all the wannabe New Romantics. Directly opposite Kensington Market, a swanky emporium appeared called Hyper Hyper, a kind of New Romantic department store selling clothes by Stevie Stewart and David Holah's BodyMap, Pam Hogg, Dexter Wong and Stephen Linard. It suddenly felt a little like Chelsea in the

60s as tourists flocked to see the trendsetters in their gear and Top Shop was again full of knock-off versions of this radical new look.

But it was Soho which really felt the full force of trendification, changing from a vaguely menacing red-light district to the epicentre of cool. Jon Baker moved Axiom to Carnaby Street, selling everybody from Fiona Dealey to Melissa Caplan. Almost directly next door was Sue Clowes, who launched a shop called The Foundry, flogging her liturgical twin sets, with Boy George as her moving mannequin behind the counter. Stephen Jones shifted his glamorous millinery atelier to Lexington Street. Everything in that W1 warren of twisted streets was absolutely fabulous.

The hardcore clubbing crew behind Demob in Beak Street made it the home of newly cool sportswear attracting all the b-boys and girls. Mark Powell, who went right back to the dancefloor at Crackers, started his eponymous shop in Archer Street selling vintage menswear and tailoring. Simon Withers joined Vivienne Westwood's team as they opened their psychedelic new emporium, Nostalgia of Mud. There were boutiques aplenty. But it wasn't just fashion.

Almost every street and alley in the un-square mile now had a nightclub of note including Skin Two, a truly eye-opening, jaw-dropping fetish hangout started by the Billy's old boy David Claridge, the man behind Roland Rat, now clad head to toe in rubber. Gaz's Rockin Blues, still going to this day, took over the Wardour Street basement where our St Moritz club had been and made it a shrine to 40s jump and jive, but it was the Wag Club further down Wardour that really secured Soho's position as the home of hip.

In October 1982, Chris Sullivan and Ollie O'Donnell had combined forces to take on a seven-nights-a-week share on a three-storey nightclub above a Chinese restaurant. In the 60s, this had been the Whisky A' Go Go, one of the arch modernist hangouts of that era, and the modern world was about to be unleashed here again.

The Wag became the HQ for a whole series of scenes throughout the decade: Stephen Linard hosted the campest night in town, called Total Fashion Victims; Davina McCall helped out on the door; Tracey Emin stood in line; Bowie became a regular and Robert De Niro made it home when he was filming in town. Just about every star in the firmament could be seen there, but they were not the stars of the show.

The Wag was supremely cool. Open late, great and brutally egalitarian, it never had a VIP room, red ropes or special treatment, just Chris or Ollie and their brilliant bouncer Winston on the door. The spirit of the Blitz had passed on. Camden Palace and the Wag were the yin and yang of the scene.

Because of all those shops, and because the Wag Club ran seven nights a week, there was a perpetual stream of good-looking young people in the neighbourhood. The change was palpable; where once it had just been pervy men in dirty macs, it was now bright young things in Demob. The whole vibe in Soho began to shift.

A scuzzy old pub called the Helvetia on Old Compton Street closed down and re-opened as the Soho Brasserie, a swish Parisian-style café and just about the first fashionable restaurant of the age. Almost immediately, the Brazz, as it became known, with its long zinc bar, its waiters in white aprons and its chunky tumblers for imported bottled beer, became *the* place for all those budding hipsters to meet. You'd see Nick Logan and Julie Burchill having lunch, Dylan Jones dining with Tony Parsons, Sally Brampton with Sam McKnight, while Steve Dagger and Gary Kemp plotted in the corner. Everybody who was anybody in media, music and fashion would be buzzing at the Brazz.

I was there most evenings feeling all sophisticated and continental in my expensive new John Paul Gaultier suit before heading to the Wag to get suitably smashed. The Brazz was joined in Soho by the born-again L'Escargot with its rag-rolled eau de nil walls and then Alastair Little's eponymous ground-breaking little nouvelle cuisine restaurant in Frith Street. Suddenly we had a restaurant scene, we were no longer a hundred years behind the continent, and Soho was no longer just a seedy tenderloin – though there were still red lights aplenty.

Just round the corner, both geographically and metaphorically, from the Soho Brasserie, another club was about to open which would go on to become completely synonymous with the excesses and successes of the 1980s. The Groucho first opened its doors in May 1985, a private members' club for a new age: bohemian and funky, arty and literary, hedonistic, elitist and, for a decade or more, the beating heart of this W1derland. And among the handful of founder members were Steve Dagger and Gary Kemp, myself, Ollie O'Donnell, Chris Sullivan, Graham Ball, Dylan Jones, Jon Baker, Rusty Egan . . . The back bar at the Groucho on a Friday night was a fancier version of the old mahogany bar at the Blitz on a Tuesday five years earlier.

So much had changed from the London I first experienced as a teenager in the 1970s, and so much of *that* was down to the impetus and the energy which had begun at Billy's and then came to fruition at the Blitz. We had started a ball rolling, and now it had a momentum all its own.

17

AFTER THE DANCE

The Blitz was much more than a nightclub but, in contemporary terms, it was also much less than one, too. The clubbing culture which took off in the late 80s owed a massive debt to the nocturnal pioneers of Billy's and the Blitz. Steve and Rusty started the first themed one-night club. Chris Sullivan and I put on the first warehouse party in an old industrial space. House music was a close cousin of the electronica Rusty Egan played, with Rusty also providing the template for all the celebrity nightclub DJs to follow.

There is even an Ibiza connection. On Spandau's first European tour in 1981, they chose to play the vast outdoor Ku Club on the island, the home of Balearic beat. They were the first band to do so and it was the first time that a link was made between the British and Ibizan club scenes. A large number of the London club crowd went out to see the band and loved the vibes, and word spread.

Spandau stayed at Pikes Hotel, which was made famous when Wham! then shot the video for 'Club Tropicana' there, further advertising Ibiza's delights to a young, fashionable crowd looking for the good life. Spandau's record plugger at the time was one Paul Oakenfold, who himself went to Ibiza and became one of the prime architects of acid house. All roads lead back.

So many of the elements of the 90s clubbing phenomenon stemmed from the shenanigans of a couple of hundred passionately partying Londoners reclaiming the night as their own. But then later, under the influence of ecstasy and economics, it flew off in a wildly different direction. Clubbing and clubs became massive, and the business of clubbing became big business indeed.

Huge outdoor raves and festivals in fields round the M25 (originally organised by Dave Mahoney) or enormous inner city mega-clubs like

Ministry of Sound and Cream, with sprung floors, hi-tech sound systems and famous superstar DJs (some of them Blitz alumni) paid vast sums to swoop in and entertain faceless crowds intent upon dancing to the point of delirium. Huge fees, helicopters and egos. The rave scene was the nightclubbing equivalent of stadium rock.

Big, bombastic, anonymous and joyous, it was nightlife as mass entertainment with added ecstasy, anthemic music blasted at full volume by the turntable equivalent of rock stars. The focus of the club was the DJ booth and the dancefloor. There wasn't a lot of conversation at raves. They were exactly the opposite of the Blitz, which was essentially a youth club for a tiny crowd of voluble people, who all knew each other, to socialise in.

The stars at the Blitz were the people at the Blitz, the entertainment each other, the focus on us and ultimately, you. It was small and cheap and intimate. It was intense and incestuous and incredibly creative. And the fact that it is still being discussed and dissected, still a subject of extraordinary interest nearly half a century later, is proof that the most important element of a great night is the people you share it with. The Blitz was a series of truly great nights out in very good company.

In the early days, the crowd at Billy's and the Blitz was a self-selecting group, a few misfits and miscreants, shameless show-offs gathering to see how far they could push against the rigid norms of the time. Then, when a door policy became necessary, the room was controlled and curated by Steve Strange, which meant that the intimacy and intensity remained, while the group of chosen ones grew a little larger and broader. You always had to make an effort, had to work at it, play your part. You could never just be a consumer of the delights of the night.

In retrospect, it was like we were eager young apprentices in the academy of a professional football club or perhaps a ballet school, where skills are honed and sharpened and talents encouraged and enhanced. Those places offer the prospect of exciting careers for those who make it, but they are rigorous; you have to keep with the programme. In the case of the Blitz school of further education, the core group never let up, never eased off. A remarkable number made it. The class of 1979.

The difference between the Blitz and a football academy is that we had no coaches or teachers, no grown-ups to guide the way; we were guiding and pushing and goading each other towards whatever goal we were aiming at. Self-motivated, driven, simultaneously competitive yet co-operative kids. Just kids. It was an education like no other.

So what was it about that place which led so many of its young denizens to prominence in so many different fields? Did we know at the time that something special was happening? Is there a chemical equation or an algorithm which can be replicated? Why was the Blitz so influential and its alumni so successful?

Like everything in life, timing was crucial; there is a tide in the affairs of men (and boys and girls) and all that. Change was undoubtedly in the air, driven by new technologies, new attitudes and a new generation eager to move on. The stale, cultural doldrums of the late 70s was suffocating, a time of low horizons and meagre ambitions; sign on the dole or sign up for a dreary job. Yet it was also liberating, a vacuum full of possibilities into which we leapt feet first with no fear of failure.

Expectations and baselines were so low that you could aim high. We didn't have far to fall, and therefore had no fear of failure. We could live for free in squats, find venues for nothing, get gear from charity shops, bunk fares on the buses and Tubes, blag our way into parties, and not have to worry about money because nobody had any. Besides, we had a currency of our own: we had style, which had been in very short supply. We also had energy and time. No one took any notice of what was happening at Billy's and the Blitz for at least a year. There were no prying eyes, no shining lights, which allowed time for the picture to fully develop. It was a hermetically sealed laboratory.

We also had each other. This was a small, tightly knit, clearly defined group, all roughly the same age, many from similar backgrounds, yet diverse in so many ways, all accepting of each other, living in each other's pockets, sleeping in each other's beds, with no outside interference or Svengalis pulling strings. We were self-reliant, with Steve Strange ensuring that we had a safe space to be ourselves or be whoever we wanted. The fact that we could all just waltz in past the toughest doorman in town did wonders for our self-confidence, made us feel special, exalted, like we were the chosen ones, the in crowd. We were going places and we had a place to go. The Blitz was a hothouse where exotic flowers could bloom.

There is obviously a strength in numbers, a critical mass which amplifies and exaggerates everything you do, but let the group become too big and it dissipates, lacks focus. The Blitz was just once a week, so it didn't need to fill all those other nights and get watered down in the process. The club was the right size. It could fit the 150 or so regulars, plus a few newcomers each time, so it was never quite a closed shop. Elitist but never exclusive. We were a fearsome family, yet we welcomed like-minded souls.

Being in a group gives you an immediate support system, and so much of what was achieved by various Blitz kids was done collectively. That certainly is not Thatcherite. The whole Spandau project was a group effort, Warren Street was a communal space, every fashion show had volunteer models, every band had musicians, a manager, promoters and fans, every nightclub a DJ and an instant audience all drawn from within the confines of the club. Need a photographer, a seamstress, a designer, a writer, a hat, a blouse, a tin of hair spray, some chemicals? Well, they're all in the room. Everybody was in this together. Sort of.

There was an undoubted camaraderie, a backs-against-the-wall, all-for-one-one-for-all attitude, driven by a genuine need to look after each other. It was still a hostile city out there, and we had to have each other's backs. But just as the Blitz provided a support framework, and we climbed up on each other's extravagantly padded shoulders, it was also incredibly competitive. It could be catty, bratty and sharp of tongue, a weekly winner-takes-all bunfight of the vanities. You had to be thick-skinned and quick-witted to hold your own, and you had to have chutzpah to push yourself forward, very useful qualities when it comes to taking on the outside world.

We were all frantically trying to outdo each other while looking like it was effortless – in the style stakes, in love and sex, in the 'look at me aren't I fabulous' way that vain and ambitious young people do. Yet we also took pride in the group and sought the approval of our peers; they were a very exacting mirror to look into. And this group of dandy teenage outcasts, already toughened up by years of public animosity, were certainly vain. After a while, we realised we were also ambitious. Ambition, it turns out, is contagious.

I've long pondered the question of whether or not we really knew what we were doing at the time. And I think the answer is: of course we did and of course we didn't. We certainly talked a lot about ourselves, often deep into the night, spurred on by the heady atmosphere of the Blitz and the rapid loquaciousness of the patter, myself and Gary and Dagger, Melissa and Simon Withers, Jo Strettell, Chris Sullivan and Perry Haines, allowing ourselves ambitious flights of fancy, revelling in being pretentious, not caring a jot about upsetting outsiders, because we had us. We also had a genuine fascination with the history of youth culture and art movements of the past.

I remember a pilgrimage we made to Oxford to see an exhibition on the Russian Constructivists because we loved their graphics and their trousers. We would talk endlessly of 30s Berlin, 60s London, 70s New York; of Bertolt Brecht, Brassaï and the Bauhaus; of Charlie Parker, Pete Meaden, Nik Cohn and Andy Warhol, CBGBs, the Scene and the Factory. We were students of that stuff and unashamedly saw ourselves in a direct lineage.

I blanch and then blush now as I write this, thinking that we ever compared ourselves to such luminaries, but we certainly didn't baulk back then. One of the characteristics of the characters at the Blitz is that they were almost impossible to embarrass. If you're prepared to get on a night bus to Cricklewood dressed as Bonnie Prince Charlie or Widow Twanky, if you've been pilloried for years because of the way you look, it makes it relatively easy to stand on a stage and recite trite poetry or go on the Russell Harty show and say you prefer a cup of tea to sex. We were shameless and therefore fearless.

We were also incredibly naive, skint, still living in squats or with our mums – know-nothing herberts. We didn't know that you couldn't play gigs in warehouses and on battleships, couldn't play off every major record label against the other, couldn't just walk into a magazine and demand they print your work, or start your own magazine or your own nightclub or shop or fashion brand with no money, no backing, no outside help.

When I told my mum I wanted to be a writer, she said, 'Oh Robert, they have people who do that.' The implication was they were not people like me. But when I said that to my mates at the bar, there would be nothing but encouragement. 'Go on then,' they'd say. 'Write about us.' We didn't know the word 'no' because we were surrounded by affirmation and positivity in our little Blitz bubble. We had the all-powerful arrogance of ignorance and so we just did all that stuff anyway because there was nobody to tell us that we couldn't.

Where does talent come into all of this? That is a very tricky question. Was the Blitz stacked with an extraordinary array of pre-ternaturally talented teenagers? Matthew Syed, *Times* writer and former table tennis champion, wrote a book called *Bounce*, which is subtitled 'the myth of talent'. In it, he recounts the time when the British table tennis team almost exclusively consisted of members of his little local club outside Reading; not, he argues, because Berkshire was a hotbed of innate ping pong brilliance, but because they had a good club, a great coach and endless opportunities to practise with other enthusiastic players egging each other on. And when I read it, I thought of the Blitz.

I also thought of Anna Scher's. Gary and Martin Kemp were both products of this little after-school acting academy in a local council hall in Islington. Anna specialised in taking tearaways from the local estates and schools – very much the working-class scions of the borough – and turning them into actors. Amazingly, not just the Kemps but Phil Daniels, Kathy Burke, Linda Robson and Pauline Quirke, Reggie Yates, Daniel Kaluuya and half the cast of *Eastenders* emerged from Anna Scher's; Gary often compared his time there with the Blitz. They both produced more than their fair share of successes, largely by providing opportunity and encouragement. Some of those names are huge talents, but if it hadn't been for Anna Scher's, they might never have discovered that talent. Same as the Blitz.

The individuals who gathered at the Blitz in 1979 were the most remarkable I have encountered in a life spent surrounded by musicians and writers and artists. Clever and quick, sharp and tough, open-minded and strong-willed, they were an inspiration and a provocation. I still see many of them to this day, still revel in their shining company. But despite being a haven for individualists, it was the collective force and creativity which really made the difference. It was the combined power of a movement which propelled so many to prominence.

We learned from each other's triumphs and mishaps. Sometimes that success came years, even decades later – J. J. Connolly and Liz Fremantle with their books and films, Peter Doig with his paintings – but even years later, the attitudes and aptitudes engendered shone through. Peter, who is a good friend of Chris Sullivan's, recently appeared on *Desert Island Discs*. He is arguably the most successful of us all. He's certainly the most expensive British painter of his age, with one of his works selling for $39 million. And yet he highlighted the time he spent at the club in his teens as one of the most positive and important periods of his life. He said what we all feel.

Having been one of the original Blitz kids is a badge worn with pride. The regulars know exactly who we were, and we know why it was so pivotal in so many of our lives. Being part of that crazy cohort was liberating and it was inspiring, a rare time in any life when you are told there are no limits, you can become whoever you want and, what's more, you will be backed up and helped in that ambition. 'If it had not been for the Blitz, I would not have . . .' is a refrain I have heard time and again.

I have no doubt that those after-midnight Tuesday tutorials were far more influential in my life, in allowing me to create my persona and my career, than anything I studied round the corner at the LSE. The network of friends I made, the encouragement I received, the support I was given and gave, the opportunities which arose and the fun we had were absolutely fundamental to not only my future, but also the future of the time and place I grew up in. For good or bad, we helped determine what came next.

The influence of the Blitz spread far and wide, but it certainly influenced music and fashion to an extraordinary degree. The launch of MTV in August 1981 was an incredibly propitious piece of synchronicity, propelling acts who looked striking and made stylish videos to the fore and changing the game forever, both here and in the States. MTV were crying out for colourful, visually striking characters to fill their channel, and we provided them. They provided this bright new wave of British acts with a platform for global success.

What is now known as the second British invasion in the mid-1980s dominated the US charts with Culture Club, Bananarama and Spandau Ballet, but also Billy Idol, Duran Duran, Depeche Mode, Soft Cell, Human League, Pet Shop Boys and ABC – and later Wham!, George Michael and Sade – all having massive hits. Bowie had his most commercially successful period after his association with the scene too. Just about everybody made their hair and their sales figures higher. A Flock of Seagulls, anybody?

And what of those two cornerstone moments of 80s pop culture – Band Aid and Live Aid? Well, chances are they would not have existed without the Blitz. Bob Geldof was an occasional visitor to the club, but his right-hand man, Midge Ure, was an absolute fixture. And when Geldof first decided to do something about the Ethiopian famine, the first person he asked to join him was Gary Kemp, with Spandau consequently being the first band to commit to the record. After that, Boy George, Bananarama, George Michael and even Marilyn were recruited to sing on the charity single. That is a line-up of Blitzerati.

Then, when Live Aid took place a year later at Wembley Stadium, it was Spandau and Ultravox and Wham! and Adam Ant who opened the show, with the new girl Sade, yet again in a backless top, wowing the billions watching worldwide, and Duran Duran playing in Philadelphia. It was Queen who stole the show, but there wouldn't have been a show without that cohort of New Romantics. They were the prime movers bringing in a younger audience and bolstering the old guard.

The excesses and rampant silliness of some of the 80s style crimes can certainly be pinned on the Blitz, but not usually on the Blitz kids themselves. The great abominations, the ridiculous barnets and dodgy outfits were often down to the copyists and the band-wagon-jumpers, the Johnny- and Jenny-come-latelys who watched the Thompson Twins on *Top of the Pops*, backcombed their hair, pimped up their wardrobe and got it horribly wrong. But they had fun and the photos to prove it. Spandau went decidedly wobbly later on when they became rock stars in stadiums; everything grew too large and too flash. But in their Blitz days, when they were skint, they were as sharp as it gets.

The true originals – Steve Strange and Chris Sullivan, Melissa Caplan and Princess Julia, Andy Polaris and Kim Bowen, Christos, Linard et al., all those characters named at the front of this book – were never anything but immaculate. It was never about money; you can't buy style. The crowd on a Tuesday night in Covent Garden, most of them penniless urchins, was the best dressed I have ever seen anywhere to this day. And those people – much older now, more sober, more waistline, less hair, but no less stylish – still wear it well. They still carry the Blitz with them.

And they altered the way that our nation was perceived. All those brilliant peacock pop stars and those dashing fashionistas, the whole New Romantic gang, changed the perception of a grey and conformist, deferential and dreary old England to something much more fabulous and glamorous, but also more cultured, creative, modern, young. Cool Britannia didn't start with Blair and Blur, but with Boy George as Boadicea and Steve Strange head to toe in a Melissa Caplan creation.

Alexander McQueen, undoubtedly the most prodigiously talented British fashion designer of his age, was too young to have been at the Blitz, but as a queer, working-class, south London boy obsessed with the nocturnal London demi-monde, he was in a direct lineage that included Boy George and John Galliano, and was directly inspired by his predecessors. He was a nightclub couturier, combining the tailoring passion of Chris Sullivan and Mark Powell with the extravagant theatricality of Stephen Linard and John Galliano to create his fabulous frocks and looks, which catapulted him to international celebrity. He was a genius, but one who might never have got the opportunity to shine if others had not blazed a trail before him.

Lee Alexander McQueen's chosen nightclub was Taboo, started by the extraordinary performance artist Leigh Bowery, who arrived here from Australia desperate to become part of the Blitz crowd. He landed here just too late to have made it into the Blitz itself, so he made his own club in its image. The whole outrageous mid-to-late 80s fashion scene, of which Galliano and McQueen were the warring kingpins, was an attempt to re-ignite the spirit of the Blitz and could not possibly have occurred without that inspiration. London Fashion Week started in 1984 on the crest of an 80s wave, and London has vied with Paris and Milan as Europe's fashion capital ever since.

Andrew Logan, Duggie Fields and 'Them' were a recognised if still marginalised art group associated with the Blitz. Peter Doig, Grayson Perry and Cerith Wyn Evans went on to achieve major success in the art world, breaking down the traditional British disdain for contemporary art, but I would also argue that the next wave of stroppy art-school stars – the YBAs of the 1990s – owed a massive debt to the Blitz generation. The idea of collective self-promotion, of organising your own shows, of combining creativity with theatricality and commercial nous, of achieving success on your own terms with performative events in unusual places and attention-grabbing stunts was the credo of the New Romantics.

And when Tracey Emin, Sarah Lucas and Damien Hirst et al. launched themselves out of Goldsmiths, they did so as a group, a movement, a proactive set of ragged-arsed but brilliant young artist entrepreneurs, living in squats, exhibiting in disused fire stations in Docklands and empty shops in Bethnal Green, curating their own shows and their own careers. It was just like the Blitz, but with the emphasis moved from music and fashion to fine art. They produced a massive shift in the public perception of contemporary art, but that started with the antics of the generation before.

Architecture, too, suddenly began to look rather like a night with Steve Strange. Architectural post-modernism became the dominant style of the 1980s. Buildings which were playful, eclectic and irreverent, which referenced the past to create the future, which threw together clashing styles and celebrated colour, decoration, juxtaposition and fantasy, were all the rage. London was suddenly awash with broken pediments and pointless pillars, dressing-up-box buildings with pseudo-historic twiddly bits on – like Adam Ant in his dandy highwayman mode turned to stone and steel. Personally, I can't stand po-mo architecture; I'm an unreconstructed modernist, but I have to acknowledge the link.

It was also there in the fantastical creations of Tom Dixon CBE, for example. I'm not sure Tom ever made it to the Blitz, but he was a committed nightclubber who started his own club, The Language Lab in Soho, and his own band, Funkapolitan. His true metier though was in industrial and furniture design. His early Frankenstein pieces – found, salvaged, melded and welded together – were a distinct echo of the attitude and the clothes worn at the Blitz, a study in bricolage and brio that was emblematic of the age.

The inherent urbanism of the Blitz kids, their desire to both live and play in the centre of town, was one factor in turning the tide of urban flight and decay in London. The tide started to turn when areas which had long sat empty and forgotten were colonised by the bright young things. London's revival began in the dark. Fashionable Hoxton is testament to the power of trendification and it all started with a warehouse party, some Russian constructivist trousers and a kilt or two.

By the time Thatcher was into her second term, things were looking very different. The pop charts were buzzing with fresh talent and nightlife was thriving. 'Style' was the buzzword of the times and the Sunday papers had style sections. Adverts were full of pretty Buffalo boys and girls, and street fashion was a national obsession as *The Face* went from strength to strength, becoming the magazine of the decade, with numerous glossy new publications trying to emulate it. Channel 4 was launched in 1982 with a remit to be young, fashionable, irreverent. The Turner Prize, which has done so much to popularise contemporary art, was inaugurated two years later. The spirit of the age was now markedly different to the grim forebodings of the winter of discontent.

There was still plenty of discontent and anger out there as the resistance to Thatcher's assault on the working classes magnified, but even that has a genuine, if largely forgotten, link to the Blitz. Red Wedge, a collection of musicians, comedians and artists opposed to the Tories and vaguely aligned to the Labour Party, was founded by both Billy Bragg and Paul Weller, but also by Steve Lewis, Graham Ball and myself.

We were all present at the very first meeting when the idea of an anti-Thatcher political youth culture movement spearheaded by bands was first mooted. Andy Polaris and Animal Nightlife were one of the first groups to sign up (they are there in the first photoshoot), followed by Sade and Gary Kemp, who all played their part. The name, based on a painting by El Lissitzky called *Beat the Whites with the Red Wedge*, came from our obsession with Russian constructivism and the brilliant graphics were designed by Neville Brody from

The Face. Steve Lewis in particular played a major part in the political machinations of that time. Thatcherite? Certainly not.

Perhaps the biggest and most lasting effect of the whole Blitz/ New Romantic phenomenon was on the way that queer culture is perceived by the mainstream. Suddenly seeing all these brilliant young people defiantly and joyously flouting the rigid gender norms of the 70s, playing with preconceptions about what is and what is not normal or acceptable, not caring about boundaries and labels, and just being whoever they wanted to be, was truly liberating and also prophetic. The Blitz was vehemently non-binary. It was not a gay club or a straight club. It refused to be limited by labels. It was a celebration of diversity and tolerance, a paean to all the possibilities, a glimpse of what was to come.

The Blitz and its progenies as they spread out in so many areas of public life were a major catalyst for change, for the radical and the new. Of course, many of these things might have happened anyway, although not in the same way, not at the same pace and maybe not at all.

But for all the many things which started on a Tuesday night in 1979, it can also be seen as the end of times, the last hurrah. That extraordinary lineage of post-war stylistic youth cults – starting with the Teddy boys of the 50s, through mods, rockers, skinheads and hippies in the 60s, and glam, soul boy and punk in the 70s – effectively ends with the New Romantics. They were an amalgam and a culmination of all that had gone before, taking elements from each of those to make a post-modern melange, a summation of that story, but also its final chapter.

Few kids today define themselves primarily through what they wear and what they listen to. They don't obsess about details, don't owe their allegiance to a prescribed style tribe. The youth cults of yore are remembered by the occasional revivalist, but that list has stopped. I cannot name any significant new home-grown street fashion cults since the cult with no name. That cavalcade of haircuts and dance moves, of hosiery and hats worn with intense passion, was a twentieth-century story.

Street fashion today is largely dictated from the top down, via influencers and celebrities. It is globalised and homogenised, available at the click of a button. Labels and logos are the order of the era. Sportswear and leisure wear are the antithesis of individuality, casual is rarely cool, and a puffer jacket is not a drape coat or a zoot suit. The amazing sartorial creativity which once spilled out from the margins – in the council estates, the football terraces and the night places – is in short supply.

Young people today have so much more to express themselves by than the clothes they stand up in and the music they listen to. I remember asking Peter York in 1980 what he thought would be the next big thing in youth culture and he said, 'It's more likely to be Atari than Elvis.' Of course, he was right. Computer games, mobile phones and the internet have changed everything, made life more instant and less difficult – but therefore less intense, less visceral. Stuff matters less when you perceive it through a screen at one remove.

Kids can access any music for free and can secure their clobber online, so the considerable effort and obsessive attention to detail and adherence to tribal loyalties has long gone. So has the creativity which accompanied that, the uniquely British flair for teen brilliance which shone so brightly at the Blitz.

The class of 1979 was also the last pre-AIDs generation. I baulk at describing any of the Blitz kids as innocent – we were all guilty as hell – but there was an innocence and an optimism about the place, a wide-eyed-with-wonder delight at the endless possibilities and adventures before us. We were perhaps naive in our attitudes to sex and drugs and dressing up, but we were freer than any generation that had gone before and perhaps any that would come after. We weren't carefree; we cared far too much about what we wore, how we looked. But that was about it.

When our parents were teenagers, they were wearing uniforms and eating rations. We had only the style wars to fight. We were also free from any great need to make money, supported by the state and not burdened by high rents or the crushing consumerism to come. It was a time of glorious excess on very little money. It was also a time before we could be tracked and monitored by technology, before the narcissistic need to let everybody know what you are doing and monetise your existence. We knew no constraints and acknowledged few barriers, and certainly made the most of it. We got up to stuff.

That would all come crashing down when people started getting sick. Suddenly promiscuity was a potential death sentence. AIDS took a terrible toll, took out too many of my generation. I personally lost great friends from the club scene on both sides of the Atlantic, and neither New York nor London would ever again equal the abandon and unabashed hedonism and energy of the pre-virus years. Even for those who never got sick, AIDS caused a deep psychological malaise, casting a terrible shadow over the night.

Every generation believes things were better when they were young, because they were young. Personally, I think almost everything has improved today. Certainly my kids' generation are better people than we were in almost every respect: kinder and wiser and more caring, less prejudiced, less violent. I believe the present is seriously underrated compared to the past. But I also think that those of us who made it past Steve Strange and into the Blitz every week were blessed to have been in the right place at a unique time.

The Blitz was a blast, a series of little explosions which set off chain reactions. It was an education, it was a party, it was a ball. Tuesday night in Great Queen Street in 1979 with Steve and Rusty and all the gang dressed to the nines and living life to the full was the best of times in the worst of times.